The First Amendment

To those persons
who not only believe in freedom
but are tolerant of those
who practice it

The First Amendment, 1791–1991

Two Hundred Years of Freedom

by
James E. Leahy

McFarland & Company, Inc., Publishers
Jefferson, North Carolina, and London

British Library Cataloguing-in-Publication data are available

Library of Congress Cataloguing-in-Publication Data

Leahy, James E., 1919–
    The First Amendment, 1791–1991 : two hundred years of freedom / by
James E. Leahy.
        p. cm.
    Includes bibliographical references and index.
    ISBN 0-89950-573-2 (lib. bdg. : 50# alk. paper) ∞
        1. United States–Constitutional law–Amendments–1st–History.
    2. Freedom of religion–United States–History.   3. Freedom of
    speech–United States–History.   4. Assembly, Right of–United
    States–History.   5. Freedom of association–United States–History.
    6. Freedom of the press–United States–History.   I. Title.
    KF4558 1st.L4 1991
    342.73'0853–dc20
    [347.302853]   90-53502
                                                                         CIP

Manufactured in the United States of America

McFarland & Company, Inc., Publishers
    Box 611, Jefferson, North Carolina 28640

TABLE OF CONTENTS

PREFACE

"The very purpose of a Bill of Rights was to withdraw certain subjects from the vicissitudes of political controversy, to place them beyond the reach of majorities and officials and to establish them as legal principles to be applied by the courts. One's right to life, liberty, and property, to free speech, a free press, freedom of worship and assembly, and other fundamental rights may not be submitted to vote; they depend on the outcome of no elections."

Board of Education v. Barnette, 319 U.S. 624, 638 (1943)

This book is about real people. People like Walter Barnette, Benjamin Gitlow, Ishmael Jaffree, Jonas Yoder, and Fred Shuttlesworth, to name just a few, who, during the past two hundred years fought "to place [our freedoms] beyond the reach of majorities and officials and to establish them as legal principles to be applied by the courts."

Each case discussed herein sets one or more persons who claim their rights have been infringed upon against some branch of the government that is allegedly doing the infringement. As the cases worked their way through the courts and eventually to the Supreme Court, judges and finally the nine justices of the Supreme Court were required to make difficult choices between people's constitutional rights and interests asserted by the government.

It is because people have undertaken such challenges throughout these two hundred years that we enjoy more freedom today than do people of any other country.

This book is also about the role of the Supreme Court in this never ending struggle. A recent newspaper headline reads: "Most Americans Know Little About the High Court." The story goes on to say, "Americans are so ignorant about the U.S. Supreme Court that fewer than one in four know how many justices serve on the high court and nearly two-thirds are unable to name a single one, a poll shows."[1] Not knowing how many justices there are or who they are is just a symptom of a greater problem, which is that few people realize how much the Court's decisions affect their daily lives. The Court, through its decisions, determines how much freedom we enjoy, and the extent to which the government can legitimately burden those freedoms. Yet in another recent poll, fewer than one-third of three hundred college students could name three freedoms guaranteed by the First Amendment.

The Court also decides cases that affect us economically, socially, and politically. Noted historian Charles Warren has written of the Supreme Court:

> The vitally important part, however, which [the] Court has played in the history of the country in preserving the Union, in maintaining National supremacy within the limits of the Constitution, in upholding the doctrines of international law and the sanctity of treaties, in affecting the trend of the economic, social and political development of the United States, cannot be understood by a mere study of its decisions, as reported in the law books.[2]

While Supreme Court decisions and those of other courts are reported in the press, rarely do such reports adequately explain the constitutional issues involved, or why the case was decided the way it was. This gives an incomplete picture of what the courts have decided, and why they have done so in the way that they have. Much confusion and misplaced criticism, especially of the judiciary, is the result.

Yet, a better understanding of what the system can do, does do, and will do, is essential if the freedoms we enjoy today are to survive.

I share the concern expressed by Chief Justice Earl Warren when he wrote:

> I had often pondered, and I continue to ponder, the question of education for good citizenship because it seems clear to me that democratic rights, privileges, freedoms . . . can survive only as long as those who exercise them do so in an informed and conscientious manner. History offers many examples of experiments in democracy that perished when the people, because of the kind of ignorance that encourages indifference, neglected the obligations of citizenship.[3]

The first chapter of this book briefly discusses what the country was like prior to 1791 and relates a bit of the history surrounding the adoption of the Bill of Rights.

Because the protection of our freedoms rests with the judiciary, the second chapter is devoted to an explanation of our judicial systems. It describes them, and explains how they operate.

When the Bill of Rights was adopted, it expressly applied to Congress and the rest of the federal government. It was not until well into the twentieth century that the Supreme Court began to apply the Bill of Rights to actions of state governments, and make state officials also follow the dictates of most of the specific requirements in the amendments. Chapter III explains the process by which the Court accomplished this result.

Subsequent chapters discuss each of the freedoms guaranteed by the First Amendment, which prohibits the establishment of religion, and protects the free exercise of religion, freedom of speech, press, assembly, petition, and association.

Numerous quotations from Supreme Court opinions are included in the text so that the reader will have a feel for the thoughts of the justices as they have confronted the difficult choices each case presents.

As this is written, the members of the Supreme Court are William H. Rehnquist (Chief Justice), Byron R. White, Thurgood Marshall, Harry A. Blackmun, John Paul Stevens, Sandra Day O'Connor, Antonin Scalia, Anthony M. Kennedy, and David Souter.

James E. Leahy
November 1990

Amendment I

Congress shall make no law respecting an establishment of religion, or prohibiting the free exercise thereof; or abridging the freedom of speech, or of the press; or the right of the people peaceably to assemble, and to petition the Government for a redress of grievances.

Ratified December 15, 1791

I.

A BIT OF HISTORY

"The consequences of a lax, or inefficient government are too obvious to be dwelt upon. Thirteen sovereignties pulling against each other, and all tugging at the foederal head will soon bring ruin on the whole; whereas a liberal, energetic Constitution, well guarded, & closely watched, to prevent encroachments, might restore us to that degree of respectability & consequence, to which we had fair claim, & the brightest prospect of attaining."

Washington to Madison, November 5, 1786 (Rutland, *The Papers of James Madison*, v. 9, p. 162)

Washington's words give some clue as to the condition of the country in 1786, five years after the end of the Revolutionary War. The Articles of Confederation, which formed the basis of the federal government, simply were not working. Without the consent of all of the states, Congress had no authority to levy taxes. What funds the government received came from voluntary contributions from the states. Thus, debts of the new nation were growing rapidly.[1]

Nor did Congress have power to regulate foreign and domestic commerce. Each state was at liberty to enact such laws as it deemed appropriate to protect its own interests, and this they did with a vengeance. Although Congress had the authority to negotiate treaties with foreign nations, such treaties were not effective until ratified by the states. Even then, Congress had no authority to enforce compliance with treaty provisions.

Because there was no uniform system of currency, business transactions which crossed state lines were very difficult. A few states issued paper money, only some of which was considered legal tender. In a letter to Thomas Jefferson in August 1786 James Madison wrote,

> The value of money consists in the uses it will serve. Specie will serve all the uses of paper. Paper will not serve one of the essential

uses of specie. The paper therefore will be less valuable than specie. Among the numerous ills with which this practice is pregnant, one I find is that it is producing the same warfare & retaliation among the States as were produced by the State regulations of commerce.[2]

It was in this setting that George Washington and many of the other prominent men of that time saw that the independence they had fought so hard to win might well be lost. Prompted by these conditions which bordered on chaos, the Virginia Assembly called for a meeting of representatives from the states to meet in Annapolis, Maryland, in September 1786. This meeting was convened to explore ways of creating a uniform system of commercial regulations.

Only five states sent representatives. Among those attending were Alexander Hamilton of New York and James Madison of Virginia. The report of this meeting, written by Hamilton, did more than just seek a solution to the commercial problems of the time, but sought also to have a constitutional solution to the many other problems facing the country.

The Annapolis meeting and events that followed prompted Congress to call for a convention to be held in Philadelphia in May of 1787 for the sole purpose of amending the Articles of Confederation to "render the federal constitution adequate to the exigencies of government and the preservation of the Union."

The area that was to be the United States stretched at this time from the Atlantic Ocean to the Mississippi River, and from the Great Lakes to near the Gulf of Mexico. Only about half of this vast and little known land was actually under the control of the federal government.

Travel throughout the states was by foot, boat, horse, buggy and stagecoach. The population was estimated at 3.9 million, made up of the well-born and the poor. About 680,000 were slaves. There were, of course, still many Indians in the country, although most of them were forced to move west as the settlers began moving farther inland.

Only five cities, Philadelphia, New York, Boston, Charleston, and Baltimore, had populations over ten thousand.

The Country and the People

*"Their existence was a hard one ... but their standard of living was high..."**

Most of the people were farmers who owned small farms of one hundred acres, more or less. Some of the men who were the political

*Richard Bernstein, *Are We to Be a Nation?* (Harvard Univ. Press, 1987), p. 3.

leaders of the time such as Washington, Madison, Jefferson, and James Monroe were dependent upon agriculture for at least part of their livelihood.

There were also, of course, lawyers, doctors, clergymen, storekeepers, scientists, and merchants. And people worked as laborers in factories, construction, fishing, and transportation. There were artists, songwriters, and poets. One of the poets was Phillis Wheatley, a Negro who was sold into slavery at the age of 9 to a Boston tailor, John Wheatley. Wheatley and his wife, Susannah, recognizing that Phillis was an intelligent and talented woman, gave her an education. She started writing poetry in her late teens. The Wheatleys sent her to London where Phillis' first book of poems was published. She was then the second American woman (Anne Bradstreet was the first) to write and have published a book of poetry. Upon her return from England, Phillis became a free woman. She married and raised a family, but the marriage did not provide security. She therefore spent the last years of her life in poverty. However, her poems continued to receive acclaim.

Farming, then as now, was fraught with the problems of the unpredictability of the weather, and the uncertainty of the price of farm commodities. Madison took note of this in a letter to Jefferson in June 1786 when he wrote,

> Things have undergone little change since my last. The scarcity of money the price of Tobo. & the high price of bread continue to be topics of complaint. . . . At the date of my last we were praying for rain. Shortly after we had a deluge of it. From the 19th. of May to the 4th. of June, we scarcely saw the sun, had almost incessant rains, sometimes showers, or rather torrents that threatened to sweep away every thing. . . . A great proportion of the heads [of wheat] in this part of the country are blasted, and in many parts it is said the fields will not be worth cutting. . . . We have had no rain since the cessation of the long spell, that is since the 3rd. instant, and the earth is as dry and as hard as a brick.[3]

Among the crops grown throughout the country were wheat, corn, tobacco, rice, and cotton.

While free enterprise flourished, many people were deeply in debt and people were still being imprisoned for not being able to pay their creditors. Manufacturing was in its infancy. A postal system existed which, together with the many newspapers flourishing throughout the states, provided opportunity for the people to communicate with one another and to keep abreast of the happenings of the day.

The people were a religious people, many having come to this new frontier to escape religious persecution in their homeland. However, by 1787 the religious climate had changed substantially from a very intolerant one to one of mutual tolerance and religious liberty. Discussing the pre-revolutionary period, authors Fred W. Friendly and Martha J.H. Elliott write that "in the Massachusetts Bay Colony, Quakers, for example, were whipped, branded, sold as servants, had their ears cropped off, or were even hanged. Anyone preaching complete separation from the Church of England or separation of church and state was in danger of being punished or deported."[4]

The struggle for political freedom in the 1770s, however, brought a fight for religious freedom as well. "Toleration is not the *opposite* of Intolerance," wrote Thomas Paine in the *Rights of Man*, "but it is the *counterfeit* of it. Both are despotisms. The one assumes to itself the right of withholding Liberty of Conscience, and the other of granting it."

Madison penned his famous "Memorial and Remonstrance Against Religious Assessments" in 1785, a document which advocated a total separation of church and state. And in 1786 Thomas Jefferson wrote and the Virginia Assembly adopted a *Statute for Religious Freedom*, which provides that "no man shall be compelled to frequent or support any religious worship, place, or ministry whatsoever ... nor shall otherwise suffer on account of his religious opinions or belief...." Jefferson considered this one of the major accomplishments of his life and directed that his tombstone bear a reference to his authorship of this statute, which it does.

There were no public schools as we know them today. Some local, private and church schools were formed in the years prior to the war. Children, specifically males, were generally taught at home with the emphasis being upon religious education. It was not considered all that important to educate girls:

> ...at first home instruction and the old established type of apprenticeship training were depended upon to furnish the necessary ability to read and to participate in the home and church religious services, the great religious purposes which had brought the colonists to America being the motive which was to insure such instruction.[5]

In 1779 Jefferson proposed a multiple-point plan for public education in Virginia, which was not adopted. It called for a three-year school in each local district for white children between 7 and 10 years, and a higher three-year school in each county for the best students from the district schools.

The war years brought disaster to the schooling that did exist. Many schools were forced to close while the colonists turned their attention to winning their freedom from Great Britain. One of the stalwarts of American education at this time was Noah Webster, a 25-year-old schoolmaster at Hartford. He argued that

> "America must be as independent in *literature* as she is in politics, as famous for *arts* as for *arms*." He did his best to make her so with his famous bluebacked speller, his first American reader, and the monthly *American Magazine*, which he edited.... The *American Spelling-Book*, which simplified the king's English by omitting the *u* from words like *labour* and *colour*, and spelling *wagon* with one *g*, became an all-time best seller, and remained in print for over a century.[6]

A number of our well-known eastern colleges were in operation, including Harvard, William and Mary, Yale, Princeton, Pennsylvania, Columbia, Brown, Rutgers, and Dartmouth.

Remembering the Ladies

*"I desire you would Remember the Ladies, and be more generous and favorable to them than your ancestors."** *

The political process in Colonial America was dominated almost exclusively by the male members of society. Women did not vote, not because they were specifically prohibited from doing so but because the right to vote was generally given only to those owning property. Unmarried women enjoyed the freedom of owning property, contracting, working outside of the home, keeping their earnings, and being able to dispose of their property by will at death. However, because of a legal doctrine called "coverture," married women, for all intents and purposes, lost their legal identity. Upon entering the marriage relationship, a husband was given control over his wife's property and was entitled to collect the rents and profits therefrom. Authors Sylvia R. Frey and Marian J. Morton have succinctly summed up the predicament of married women at this time:

> Theoretically, at marriage the wife disappeared as a legal entity. The law denied to her the ability to to enter into legal relationships with others, including the ability to borrow money or to buy tangible goods, and it limited her liability for contracts entered into.[7]

*Letter from Abigail Adams to John Adams, March 31, 1776. Butterfield, et al., eds. *The Book of Abigail and John Adams, Selected Letters of the Adams Family* (Harvard Univ. Press, 1975), p. 121.

It would, however, be a gross oversimplification to say that women at this period in our history were expected to do no more than take care of home, family, and childbearing. Many women, of course, did just that. They cooked, kept house, washed and ironed clothes, milked the cows, made butter and cheese, and maintained a garden. They sewed, spun yarn and thread, and weaved. If the family consisted of children, the mother most likely taught them to read and write, and saw to it that they were instructed in their religious faith.

To pay homage to his wife, one husband listed her household activities in 1778 as

> getting prepared in the kitchen, baking our own bread and pies, meat &c. . . . cutting and drying apples . . . making of cider without tools . . . seeing all our washing done, and her fine clothes and my shirts, the which are all smoothed by her . . . her making of twenty large cheeses, and that from one cow, and daily using milk and cream, besides her sewing, knitting &c.[8]

That women, especially young girls, were also becoming factory workers is evidenced by Washington's visit to a factory in Boston in 1789, and his later writing about it.

> Went after an early breakfast, to visit the duck [cloth] manufacture, which appeared to be carrying on with spirit, and is in a prosperous way. They have manufactured 32 pieces of duck of 30 or 40 yards each in a week and expect in a short time to increase it. They have 28 looms at work, and 14 girls spinning with both hands (the flax being fastened to their waist). Children [girls] turn the wheels for them, and with this assistance each spinner can turn out 14 lbs. of thread a day when they stick to it, but as they are paid by the piece for work they do, there is no other restraint upon them but to come at 8 o'clock in the morning and return at 6 in the evening. They are daughters of decayed families, and are girls of character. None other are admitted.[9]

Our history books have given us the names of many male patriots of the day and told us much about the part each played in securing our independence; in forming the new federal government; and in the adoption of the Bill of Rights. For example, the names of the first six presidents of the United States—George Washington, John Adams, Thomas Jefferson, James Madison, James Monroe, and John Quincy Adams—are indelibly etched upon the minds of all schoolchildren. The names of the women who were an important part in this struggle, however, have not been as well chronicled. But the fact that they were there, and assumed essential roles in the prewar period, during the war, and thereafter cannot be denied.

Two women who were active observers and participants in the efforts to gain political freedom during the 70s and 80s were Abigail Adams, wife of John Adams, and Mercy Otis Warren. Abigail wrote to husband John, in March of 1776, at the time the Continental Congress was considering whether the colonies should seek independence from England, "not [to] put such unlimited power into the hands of Husbands. Remember all Men would be tyrants if they could. If perticuliar care and attention is not paid to the Laidies we are determined to foment a Rebellion, and will not hold ourselves bound by any Laws in which we have no voice or Representation."[10]

In response, John, whether with tongue in cheek or not we do not know, pointed out that the spirit of independence had "loosened the bands of Government" to such an extent that "Children and Apprentices were disobedient — that schools and Colleges were grown turbulent — that Indians slighted their Guardians and Negroes grew insolent to their Masters. But your Letter was the first Intimation that another Tribe more numerous and powerful than all the rest were grown discontented...."[11] He was, of course, referring to women.

Mercy Otis Warren, a poet and a playwright, was also a strong advocate of political independence. She wrote a three-volume *History of the Rise, Progress, and Termination of the Revolution,* which evidences a keen insight into the challenges which faced the new nation.

Many women whose names will never be known followed the army during the war and provided many services, such as food, clothing, nursing care, laundry and shelter that were essential to the soldier in the field.

Two women who actually fought side by side with the soldiers were Deborah Sampson (Gannet) and Mary Ludwig Hays, known as Molly Pitcher.

Deborah Sampson (Gannet) at the age of nineteen dressed as a man and enlisted in the army under the name of Timothy Thayer. Although she served for a while without it being known that she was a female, her identity was discovered and she was discharged. Not one to be denied, however, she later enlisted in a Massachusetts regiment as a private, saw action, and was wounded. She contracted yellow fever and was hospitalized, and again it was discovered that she was female, and she was discharged. In 1792 her war service was recognized by the state of Massachusetts, which granted her thirty-four pounds compensation for her services. The legislature noted at that time:

The said Deborah exhibited an extraordinary instance of female
heroism, by discharging the duties of a faithful, gallant soldier, and
at the same time preserving the virtue and chastity of her sex un-
suspected and unblemished, and was discharged from the service
with a fair and honorable character.....[12]

Mary Ludwig Hays "earned her nickname Molly Pitcher at the battle of Monmouth, on June 28, 1778, when she used a pitcher or pail
to carry water . . . to the thirsty and exhausted soldiers. When her husband fell in battle, . . . she was said to have loaded his cannon, missing
not a single round, and helping win the American victory."[13] She was
given a pension for her service during the war, and her statue appears
on the Monmouth, New Jersey, battlefield monument "showing her
barefoot, tending the cannon, with a pitcher at her side."[14]

Slavery — A Debasement of Human Nature

"Slavery is such an atrocious debasement of human nature . . ."*
With the above words, Benjamin Franklin discussed the enslave-
ment of Negroes, a practice which had been introduced into the Colonies in 1619 when a Dutch ship anchored at the Jamestown, Virginia,
settlement. The ship's captain agreed to trade twenty Africans, who
were aboard the ship, for food and water. Included in the twenty were
three women. Because English law prohibited baptized persons from
being slaves, these Africans were taken into the colony as indentured
servants and treated in the same manner as many of the colonists who
had come to the new country under contracts of indenture. Indentured
servants were generally required to work for an employer for a period
of four years. As the demand for laborers for plantations, farms, and
domestic servants increased, the indenture system could not keep pace.
Further, when the contracted time expired, the indentured person was
no longer obligated to perform services, thus creating a constant turn-
over of laborers.
Gradually the time of indenture increased for Negroes until it was
extended to life, and they were thereafter considered slaves. Slaves were
property and subject to purchase and sale like any other property.

*Benjamin Franklin, President, Pennsylvania Society for Promoting Abolition
of Slavery, November 9, 1789, Bigelow, *The Works of Benjamin Franklin*
(Federal Edition, 1904) v. 12, pp. 157–59.

Most slaves lived a harsh life. They were regulated by strict codes of laws and severely punished for any violation. In the South, both slave men and slave women were required to work in the field. In addition the women were required to provide a home and take care of their husbands and children. Some of the women were put to work in their master's household as maids, cooks, nursemaids, etc. And many were forced into sexual relations with their white owners.

Whether and in what manner the slaves were allowed to marry depended upon the whim of the owner. Some encouraged marriage and having children, believing that this made for a happier slave. And, of course, the birth of a child increased the property of the owner.

Barbara Mayer Wertheimer describes the life of slave women as follows:

> Since slaves could not legally marry and could be sold at the whim of the master, close family relationships among slaves could be broken up at any time, with men sold to new owners more often than women. Thus the reponsibility not only for raising the children but for any continuity in family life often fell upon the women. The pattern of the extended family was vital, since mothers worked all day, and their young children were left to the care of grandmothers or old or disabled slaves, except on larger plantations where informal slave nurseries were run by older slave women called "aunties."[15]

Negroes in the North were treated better than in the Southern states. Some were free, and those that were considered slaves worked as domestic servants and on small farms. The movement to abolish slavery started early here, and eventually spread to all the Colonies, including those in the South. The Society of Friends (Quakers) were at the forefront of this struggle, having voiced their objection to slavery as early as 1652.

In 1781, Quork Walker, a slave, was given his freedom by a court because the Massachusetts Constitution contained the statement that "All men are created equal." This decision brought an end to slavery in that state.

Negroes served in both the Continental and British armies during the war. The disruption caused by the war gave slaves an opportunity to run away. Many of them did, seeking refuge with the British troops.

Among the five Americans who died during the Boston Massacre was a Negro, Crispus Attucks. Thereafter the acceptance of Negroes as soldiers was an on-again, off-again, and on-again affair. In July 1775, Congress sent out a call that military units should be organized, but whether these units were to contain Negroes was not specified. Negroes were allowed to enlist. However, this practice was soon discontinued because of the fear that some of the slaves might turn their guns upon their masters. When it was decided to exclude free Negroes from serving, a number of them protested and General Washington changed the policy allowing them to enlist, and many did.

Among those who did was Peter Salem, who took part in the battle of Bunker Hill. Salem was a slave but may have become a free man when he joined the Continental Army in Massachusetts. His participation in the battle of Bunker Hill is described by Merl R. Eppse:

> Peter Salem was a private in Colonel Nixon's regiment. Major Pitcairn of the British marines suddenly appeared, and led an attack on the Continental Army. The men were startled by his sudden attack, and during the tense moment, Peter Salem stepped forward, aimed his musket at the Major's bosom and killed him, thus being the first in this battle to open fire on the enemy of the colonies.[16]

The movement for the abolition of slavery accelerated after the war. Many societies dedicated to that goal were organized in most of the states, including some in the South. Slave trade was prohibited by all of the Northern states by 1783.

Among the strong voices against slavery were Franklin and Benjamin Rush in Pennsylvania, James Otis of Massachusetts, and the Reverend Samuel Hopkins of Rhode Island. Although many of the prominent men in the political life of the country were slave owners, some of these ultimately became vigorous opponents.

Washington wrote to Robert Morris in April 1786 that he could "only say, that there is not a man living, who wishes more sincerely than I do to see a plan adopted for the abolition of it [slavery]...."[17] Jefferson expressed the same feeling in a letter addressed to a friend in Paris to the effect that "you know that nobody wishes more ardently to see an abolition not only of the trade but of the condition of slavery...."[18]

The movement toward the abolition of slavery did not fare well in the Constitutional Convention. The delegates were caught between the proslavery position of the Southern states and the abolitionist movement taking place in the North. This dilemma forced the Convention to adopt a compromise whereby Congress was prohibited by Article I, Section 9, Clause 1 from legislating on the "migration" or "importation" of persons until 1808. This left the slave trade intact until that date. Further, Article I, Section 2, Clause 3 required that in the apportionment of population for determining the makeup of the House of

Representatives, all free persons but only three-fifths of all others were to be counted. The "all others," of course, were the slaves. These two clauses were nullified by the Fourteenth and Thirteenth Amendments, respectively, to the Constitution. The Fourteenth Amendment requires "counting the whole number of persons in each State," and the Thirteenth prohibits all slavery.

One outright concession that was made at the Convention to slave owners was Article IV, Section 2, Clause 3, which required that persons held in service in one state and escaping to another were to be returned by the latter to the former, thus assuring the return of runaway slaves who were apprehended in another state. This clause also became void with the adoption of the Thirteenth Amendment.

During the debate over prohibiting Congress from legislating on the importation of persons into the country until 1808, Madison said that "Twenty years will produce all the mischief that can be apprehended from the liberty to import slaves. So long a term will be more dishonorable to the National character than to say nothing about it in the Constitution."[19] He "thought it wrong to admit in the Constitution the idea that there could be property in men."[20]

The Constitutional Convention

*They met to "form a more perfect union."**

Although the delegates were slow in assembling in Philadelphia in May 1787, eventually all states were represented except Rhode Island, which never did send delegates. Washington, who had been selected as a delegate from Virginia, was elected presiding officer.

Among those in attendance were Madison, Franklin, George Mason, Gouverneur Morris, Edmund Randolph, and Elbridge Gerry. Hamilton, who was a delegate and an advocate of a strong federal governmemt, left at the end of June because of disagreements with his fellow New York delegates who were strong supporters of states' rights. He also became disenchanted with the whole process because it appeared to him that the possibility that the Convention would create a strong central government was quite remote. "I own to you sir," he wrote General Washington on July 3, "that I am seriously and deeply distressed at the aspect of the counsels which prevailed when I left Philadelphia. I fear that we shall let slip the golden opportunity of

*The Preamble to the Constitution.

rescuing the American empire from disunion, anarchy, and misery."[21] Hamilton, however, returned for the closing days of the Convention.

Jefferson did not attend; he was in Paris at the time as the nation's minister to France. His voice, however, was heard by the other delegates through letters he wrote to some of them. John Adams was also away on business for the United States in London. Patrick Henry had declined to be a delegate from Virginia. One of the real freedom fighters of the time, Sam Adams, was unable to be present because of age.

The fact that so many of the prominent men in the political and economic life of the country were willing to attend and devote their time to finding a solution for the crisis in government then existing, attests to the importance they believed this meeting to have. Madison, in a letter to Jefferson dated June 6, 1787, discussed the atmosphere surrounding the Convention at its beginning: "The names of the members will satisfy you that the States have been serious in this business. The attendance of Genl. Washington is proof of the light in which he regards it. The whole Community is big with expectation. And there can be no doubt but that the result will in some way or other have a powerful effect on our destiny."[22]

It was determined that the meeting would be held in strictest secrecy. The delegates were admonished not to talk about the proceedings outside of the meeting hall. The windows were tightly closed, making the temperature inside almost unbearable during the hot Philadelphia summer.

Voting at the Convention was done by states. Two issues that permeated the whole debate were the question of a strong national government versus strong state governments, and the concern of the smaller states not to be left to the mercy of the larger states in representation in any newly formed government.

What ultimately came out of the Convention was a proposal for a strong central government yet one which left the states with much of their sovereignty. And the fears of the smaller states were allayed by the so-called Connecticut Compromise whereby membership of the lower house of the Congress, the House of Representatives, would be based upon population and the upper chamber, the Senate, would be composed of two representatives from each state.

Of course, not everyone was happy with the result. Three delegates—Gerry of Massachusetts, and Mason and Randolph of Virginia—refused to sign the Constitution, and became vigorous foes of its adoption. Franklin, then in his eighties, had some misgivings about the proposed new government, but believed that it was the best that could be obtained under the circumstances. During the closing days of the Convention, in an address read for him by James Wilson, Franklin said:

> Mr. President: — I confess that I do not entirely approve of this Constitution at present; but, sir, I am not sure that I shall never approve it; for, having lived long, I have experienced many instances of being obliged, by better information or fuller consideration, to change opinions even on important subjects, which I once thought right, but found to be otherwise.[23]

No Protection for Civil Rights

*"It would give great quiet to the people..."**

Protection for civil rights did not play an important part in the formation of the Constitution. This seems strange because the colonists, especially those who came from Great Britian, were accustomed to enjoying some civil rights in their homeland. They were, of course, familiar with the Magna Carta of 1215, wherein "every person . . . was protected in the enjoyment of his life, liberty and property, except as they may be declared to be forfeited by the judgment of his peers or the law of the land. . . ." Also the Petition of Right, adopted by the English Parliament in 1628 in the reign of Charles I, contained a declaration of liberties.

The rights guaranteed in these documents, together with those in practice under the English common law, provided the background for Colonial legislatures in setting up their own legal systems. Further, many of the Colonies had adopted declarations of rights prior to the convening of the Constitutional Convention in 1787. Virginia adopted a comprehensive declaration in June of 1776. In the ensuing years, Pennsylvania, Delaware, Maryland, North Carolina, Vermont, Massachusetts, and New Hampshire did likewise, modeling their declarations after the Virginia Declaration.

This background, however, did not necessarily guarantee protection for civil rights during the period leading up to the Revolutionary War, because the colonists had to contend with George III, king of England. Although much of this discontent was over taxation and economic regulations imposed on them, the agents of the Crown were guilty of numerous violations of people's rights. Therefore, coupled

---

*Words of George Mason, *Notes of Debates in the Federal Convention of 1787*, reported by James Madison, p. 630.

with their protests of the tax laws, the colonists listed these violations. One such listing was drawn up by a Boston town meeting in 1772. The Bostonians complained that "our houses and even our bed chambers, are exposed to be ransacked, our boxes chests & trunks broke open ravaged and plundered by wretches, whom no prudent man would venture to employ even as menial servants. . . ."

The Stamp Act Congress, in 1765, sought to alleviate some of the oppressive measures of the Crown by a Declaration of Rights and Grievances. While here too the complaints centered around taxation and trade, the Twelfth Article of the Declaration reads: "That the increase, prosperity and happiness of these colonies depend on the full and free enjoyment of their rights and liberties, and an intercourse, with Great Britain, mutually affectionate and advantageous."

As the relationship between the Colonies and England deteriorated in the 1770s, Congress found it necessary to put forth its own Declaration and Resolves, which it did on October 14, 1774. At this time the colonists' complaints against the king were more than just economic. They listed among their rights "life, liberty, and property." They asserted that "the foundation of English liberty, and of all free government, is a right in the people to participate in their legislative councils. . . ." And they insisted that "they . . . [were] entitled to the benefit of such of the English statutes as existed at the time of their colonization. . . ." They specifically argued that they were entitled to "peaceably assemble, consider their grievances, and petition the King. . . ."

These declarations of rights seemed to have little effect upon the king, for in July 1776 Congress adopted The Declaration of Independence, cutting the Colonies loose from Great Britain. This Declaration, written by Jefferson, contains a long list of grievances against the Crown, some of which deal directly with violations of civil rights.

So with this background, it is surprising that the Constitution did not contain a detailed list of rights. A few attempts were made, during the Convention, to include some protections, but these proved futile.

No doubt the princpal reason for this was that it was generally thought that protection for civil rights rested with the states, and their respective declarations of rights, and as long as the states were strong such rights were well protected. It was also argued that because the new federal government would be one of limited powers, it had no power to infringe upon people's rights.

Near the end of the Convention, in early September 1787, Mason, who authored the Virginia Declaration of Rights in 1776, made an attempt to have a bill of rights included in the Constitution: "it would give great quiet to the people. . . ."[24] His attempt failed. The failure to include a bill of rights in the proposed Constitution provided considerable ammunition for those opposed to ratification.

The Battle for Adoption

*"But I sincerely believe it is the best that could be obtained at this time"**

In spite of Washington's belief that the new Constitution was "the best that could be obtained at this time," a long and hard-fought battle for ratification ensued, lasting through the end of 1787 and well into 1788. Those in favor were called Federalists, supporters of a strong central government. The opposition, which became known as the Antifederalists, fought to preserve the power of the states. They embellished their arguments against ratification by pointing out that there was no protection against violation of citizens' rights by the proposed new federal government.

At the forefront of the ratification battle were Hamilton, Madison, Franklin, and John Marshall, who later became Chief Justice of the United States. Jefferson and John Adams ultimately gave their approval, although both were concerned that no bill of rights was included in the document. Washington saw the argument over the lack of a bill of rights as a smoke screen being used by the opponents of ratification. He chose not to take an active part in the debate.

Among the most ardent opponents were Henry, Randolph and Mason of Virginia, and Sam Adams and Gerry of Massachusetts.

Henry, who had refused to be a delegate to the Convention, was suspicious of the attempt to amend the Articles of Confederation, fearing that there would be an erosion of the power of the states. He saw the proposed Constitution as doing just that.

While Mason, Randolph and Gerry were concerned over some of the provisions in the new Constitution, they argued that the lack of a bill of rights was one of its main defects.

Although Delaware was the first state to ratify the Constitution, it was on December 12, 1787, when the Pennsylvania Convention gave

*Washington to Patrick Henry; Bowen, *Miracle at Philadelphia,* p. 280.

its approval, that the Federalists won a significant victory. New Jersey, Georgia, and Connecticut followed in rapid succession. Another crucial state was Massachusetts, which ratified in February 1788. With ratification, Massachusetts sent along certain amendments that it recommended for adoption by the new Congress. New Hampshire did the same.

By the time the ratification struggle came before state conventions in Virginia and New York, much of the battle centered around amendments that would protect citizens' rights. An attempt was made at the Virginia Convention to attach a number of such amendments. At this time, Madison opposed adding a bill of rights for two reasons. He did not believe it necessary because the Constitution did not give the new federal government any power whatsoever to deal in people's rights. He was also concerned that an enumeration of some rights might be understood as being an exclusive listing thereof. In a speech before the Virginia Ratifying Convention he expressed his views as follows:

> There cannot be a more positive and unequivocal declaration of the principles of the adoption—that every thing not granted, is reserved. This is obviously and self-evidently the case, without the declaration [of rights]. Can the general government exercise any power not delegated? If an enumeration be made of our rights, will it not be implied, that every thing omitted, is given to the general government?[25]

The attempt to add amendments in the Virginia Convention failed, and the Constitution was ratified. The Convention subsequently appointed a committee, however, to draft amendments to be sent to the governors and legislatures of the other states. The fight them moved on to New York where it was bitterly fought. The New York Convention finally ratified the Constitution in July 1788. It, too, proposed amendments that would include protection for civil rights. By this time eleven states had approved the Constitution and the wheels were set in motion for its implementation.

A Bill of Rights Is Adopted

"The Bill of Rights is what the people are entitled to against every government on earth, ... and what no just government should refuse..."*

*Jefferson to Madison, December 20, 1787. Fred W. Friendly and Martha J.H. Elliott, The Constitution: That Delicate Balance (New York: Random House, 1984), p. 12.

In spite of the fact that several of the states had submitted amendments at the time of ratification, and even though the Federalists had pledged to introduce such amendments when the first Congress met, Congress did not seem in a hurry to consider them. After Congress convened in April 1789, much time was taken just getting the government organized. To fulfill what he thought was the commitment of the Federalists, Madison, then a member of the House of Representatives, offered a number of amendments in May 1789. The House took no action at that time. He tried again in June and at that time told the members of the House that

> the applications for amendments come from a very respectable number of our constituents, and it is certainly proper for congress to consider the subject, in order to quiet that anxiety which prevails in the public mind: Indeed I think it would have been of advantage to the government, if it had been practicable to have made some propositions for amendments the first business we entered upon; it would stifle the voice of complaint, and make friends of many who doubted its [the Constitution's] merits.[26]

Madison tried again in late July to secure action, but the matter was tabled. Finally, after more delay, the House debated the matter and in August sent to the Senate seventeen amendments. It was not until early in September, however, that these were debated by the Senate. It cut the number down to twelve, which it sent back to the House for approval. Upon being approved by the House in September 1789, these amendments were then submitted to the states for adoption. It was not until December 15, 1791, that ten of the amendments were ratified by the required number of states and became that part of the Constitution we know as the Bill of Rights.

While those ten amendments contain written guarantees of personal freedom and individual justice, it is the decisions of the United States Supreme Court these past two hundred years that have given the amendments life. These decisions not only discuss and decide the issues of freedom and justice for the individuals involved but are the basis for the kind of freedom and justice all Americans are guaranteed and enjoy.

One of the reasons that the Constitution is what the Supreme Court says it is, is that history provides little assistance in determining what the various provisions mean, especially those in the Bill of Rights. As to some of the guarantees, one can only speculate as to what the drafters really meant by the language actually used. Furthermore, the

Court has the last word on the meaning of the Constitution—subject, of course, to the right of the people to amend it.

As Chief Justice Charles Evans Hughes said when he was governor of New York: "We are under a Constitution, but the Constitution is what the judges say it is, and the judiciary is the safeguard of our liberty and of our property under the Constitution."[27]

II.
GUARDIANS OF OUR RIGHTS

"If they [the proposed amendments] are incorporated into the Constitution, independent tribunals of justice will consider themselves in a peculiar manner the guardians of those rights; they will be an impenetrable bulwark against every assumption of power in the Legislative or Executive; they will be naturally led to resist every encroachment upon rights expressly stipulated for in the Constitution by the declaration of rights."

James Madison, 1 *Annals of Congress* 439 (1789)

There are fifty-two separate judicial systems in our country. One is created by the Constitution; that's the federal system. Another has been established by Congress for processing of crimes committed by military personnel. The other fifty are created by individual state constitutions and will hereinafter be referred to as state systems.

These systems are staffed by judges, bailiffs, court clerks, court reporters, and other support personnel. The key to the successful operation of a judicial system, however, are the judges, and tens of thousands of men and women have served our country well as such.

Paraphrasing a statement of what makes a good judge, one might say: "'First, he [or she] must be honest. Second, he [or she] must possess a reasonable amount of industry. Third, he [or she] must have courage. Fourth, he [or she] must be a gentleman [or a lady]. And then, if he [or she] has some knowledge of law, it will help.'"[1]

While all judges are important factors in the administration of justice and the protection of freedom, it is in the trial courts where most people experience the judicial system in action. It would take many volumes to list the names of all those who have performed outstanding service in these courts. Such a list would, however, include Florence E. Allen of Ohio, Samuel S. Leibowitz of New York, and Isaac Charles Parker of the territory of Arkansas. And then there was Justice of the

Peace Roy Bean, who was the "law west of the Pecos" in the late 1800s.
Judge Bean owned the Jersey Lily Saloon in Langtry, Texas, where he
held court, sometimes in the saloon and sometimes outside on the
veranda. His antics became so legendary that a song was written about
him, "The Song of Roy Bean."

It was said of him that "all the law he knew was a crude system of
what he thought was equity, and [he] let it go at that."[2] And although
many tales have been told about him, "We may smile at his decisions
and question some of his actions, . . . [nevertheless] he succeeded in
winning respect for his home-spun justice where more refined methods
might have failed."[3]

The Federal Judicial System

In establishing the federal judicial system, Article III of the Constitution specifically creates a Supreme Court but leaves to Congress the
establishment of inferior courts. Acting under this authority, Congress
has created thirteen federal circuit courts of appeals and ninety-four
district courts. It has also established courts for special purposes, such
as the Tax Court, Claims Court, Court of International Trade, Bank-
ruptcy Court and, as noted, courts for the military.[4]

Section 2 of Article III spells out the kind of cases over which the
federal system has jurisdiction. Generally speaking, federal courts deal
with cases "arising under this Constitution, the laws of the United
States, and treaties made, or which shall be made, under their authority. . . ." This means that cases involving constitutional rights and cases
involving laws made by Congress may be brought in a federal court.

The United States District Courts

Federal cases start in a district court, except for the person who is
charged with violating a federal criminal law. That person will first appear before a federal magistrate and be given an opportunity to enter
a plea to the charge. Unless the person charged pleads guilty, he or she
will usually be "bound over" for trial in the district court.

The careers of only a few district judges have had as auspicious a
beginning as that of Judge Parker, who took office May 2, 1875, in Fort
Smith, Arkansas. When he opened court eight days after assuming the
bench, "eighteen persons came before him charged with murder and
fifteen were convicted. Eight of these he sentenced to die on the gallows

on September 3."[5] Six of the defendants were actually hanged, one was shot trying to escape, and one had his sentence commuted to life imprisonment.

In the federal system, judges must preside over both civil and criminal cases, sometimes with and sometimes without a jury. In discussing presiding in a criminal case, Judge Leibowitz, a New York state judge, summed up the judge's responsibility as follows:

> You sit there on the bench and they parade before you; the vicious, the frightened juvenile, the degenerate, the cold-blooded criminal, the moral cripple, the spiritual consumptive. You have the frightening power of life and death over these men and women. What is justice in this case? You ask yourself that a dozen times each week. Which door will you open to this defendant?[6]

It is not only in criminal cases, however, that judges face great challenges. As guardians of the rights of Americans, they stand between us and our government. And although government infringement upon those rights is ever-present, there are times when the threat is greater than usual. It is then that judges with courage are especially needed. One such time occurred during World War I when many people, especially Germans or German sympathizers, were being wrongfully prosecuted for allegedly subversive activities. During this critical period of our history, Judge Charles F. Amidon, of the Federal District Court of North Dakota, emerged as one of the strong defenders of the First Amendment. While many judges were upholding government restriction of free speech, Judge Amidon was characterized as one of "a few judges . . . [who] swam against the tide."[7]

One of the great champions of civil liberties, Zechariah Chafee, wrote Judge Amidon that

> not many men kept their heads cool during the war, and most of those had all they could do to accomplish that; but you and a few others did much more — you had the courage to try to get the crowd to keep cool as well. . . . Unlike the pacifists, you knew we had to beat Germany, but never forgot that the freedom we won in 1776 must not be melted down in the process.[8]

Another time when a strong judicial response was required was during the struggle for civil rights by blacks during the 1950s, 60s and 70s. The federal courts in Alabama and the other Southern states became legal battlegrounds for the establishment of the rights of all citizens regardless of color. All other avenues normally open for vindication of civil rights, such as legislatures and state courts, offered little help.

Although all judges are sworn to uphold the Constitution of the United States, Judge Frank Johnson of Alabama Federal District Court surely gave that oath real meaning.

> Johnson's ability and willingness to exert authority, his passionate dedication to the supremacy of the law and his activist inclinations plunged him headlong into sensitive constitutional controversies and embroiled the entire state in an emotional turmoil over questions of human and civil rights. Johnson applied his concepts to some of the toughest racial problems in the nation's history. He played an aggressive role in dealing with every human rights controversy that came under his jurisdiction. In the process he broke new constitutional ground in requiring a state to take affirmative action to bring the lives of all its citizens up to minimum constitutional standards.[9]

In 1955 Judges Johnson and Richard Rives held that segregation on buses in the city of Montgomery was unconstitutional, and subsequently Judge Johnson struck down segregation in Montgomery's libraries and museums. When the city decided to close its parks and swimming pools to everyone, he issued an order to city officials to abandon its policy of denying blacks use of city facilities.

The Judicial Power

*"The judicial power shall extend to all cases . . . arising under this Constitution . . ."**

Governments, both federal and state, enact laws, rules and regulations which specifically regulate, prohibit or punish the exercise of constitutional rights. For example, there are many laws that regulate the time, place and manner of parading, distributing literature, or picketing, all of which are forms of speech and protected by the First Amendment. If a person believes that such a law violates the right to picket or demonstrate freely, that person may bring an action in a federal court (state courts too) to have the law declared unconstitutional.

This was the situation in *United States v. Grace.*[10] About noon on

*Article III, Section 2 (1), United States Constitution.

March 17, 1980, Mary Grace went to the sidewalk in front of the Supreme Court Building in Washington, D.C. She carried a four-foot sign upon which she had printed the text of the First Amendment. Shortly after she arrived on the sidewalk, Mary was approached by a police officer who told her that it was against the law to display such a sign on this sidewalk and that if she did not move to the other side of the street, she would be arrested. The officer told her that a federal law made it unlawful "to parade, stand, or move in procession or assemblages in the Supreme Court Building or grounds," or "to display therein any flag, banner or device designed or adapted to bring into public notice any party, organization, or movement."

Mary left the area and shortly thereafter filed an action in the federal district court against the United States seeking a declaration that the law was unconstitutional under the First Amendment.

Mary's case eventually reached the Supreme Court. The justices agreed that this law was unconstitutional as applied to her because she was exercising her right to free speech on a public sidewalk, a place traditionally open and available for making speeches. Commenting upon the use of streets for the purpose of making a speech, the Court pointed out that "it is also true that 'public places' historically associated with the free exercise of expressive activities, such as streets, sidewalks, and parks, are considered, without more, to be 'public forums.'"[11]

The United States Circuit Courts of Appeals

When either a civil or criminal case has been tried in the district court, and an appeal is taken, that appeal most often will be to the federal circuit court of appeals of the circuit in which the district court is located. Only in a few instances can the circuit court be bypassed and an appeal be taken directly to the Supreme Court.

Although there are several judges in each circuit, a case on appeal will most often be heard by a panel consisting of three judges. The issues on appeal are questions of law. A question of law would be: Did the district judge make any erroneous rulings during the trial, such as in the selection of the jury or on the admission of evidence? Or did the judge wrongfully instruct the jury? Is the law or court procedure a violation of any constitutional right?

If there had been a trial, the questions of fact would have been decided by a jury or by the judge sitting without a jury. As a general rule, but not always, the facts found at the trial are not contestable on appeal.

Concerning the role of an appellate court, Judge Joseph Ulman has written that "an appellate court does not substitute its opinion upon every phase of an appealed case for that of the original tribunal, but limits itself to a review of the questions of law decided by the trial judge."[12] And further, "appellate courts, then, do not reverse decisions simply because they disagree with them. Reversal must proceed from error of law and such error must be substantial."[13]

The case of *Creamer v. Porter*,[14] is an example of the federal appellate process in action. In this case Robert N. Creamer claimed that his constitutional rights had been violated by members of the local police department when they searched his store. He brought an action against the officers in the federal district court. As a person suing to vindicate his constitutional rights, he was entitled to ask for damages for such violation, and/or for different orders from the court, such as an order prohibiting the perpetrator from doing the same thing again, or for an order just declaring his constitutional rights.

Creamer's case arose when a man walking by the window of Creamer's furniture store noticed a television set that had been stolen from his residence. The man went into the store where he saw a second set that was also his. He left the store and contacted the local police department. Officer Lewis Porter, after securing a search warrant, proceeded to search the store, together with Officer J.L. Sampson. Creamer, however, was not present at the time.

After finding the two televisions and placing them near the front door, Officers Porter and Sampson continued to search the premises, including Creamer's office, where they opened file drawers, the safe, and a desk. In all, the officers took twenty-nine items, even though the search warrant authorized them to seize only the two sets.

When Creamer learned that his store had been searched and that a number of items had been taken, he brought the action against Porter and Sampson for violating his Fourth Amendment right to be free of unreasonable searches and seizures. He claimed that the officers had no authority to make a general search of the store nor to take anything more than the two television sets. The jury agreed and awarded him $7,000 in damages.

The officers appealed to the court of appeals. In upholding the jury's award of damages to Creamer, the court wrote:

> A general, exploratory search through personal belonging is the precise evil sought to be eliminated by the Fourth Amendment's requirement that things to be seized and places to be searched be

described with particularity. Standing alone, the clear language of the Fourth Amendment imparts this message. Under no circumstances could the officers justify their intrusion into an area such as a desk drawer, a filing cabinet, or a night stand to search for a television set. There was no conceivable justification for the officers to continue the search after the items described in the warrant had been seized. Absolutely no regard was shown for Mr. Creamer's privacy.[15]

Many eminent individuals have served on the circuit courts of appeals. And some of those, after distinguishing themselves on that court, were appointed to the Supreme Court. The latter include William Howard Taft, Fred M. Vinson, and Warren Burger—who served as Chief Justice—and Wiley B. Rutledge, John M. Harlan, and Potter Stewart. Further, of the nine justices now on the court, six were formerly court of appeals judges—Harry A. Blackmun, Thurgood Marshall, John P. Stevens, Antonin Scalia, Anthony M. Kennedy, and David H. Souter.

Judge Allen, who was the first woman to be elected to a state supreme court, was also the first woman appointed to the court of appeals when she was nominated by President Franklin D. Roosevelt in 1934. At the time of the acceptance of her portrait for the court of appeals, Judge Thomas F. McAllister, speaking for the court, said:

> The heart and mind of Florence Allen will flame for generations as a beacon for thousands of young women who will take their rightful places in government, in the practice of the law, and in judicial service—and lawyers and judges yet unborn will read the words she has written, in the endless, ever-old and ever-new quest for justice.[16]

Not only did Judge Allen serve with great distinction on the bench, she was an active participant in the women's suffrage movement, a frequent lecturer, and an author. In a book entitled *This Constitution of Ours* she wrote:

> Liberty cannot be written ready made into a character. It must be written into our hearts, and thus sent on by us as a living force to the next generation. Here in America we do have great and living traditions. But only by [en]graving them as articles of faith on the hearts of the people can they be realized.[17]

The United States Supreme Court

A party who is not satisfied with the decision of the court of appeals may petition the Supreme Court to hear the case. Again, the issues to be decided are questions of law.

Although Article III of the Constitution creates a Supreme Court, it does not specify the makeup of that Court. By the Judiciary Act of 1789 Congress set the number of justices at six, including the Chief Justice. The number was changed to nine in 1869.

In 1937 President Roosevelt proposed a plan that would have allowed him to appoint an additional justice for each justice who had served on the Court for at least ten years and who was 70 years of age. At this time the adoption of the plan would have added six new justices. The president proposed this rearrangement of the justices in hopes that an expanded Court would look more favorably upon his New Deal legislation aimed at solving the economic crisis in the country. The plan met with stiff opposition in and out of Congress and was never adopted.

President Washington's original appointments to the Supreme Court included three men who had been delegates to the Constitutional Convention and had signed the Constitution — John Blair, John Rutledge, and James Wilson, He also appointed John Jay as Chief Justice, James Iredell, and William Cushing.

Although Chief Justice Jay had had a very distinguished career as a member of the Continental Congress, as Minister to Spain and as a member of the Peace Commission, he was unhappy serving on the Court. He disliked riding circuit, as the justices were required to do at that time, and did not think that being a member of the Court carried much weight or was held in much esteem by the public. He resigned in 1795 to become governor of New York.

The task of defining the role of the Court in our constitutional system fell to John Marshall who was appointed Chief Justice by President John Adams in 1801. Marshall, who served until 1835, was one of the leading citizens of the country — an army officer, leader of the Bar of Virginia, diplomat, statesman and public servant. He was a strong supporter of the Constitution and a friend of Washington and Madison.

Henry J. Abraham has written of Chief Justice Marshall:

> It is simply beyond dispute that he, more than any other individual in the history of the Court, determined the character of America's federal constitutional system. It was Marshall who raised the Court

from its lowly if not discredited position to a level of equality with the Executive and the Legislative branches—perhaps even to one of dominance during the heyday of his Chief Justiceship.[18]

One of the most important constitutional principles proclaimed by the Supreme Court is the principle of judicial review of actions of the other two branches of government—the executive and the legislative. This principle, which was announced by the Marshall Court in 1803, will be discussed in full later.

While the Marshall Court firmly established the role of the Supreme Court in our governmental system, at no time has the Court given more judicial protection to freedom, justice and equality than did the Court under the leadership of Chief Justice Earl Warren.

Chief Justice Warren was appointed to the Court in 1953 by President Dwight Eisenhower and served until 1969. In a memorial to the Chief Justice, Justice William J. Brennan said of him, "His concern with fairness was also the hallmark of his jurisprudence. People were his concern, especially ordinary people—the disadvantaged, the downtrodden, the poor, the friendless."[19]

Although deeply committed to the principles of the First Amendment, Warren found himself on the losing side of many cases during the 1950s. This was a period in our history when those holding socialist or communist views concerning government were prosecuted and punished even though they asserted that the right to hold and express such views were protected by the First Amendment. By the early 1960s, however, the makeup of the Court had changed to the extent that there were then at least four other justices who shared Warren's view of the meaning of the Bill of Rights. And from that time on until Warren's retirement in 1969, the guarantees of just treatment for those accused of crime, freedom for unpopular speech, the right to join associations that were shunned, freedom to practice one's faith, and freedom from discrimination because of one's race became realities and not just ethical principles on paper.

Chief Justice Warren's views of the Bill of Rights are summed up in his *A Republic, If You Can Keep It.*

THE FOUNDATION for "Life, Liberty and the Pursuit of Happiness" resides in the Bill of Rights. Were it not for the freedoms of speech, of the press, of religion, of association, of the right to petition the government, of the right of the accused to a public jury trial, to counsel and to be confronted by any witnesses against him, as well as freedom from unreasonable searches and seizures, our Constitution could, indeed, be a sterile document.[20]

Supreme Court justices, and most other federal judges, are appointed by the president for life, subject to good behavior, thus assuring an independent judiciary. As civil officers of the United States, however, they are subject to impeachment under Article II, Section 4, of the Constitution.

One hundred four men and one woman have served as Supreme Court justices since 1789. Most have served with distinction. Some, however, have stood rock solid as the "impenetrable bulwarks" against infringement upon our freedoms, as envisioned by Madison. These include Oliver Wendell Holmes, Jr., Louis D. Brandeis, Benjamin N. Cardozo, Hugo L. Black, William O. Douglas, Earl Warren, William J. Brennan, Thurgood Marshall, and Harry Blackmun. No justice who ever served on the Court, however, was more dedicated to protection of First Amendment freedoms than Justice Black, who carried a copy of the Constitution with him. For him, the First Amendment contained immutable principles—absolute principles. He believed that because the Amendment reads "Congress [i.e., the government] shall make no law...," that meant no law. He wrote:

> But governmental suppression of causes and beliefs seems to me to be the very antithesis of what our Constitution stands for. The choice expressed in the First Amendment in favor of free expression was made against a turbulent background by men such as Jefferson, Madison, and Mason—men who believed that loyalty to the provisions of this Amendment was the best way to assure a long life for this new nation and its Government.[21]

Article III provides that the jurisdiction of the Supreme Court will generally be appellate only. The only cases that can be started in the Court are "cases affecting ambassadors, other public ministers and consuls, and those in which a State shall be a party."

The Court is not required to hear every case filed with it. Congress has enacted statutes which require that certain cases be heard on appeal, but gives the justices discretion with regard to most other cases.

Although there are thousands of cases filed in the Supreme Court each year, it actually hears, decides, and issues opinions in somewhat fewer than two hundred. In the exercise of its discretion as to which cases to hear, only those cases in which at least four justices agree an important constitutional or legal issue is involved are placed on the calendar.

Once a determination has been made that a case is to be heard, lawyers representing each side are required to file written briefs.

Amicus curiae (friend of the court) briefs are sometimes accepted from other parties having an interest in the outcome of the litigation.

The case will almost always be argued before all members of the Court. Leon Jaworski, discussing what it is like for a lawyer to appear before the justices, wrote:

> The justices do not sit on ceremony. They tear into the arguments. They may wish to bring out the strength of your point. Sometimes they do so solely for the purpose of forcing you to proceed to the heart of your case, even though you may be trying to lay the ground-work for another issue. There are nine justices . . . all free to ask any questions, whenever they wish.[22]

Jaworski goes on to point out that he was "interrupted by the justices a total of 115 times in an hour," and that "the questions came so fast that a notebook I had prepared, containing my handwritten notes, transcripts, and sources, was never opened. Some were piercing, in one or two instances disquieting, but no more for me than for Jim St. Clair [the opposing attorney]."[23]

After oral arguments the justices meet and reach a decision, and one justice is assigned to write an opinion giving the decision and explaining the Court's reasoning. Often one or more of the justices do not agree with the result reached, or if they agree with the result, they may not agree with the Court's reasoning for reaching that result. If a justice agrees with the decision but not with the reasoning, he or she may write a concurring opinion. Frequently one or more of the justices will disagree with both the result and the reasoning, and will write an opinion dissenting from both.

The case of *New York Times Co. v. United States,*[24] illustrates how a majority may reach a decision but not agree on the reasoning for reaching the result. This case is commonly referred to as the Pentagon Papers Case because the *New York Times* and the *Washington Post* had printed parts of a classified Pentagon study entitled *History of U.S. Decision-Making Process on Viet Nam Policy.*

As soon as the material was published, the government went to court requesting court orders to prevent further publication, claiming that dissemination of this classified material would be harmful to the interests of the United States. District Judge Murray I. Gurfein in New York refused to restrain the *New York Times* permanently from further publication, but he was reversed by the court of appeals. In Washington, D.C., Judge Gerhard A. Gessel denied an injunction against the *Washington Post* on the ground that such an order was a prior restraint on freedom of the press and therefore unconstitutional under the First Amendment.

The Supreme Court agreed with judges Gurfein and Gessel that to prohibit the press from publishing this material was an infringement upon freedom of the press. This case spawned one opinion which contains just the Court's decision—six concurring and three dissenting opinions.

The justices reach unanimous decisions in only a few cases each year. This is particularly true in cases involving constitutional rights because of deep philosophical differences among the justices as to the meaning of the Bill of Rights, and the role of the judiciary in their implementation. One must keep in mind that the justices are nine individuals whose backgrounds, education, religious beliefs, life experiences, and ideology are very different.

The task of the Court is to interpret the language of the Constitution in light of history and precedent, taking into consideration the changes in our society since the beginning of the country in 1787.

An unusual case that brought forth a unanimous decision in both the reasoning and the result is a case involving former President Richard M. Nixon.[25]

During the early part of 1974 a grand jury in the District of Columbia conducted an investigation into events following a break-in at the Democratic party's headquarters in a building known as Watergate. As a result of this investigation, seven individuals on President Nixon's staff were indicted for various offenses, including conspiracy to defraud the United States and to obstruct justice. Shortly thereafter, in preparation for trial, Leon Jaworski, the special prosecutor, requested the district court to issue a subpoena to President Nixon ordering him to produce "certain tapes, memoranda, papers, transcripts, or other writings relating to certain precisely identified meetings between the President and others."

The president responded, through his counsel, James St. Clair, that as president of the United States he had an absolute privilege not to reveal "confidential conversations between a President and his close advisors . . . [and that to do so] would be inconsistent with the public interest. . . ." District Court Judge John J. Sirica disagreed and ordered the president to deliver the material requested. The president appealed to the court of appeals. However, before that court could hear the case, the special prosecutor petitioned the Supreme Court to accept the case immediately, arguing that the case was of great importance and a prompt final adjudication was essential. The justices agreed, heard the case, and unanimously upheld Judge Sirica. They ordered the president to deliver the materials to the special prosecutor.

While the justices recognized that a president may, under some circumstances, have a privilege not to disclose confidential communications between high government officials and those who advise the president, it was not an absolute privilege. The Court wrote:

> In this case we must weigh the importance of the general privilege of confidentiality of Presidential communications in performance of the President's responsibilities against the inroads of such a privilege on the fair administration of criminal justice.[26]

The Supreme Law of the Land

"This Constitution ... shall be the supreme law of the land..."

Decisions of the Supreme Court on constitutional and federal legal issues are binding in all of the United States. The case of *Gideon v. Wainwright*[27] illustrates this principle.

Clarence Earl Gideon had been in and out of prison much of his adult life. He was not a man of violence, but because of a combination of hard times, gambling, drinking, domestic, and health problems, he often turned to petty thievery.

In June 1961 Gideon was arrested and charged with having broken into a poolroom, allegedly to steal something. When his case was called for trial, Gideon told the judge that he did not have a lawyer and requested the judge to appoint one for him. The following colloquy then took place:

> The Court: Mr. Gideon, I am sorry, but I cannot appoint Counsel to represent you in this case. Under the laws of the State of Florida, the only time the Court can appoint Counsel to represent a Defendant is when that person is charged with a capital offense. I am sorry, but I will have to deny your request to appoint Counsel to defend you in this case.
> The Defendant: The United States Supreme Court says I am entitled to be represented by Counsel.[28]

He was, of course, wrong. The Court in 1942 had held just exactly the opposite—that the Sixth Amendment's right to counsel was not

*Article VI, Section 2, United States Constitution.

applicable to the states and that there was no constitutional violation of due process in trying a person for a crime who does not have a lawyer to represent him.

Gideon, acting as his own lawyer and defending himself as best he could, was convicted and sentenced to five years in prison.

While in prison, Gideon attempted to secure a reversal of his conviction by appealing to the Florida Supreme Court, but to no avail. He then sent a penciled, handwritten petition to the U.S. Supreme Court arguing that his conviction violated due process because he did not have the assistance of counsel at his trial.

The Court accepted the petition and appointed attorney Abe Fortas to represent him. Fortas, some years later, was appointed a justice of the Court.

The issue squarely presented by Gideon's petition was whether the Sixth Amendment's requirement that the accused have assistance of counsel required the state of Florida to appoint one for him.

Although all of the justices agreed that Gideon was entitled to counsel at his trial, and that therefore his conviction must be reversed, they did not all agree on the reasoning. The majority opinion states:

> The right of one charged with crime to counsel may not be deemed fundamental and essential to fair trials in some countries, but it is in ours. From the very beginning, our state and national constitutions and laws have laid great emphasis on procedural and substantive safeguards designed to assure fair trials before imparital tribunals in which every defendant stands equal before the law. This noble ideal cannot be realized if the poor man charged with crime has to face his accusers without a lawyer to assist him.[29]

Now, of course, we accept the decision in *Gideon* without reservation, and no matter whether a defendant is charged with a federal or state crime, he or she is entitled to appointment of counsel if he or she cannot afford to hire one. This is now the law of the land.

As a result of the reversal of Gideon's conviction, the Florida Supreme Court ordered a new trial. This time Gideon had a lawyer, and the jury found him not guilty.

Judicial Review

*"A law repugnant to the constitution is void."**

One of the unique features of our judicial systems is that a court may review the actions of the executive and legislative branches of either the federal or state governments. In the landmark case of *Marbury v. Madison,*[30] the Court held that the judiciary had the power to review actions of the other branches of the government when those actions are challenged as being in violation of the Constitution.

Marbury arose when Federalist President John Adams, just before his term ended, made a number of last-minute judicial appointments. Jefferson, who had been elected to succeed Adams, and his supporters, not being Federalists, did not take kindly to these appointments, and the commissions therefore were not delivered to the appointees.

William Marbury's appointment as justice of the peace for the District of Columbia was one of these late selections. The commissions for the appointments had been signed by President Adams and sealed by John Marshall, then secretary of state, but had not been delivered when President Jefferson took office March 4, 1801.

Marbury, together with several others who had not received their commissions, petitioned the Supreme Court for an order, called a writ of mandamus, requiring Jefferson's secretary of state, James Madison, to deliver the commissions to them. The petitioners' lawyer, Charles Lee, chose to start the proceedings in the Supreme Court because the Judiciary Act of 1789 authorized that Court "to issue writs of mandamus in cases warranted by the principles and usages of law, to any courts appointed, or persons holding office, under the authority of the United States."

If Lee's reading of the Judiciary Act was correct, then that act granted power directly to the Supreme Court to issue writs in any and all cases brought to that Court. This put the act in direct conflict with Article III, Section 2, of the Constitution, noted above, which limits the kinds of cases which the Supreme Court can hear. *Marbury,* therefore, gave the Court the opportunity to define the power of the judiciary in relation to the powers of Congress. The justices, through the strong leadership of Chief Justice Marshall, seized that opportunity.

The Chief Justice framed the questions to be answered as follows: "In the order which the court has viewed this subject, the following questions have been considered and decided: 1st. Has the applicant a

*Marbury v. Madison, 1 Cranch 137, 180 (1803).

right to the commission he demands? 2d. If he has a right, and that right has been violated, do the laws of his country afford him a remedy? 3d. If they do afford him a remedy, is it a *mandamus* issuing from this court."[31]

Affirmative answers were given to the first and second questions. Even though the commissions had not been delivered, they had been signed by President Adams and certified by the secretary of state. That made them valid, and the petitioners were entitled to them. Insofar as whether there was a judicial method of securing the commissions, the Court stated that "the very essence of civil liberty certainly consists in the right of every individual to claim the protection of the laws, whenever he receives an injury. One of the first duties of government is to afford that protection." Furthermore, "the government of the United States has been emphatically termed a government of laws, and not of men. It will certainly cease to deserve this high appellation, if the laws furnish no remedy for the violation of a vested legal right."[32]

After a lengthy discussion of writs of mandamus, Justice Marshall concluded that "this, then is a plain case for a *mandamus* . . . and it only remains to be inquired, whether it can issue from this court?"

The last question is what *Marbury* is all about. If the Judiciary Act conflicts with Article III of the Constitution, to whom falls the authority to decide whether that conflict makes the act unconstitutional? A unanimous Court held that it was the judiciary that had that power.

> It is, emphatically, the province and duty of the judicial depart-
> ment to say what the law is. Those who apply the rule to particular
> cases, must of necessity expound and interpret that rule. . . . So, if
> a law be in opposition to the constitution; if both the law and the
> constitution apply to a particular case, so that the court must either
> decide that case, comformable to the law, disregarding the constitu-
> tion; or conformable to the constitution, disregarding the law; that
> court must determine which of these conflicting rules governs the
> case: this is the very essence of judicial duty. If then, the courts are
> to regard the constitution, and the constitution is superior to any or-
> dinary act of the legislature, the constitution, and not such ordinary
> act, must govern the case to which both apply.[33]

The *Marbury* decision has brought forth much criticism and scholarly comment ever since it was handed down in 1803. Never-theless, review by courts of the acts of the legislative and executive branches of government is today firmly established in both federal and state judicial systems.

Stare Decisis Demands Respect

"Nonetheless, the doctrine of stare decisis, ... demands respect in a society governed by the rule of law."

Stare decisis means "to stand by things decided." Cases previously decided become precedents to be used by judges in later cases. When the Supreme Court decides a case involving constitutional questions, its decision becomes a binding precedent on all other courts, federal and state.

Commenting on the doctrine of *stare decisis,* the Court has declared:

> Very weighty considerations underlie the principle that courts should not lightly overrule past decisions. Among these are the desirability that the law furnish a clear guide for the conduct of individuals, to enable them to plan their affairs with assurance against untoward surprise; the importance of furthering fair and expeditious adjudication by eliminating the need to relitigate every relevant proposition in every case; and the necessity of maintaining public faith in the judiciary as a source of impersonal and reasoned judgments.[34]

But even though "very weighty considerations underlie the principle that courts should not lightly overrule past decisions," that does not mean that they do not and should not do so. When considering *Gideon,* the Court was confronted with the case of *Betts v. Brady*[35] in which, twenty-one years earlier, it had held that the Sixth Amendment's requirement of right to counsel did not apply in state criminal cases. Justice Black, writing for the *Gideon* majority, held that *Betts* had been wrongfully decided and should be overruled.

The State Judicial Systems

Each state by virtue of its own constitution has its own judicial system. Although these systems create a court structure similar to the federal system, the number of tiers of courts and their names are not the same. Generally each state will have one or more trial courts where cases can be started. These are sometimes called district courts or superior courts. In New York State this trial court is named the Supreme Court.

Akron v. Akron Center for Reprod. Health, 462 U.S. 416, 419–420 (1983).

Trial judges, both state and federal, are the unsung heroes of our judicial systems. Louis Nizer, a well-known trial attorney, has written "how little the public understands that conscientious judges work evenings and weekends studying voluminous briefs and trying desperately to stay afloat on the ever-increasing flood of litigations which inundate them."[36] And Judge Leibowitz has said of his work on the Kings County Court of New York:

> My present office is by no means an easy one—not when you are dealing with the lives and liberties of your fellow men and women. It is no simple thing to pronounce those words that doom a human being to a long prison term or to the death chair. Even the run-of-mill case fascinates me for the simple reason that all cases, both big and small, are made up of human beings.[37]

Some states have an intermediate appellate court and a final court of appeal. Some states call this final appellate court the supreme court, while others, such as New York, designate it the court of appeals.

State courts deal with state constitutional and legal issues, and crimes committed in violation of state law. These include cases arising under the state constitution and cases involving automobile accidents, divorces, adoption, and contracts, to name just a few.

State courts may also process cases involving federal constitutional and legal issues, but not violations of federal criminal laws. For example, the storeowner whose store had been subjected to an unreasonable search, as noted above, could have brought the action against the officers in a state court if he had chosen to do so.

In a tribute to Illinois Supreme Court Chief Justice Walter V. Schaefer, Supreme Court Justice Brennan noted, "I suppose that the state courts of all levels must annually hand down millions of decisions that do not rest on federal law, yet determine vital issues of life, liberty and property of countless citizens of our nation."[38] Justice Schaefer was one of those judges who were part of that "ever-old and ever-new quest for justice." "I take great pride," Justice Brennan wrote of Justice Schaefer, "that every list of the great judges of our time has his name near the top."

Roger J. Traynor was also one of those state judges who was at the forefront of the progress made in civil rights during the past fifty years. In a memorial to him he was described as the "Ablest Judge of His Generation," "A Judicial Giant," and "Master of Judicial Wisdom."[39]

Even before the Supreme Court had fully developed First Amendment jurisprudence, Justice Traynor and the California Supreme Court left no doubt where they stood on the issue in a case involving the use of a junior high school auditorium for a series of meetings about the Bill of Rights. Before the school district would grant permission to the Civil Liberties Committee (CLC) for the auditorium's use, it demanded that they subscribe to an oath, pledging that they did "not advocate . . . [nor were they] affiliated with any organization which advocates or has as its object . . . the overthrow of the present Government of the United States or of any State by force or violence, or other unlawful means."[40]

The CLC, believing that the oath requirement was a violation of the First Amendment, brought an action against the school district seeking a court order granting them permission to use the auditorium. They argued that the Constitution guaranteed them the right to believe in whatever political philosophy they wanted to, even one that included the belief that the government should be overthrown, and that their right to associate together for the furtherance of these views was also protected.

The California Supreme Court, in an opinion written by Justice Traynor, agreed with the Committee and granted the order. The court acknowledged that a school district does not have to make school buildings available to the public, but that if it does, "it cannot arbitrarily prevent any members of the public from holding such meetings."

> The convictions or affiliations of one who requests the use of a school building as a forum is of no more concern to the school administrators than to a superintendent of parks or streets if the forum is the green or the market place. The ancient right to free speech in public parks and streets cannot be made conditional upon the permission of a public official, if that permission is used as an "instrument of arbitrary suppression of free expression."[41]

Once a case has proceeded through the state system, including the state's highest court of appeal, a petition may be filed with the U.S. Supreme Court only if the case involves *federal* constitutional or legal issues. As noted above, however, even if the case involves a federal question, the justices have wide discretion in choosing the cases they will hear. If the case deals only with state constitutional and legal issues, the decision of the state's highest court of appeal is final.

As a general rule, cases cannot be transferred between the federal and state judicial systems. Once a case is started in one of the systems, it must proceed through that system to final conclusion, except that, as noted above, the U.S. Supreme Court is the court of last resort on federal constitutional and legal issues.

The Constitution provides one exception to the general rule. Article III gives the federal courts the power to hear cases between citizens of different states. If a citizen of Minnesota starts a case in a Minnesota court against a citizen of North Dakota, the North Dakotan may have the case transferred to the federal district court in Minnesota if he or she chooses to do so.

As noted at the beginning of this chapter, it is to our judicial systems and ultimately to the Supreme Court that we look for protection of our constitutional rights. Justice Potter Stewart, speaking to members of the press, eloquently described the place judges play as guardians of our rights:

> Where, ladies and gentlemen, do you think these great constitutional rights that you were so vehemently asserting, and in which you were so conspicuously wallowing yesterday, where do you think they come from? The stork didn't bring them. These came from the judges of this country, from the villains here sitting at the table. That's where they came from. They came because the courts of this country at some time or place when some other agency of government was trying to push the press around or, indeed, may be trying to do you in, it's the courts that protected you. And that's where all these constitutional rights came from.[42]

III.
THE BILL OF RIGHTS
AND THE STATES

"The Constitution was ordained and established by the people of the United States for themselves, for their own government, and not for the government of the individual states. Each State established a constitution for itself, and in that constitution provided such limitations and restrictions on the powers of its particular government as its judgment dictated."

Barron v. Mayor and City Council of Baltimore, 32 U.S. 243, 247 (1833)

The above quotation is from a case in which the owners of a wharf in Baltimore harbor brought suit against the city for damages done by a city construction project. The wharf, which had been very profitable because of deep water surrounding it, became useless when the city reconstructed grades and paved the streets. By so doing, runoff water from the surrounding hills was diverted into the harbor near the wharf. This runoff carried considerable soil and sand, and caused the depth of the water around the wharf to be gradually reduced until finally ships could no longer tie up there.

The owners, John Barron and John Craig, claimed that by causing this damage the city had taken their property for public use and that they were therefore entitled to compensation under the Fifth Amendment, which provides that "private property [not] be taken for public use, without just compensation. . . ." Barron and Craig argued that "this amendment being in favor of the liberty of the citizen, ought to be so construed as to restrain the legislative power of a state, as well as that of the United States."[1]

Because a city is part of state government, this case presented the justices with the question of whether the Fifth Amendment (and all the other amendments in the Bill of Rights) were restrictions upon states as well as the federal government. The Court concluded that neither the Fifth Amendment nor any other part of the Bill of Rights applied to actions of state governments.

After reviewing the history of the Constitutional Convention and the ratification of the Constitution, Chief Justice Marshall wrote for the Court:

> We are of the opinion, that the provision in the fifth amendment to the constitution declaring that private property shall not be taken for public use, without just compensation, is intended solely as a limitation on the exercise of power by the government of the United States, and is not applicable to the legislation of the states.

The effect of this decision was to leave state governments free to establish a religion, restrict the press, deny jury trials, punish free speech, and take private property without just compensation, etc., unless prohibited from doing so by their own constitutions. This situation continued into the twentieth century.

Following the adoption of the Fourteenth Amendment in 1868 lawyers began to argue that that amendment required the states also to comply with the Bill of Rights. The Fourteenth Amendment provides:

> No State shall make or enforce any law which shall abridge the privileges or immunities of citizens of the United States; nor shall any State deprive any person of life, liberty, or property, without due process of law; nor deny to any person within its jurisdiction the equal protection of the laws.

Whether the Fourteenth Amendment was intended to make the Bill of Rights applicable to state actions has been hotly debated on and off the Court, almost from the time of its adoption, and that debate continues today.

Justice Black, who served as a justice from 1937 to 1971, contended that history supported the view that the Fourteenth Amendment was intended to be a "shorthand" method of requiring all state governments to abide by the Bill of Rights in the same manner that the federal government was always required to do. Justice John M. Harlan, a member of the Court during the last fifteen years of Justice Black's term, studiously disagreed with him. Even though Justice Harlan was reading the same history, he could find nothing therein to support Justice Black's position.

Long before justices Black and Harlan became justices, the Court had begun to say something about this question. Commencing in 1897 it began to require states to abide by some provisions of the first ten amendments. In a case decided that year the Court considered a question similar to that in the *City of Baltimore* case. A railroad had sued the city of Chicago for taking some of its land. The city had condemned a right of way over the railroad's tracks for a street crossing. At the conclusion of the trial, the jury agreed there had been a taking and awarded the railroad one dollar as compensation. The railroad appealed, and the case eventually reached the Supreme Court.[2]

Among the legal arguments made by the railroad against the taking was that it was a violation of the Fifth Amendment. The city, however, referring to *Barron v. Mayor and City Council of Baltimore,* argued that the Fifth Amendment did not apply to it, as part of a state, and that therefore no compensation was necessary. While the justices agreed that the Fifth applied only to the federal government, they also held that for a state to take private property without paying compensation would be unfair and therefore would be a violation of "due process" as guaranteed by the Fourteenth Amendment. The Court also held that one dollar in compensation was sufficient because even with the crossing there, the railroad had almost full use of its tracks.

The railroad case did not specifically hold that the Fifth Amendment (and the other amendments) were thereafter going to be applicable to state action. It was, however, the start of a process lasting over many years which eventually resulted in states being required to abide by almost all of the requirements of the Bill of Rights. This process has been called "selective incorporation" of the Bill of Rights into the Fourteenth Amendment. It is "selective" because it was done case by case over a period lasting more than forty years. Furthermore, the Court has not required the states to respect all of the guarantees in the first ten amendments.[3]

States and the Bill of Rights

*"Fundamental personal rights and 'liberties' [are] protected by the due process clause of the Fourteenth Amendment from impairment by the States . . ."**

It was not until 1925 that the Supreme Court acknowledged that states were required to comply with the commands of the First Amendment provision protecting free speech. The Court had before it the case of Benjamin Gitlow, who was charged with violating a New York

*Gitlow v. New York, 268 U.S. 652, 666 (1925).

statute making "criminal anarchy" a crime.[4] Under this New York law a person was guilty of committing "criminal anarchy" if he orally or in writing "advocates, advises or teaches the duty or necessity or propriety of overthrowing or overturning organized government by force or violence...."

Gitlow, who was a member of the Left Wing Section of the Socialist Party, was charged with violating this law because he had arranged for the printing of a paper entitled "The Left Wing Manifesto." This manifesto advocated, in plain and unequivocal language,

> the necessity of accomplishing the "Communist Revolution" by a militant and "revolutionary Socialism," based on "the class struggle" and mobilizing the "power of the proletariat in action," through mass industrial revolts developing into mass political strikes and "revolutionary mass action," for the purpose of conquering and destroying the parliamentary state and establishing in its place, through a "revolutionary dictatorship of the proletariat," the system of Communist Socialism.

Because this was a state proceeding, one of the questions confronting the justices was whether the defendant's advocacy of the overthrow of the government was protected by the First Amendment. The Court answered that it was, and noted:

> For present purposes we may and do assume that freedom of speech and of the press—which are protected by the First Amendment from abridgement by Congress—are among the fundamental personal rights and "liberties" protected by the due process clause of the Fourteenth Amendment from impairment by the States....

A majority, however, voted to uphold Gitlow's conviction, being of the opinion that even though he was exercising his right to speak, speech that involves risk of substantial evil, in this case the possible overthrow of the government, can be punished.

Justices Holmes and Brandeis disagreed. They were of the opinion that because there was no evidence that the manifesto would cause the overthrow of the government, the defendant's speech was fully protected.

Writing for himself and Justice Brandeis, Holmes pointed out:

> It is said that this manifesto was more than a theory, that it was an incitement. Every idea is an incitement. It offers itself for belief and if believed is acted on unless some other belief outweighs it or some

failure of energy stifles the movement at its birth. The only difference between the expression of an opinion and an incitement in the narrower sense is the speaker's enthusiasm for the result. Eloquence may set fire to reason. But whatever may be thought of the redundant discourse before us it had no chance of starting a present conflagration. If in the long run the beliefs expressed in proletarian dictatorship are destined to be accepted by the dominant forces of the community, the only meaning of free speech is that they should be given their chance and have their way.

Twenty-two years passed before all the other freedoms in the First Amendment were applied to state governments; freedom of the press in 1931; the right to assemble and petition in 1937; free exercise of religion in 1940; and the establishment of religion in 1947. And it was not until 1969 that most of the criminal justice protections in the other amendments were also held to apply to state actions.

No Watered-down Bill of Rights

Not a "watered down subjective version of the individual guarantees of the Bill of Rights."*

By requiring that states abide by most of the guarantees of the Bill of Rights, the Court has been emphatic in its declaration that the states are bound in the same way as the federal government is bound. For example, "The court ... has rejected the notion that the Fourteenth Amendment applies to the States only a 'watered down subjective version of the individual guarantees of the Bill of Rights.'"[5]

That statement appears in a case about the Fifth Amendment privilege against self-incrimination being applied in a state inquiry into gambling and other criminal activities. During the inquiry, William Malloy, who had previously been convicted for gambling, was called as a witness. "He refused to answer any question 'on the grounds it may tend to incriminate me.'"

Because he would not answer the questions, he was adjudged to be in contempt and was sent to jail until he was willing to do so.

Malloy petitioned the state court to be released, contending that he was being unlawfully imprisoned because he invoked the Fifth Amendment privilege not to testify against himself. The court denied the peition, holding that the Fifth Amendment was not available in a state proceeding.

*Malloy v. Hogan, 378 U.S. 1, 10–11 (1964).

Upon appeal, the Supreme Court reversed and ordered Malloy freed. In so doing, a majority stated: "We hold today that the Fifth Amendment's exception from compulsory self-incrimination is also protected by the Fourteenth Amendment against abridgement by the States."

As further explanation, the Court noted:

> The Fourteenth Amendment secures against state invasion the same privilege that the Fifth Amendment guarantees against federal infringement—the right of a person to remain silent unless he chooses to speak in the unfettered exercise of his own will, and to suffer no penalty . . . for such silence.

Those rights not "selectively incorporated" include those of the Second Amendment, which is a guarantee against federal government restrictions upon a well-regulated militia; the Third Amendment's guarantee against quartering soldiers in a private home; and the Seventh Amendment, which guarantees a right to a jury trial in civil actions where the alleged damages are in excess of twenty dollars. Also not applicable to the states is the provision of the Fifth Amendment requiring that in certain crimes the accused be indicted by a grand jury.

The Ninth Amendment is simply a declaration that there are other rights retained by the people. And the Tenth Amendment reserves to the states all powers not delegated to the federal government.

The importance of having the Bill of Rights applicable to both the federal and state governments was eloquently stated by Justice Black as follows: "In my judgment the people of no nation can lose their liberty so long as a Bill of Rights like ours survives and its basic purposes are conscientiously interpreted, enforced and respected so as to afford continuous protection against old, as well as new, devices and practices which might thwart those purposes."[6]

IV.
THE ESTABLISHMENT
OF RELIGION

"The 'establishment of religion' clause of the First Amendment means at least this: Neither a state nor the Federal Government can set up a church. Neither can pass laws which aid one religion, aid all religions, or prefer one religion over another."

Everson v. Board of Education, 330 U.S. 1, 15 (1947)

The First Amendment begins: "Congress shall make no law respecting an establishment of religion...." As noted in Chapter III, from the time of the adoption of the Bill of Rights until well into the twentieth century this prohibition and all of the other provisions of the Bill of Rights applied only to the federal government.

In 1947, in the *Everson* case noted above, the Court held that the prohibition against the establishment of religion was one of the liberties early Americans wished to preserve for themselves and therefore was within the meaning of the word *liberty* in the Fourteenth Amendent, which applies to actions of state and local governments. In this case, a taxpayer challenged a state law which authorized local school districts to "make rules and contracts for the transportation of children to and from schools," including nonpublic schools. The taxpayer "contended that the statute ... violated both the State and Federal Constitutions." When the case came before the U.S. Supreme Court it held that the transportation program was not unconstitutional under the Establishment Clause.

In discussing the background of the religious clauses, the justices took note of the fact that many of those who emigrated to this country as original settlers came from countries where governments had supported religious persecution. Furthermore, some of the Old World practices were repeated in the colonies. At the time of the Revolutionary War, twelve of the colonies had some form of established religion, and taxes were used to pay ministers' salaries and to help build and maintain churches. In referring to the situation as it existed in the colonies, the Court wrote:

> These practices became so commonplace as to shock the freedom-loving colonials into a feeling of abhorrence. The imposition of taxes to pay minsiters' salaries and to build and maintain churches and church property aroused their indignation. It was these feelings which found expression in the First Amendment.[1]

In 1784, with Patrick Henry one of its principal sponsors, a bill was introduced into the Virginia Assembly that would have created a tax for support of Christian teachers. Jefferson and Madison fought against the tax. It ultimately died without reaching a vote. It was this struggle that prompted Jefferson to write and the assembly to pass a Statute for Religious Freedom. This bill declared that "all men shall be free to profess, and by argument maintain, their opinions in matters of religion." Jefferson considered this one of the major accomplishments of his life and directed that his tombstone bear a reference to his authorship of this law, which it does.

The fight for religious freedom in Virginia, and throughout the colonies prior to 1789, had a substantial influence upon the framing and adoption of the First Amendment. Of this struggle, the *Everson* opinion states:

> The people there, as elsewhere, reached the conviction that individual religious liberty could be achieved best under a government which was stripped of all power to tax, to support, or otherwise to assist any or all religions, or to interfere with the beliefs of any religious individual or group.

The majority, in acknowledging that the transportation of parochial school children was of some benefit to the religious institutions to which the children belonged, nevertheless concluded that it was only an indirect benefit, the real beneficiaries being the children. With this case, the justices began to equate "aid" to religion with the "establishment" of religion, at the same time recognizing that there would always be some government assistance to religious activities. For example, religious institutions enjoy police and fire protection, sewage disposal, and public highways and sidewalks. There are chaplains in both the House of Representatives and the Senate, the school lunch program is available to children attending private as well as public schools, and contributions to religious organizations are deductible for federal tax purposes. And the words *In God We Trust* appear on our pennies and nickels. These incidental aids to religion have not been found to be a violation of the First Amendment.

Thus the question to be decided was not whether there was "aid" to religion but whether there was "too much" aid. Because the transportation of the parochial schoolchildren did not provide very much direct aid to the church, according to the majority, there was no constitutional violation.

Building a Wall of Separation

"Building a wall of separation between Church and State."*

Everson did not provide much help for lower courts when called upon to solve the aid to religion issue. Even a statement by Jefferson made in 1802 that the purpose of the First Amendment was to build "a wall of separation between Church and State," did not provide much of a definitive test. The Court pointed out, however, that the First Amendment "requires the state to be a neutral in its relations with groups of religious believers and non-believers; it does not require the state to be their adversary. State power is no more to be used so as to handicap religions than it is to favor them."

Four justices dissented. While they disagreed with the decision approving the use of tax money for parochial school bus transportation, they did agree with the majority's discussion of the meaning of the Establishment Clause. Justice Wiley B. Rutledge, writing for the minority, stated:

> The Amendment's purpose was not to strike merely at the official establishment of a single sect, creed or religion, outlawing only a formal relation such as had prevailed in England and some of the colonies. Necessarily it was to uproot all such relationships. But the object was broader than separating church and state in this narrow sense. It was to create a complete and permanent separation of the spheres of religious activity and civil authority by comprehensively forbidding every form of public aid or support for religion.

Two cases involving the constitutionality of school programs releasing students for religious instruction were considered by the justices in

---

*Words of Jefferson quoted in *Reynolds v. United States,* 98 U.S. 145, 164 (1878).

1948 and 1952. In the first case, *McCollum v. Board of Education*,[2] religious teachers were permitted to go into the Champaign, Illinois, schools every week to provide religious instruction to those students whose parents permitted them to attend. Students who were excused by their parents were assembled in another part of the school building. Although attendance was taken at the religion classes, there was no direct monetary assistance to the religious institutions.

Vashti McCollum, a resident-taxpayer in Champaign and a parent of a child in school, brought an action against the board of education seeking an order of the court prohibiting "all instruction in and teaching of religious education in all public schools in Champaign...."

The second case was *Zorach v. Clauson*.[3] In this case the children were released from school with permission of their parents to go to off-campus religious centers for instruction. Attendance was taken and reported to the schools. Children who were not attending the instructions remained at the school and continued their classes.

A majority of the justices held that the factual difference between these two cases required a different result. In *McCollum* they struck down the program because of the use of public property (i.e, the school) for the religious instruction. This, the Court said, was "not a separation of Church and State," and therefore violated the First Amendment. Allowing children to leave the school for the religious instruction, however, as in *Zorach*, distinguished that case from *McCollum*, and therefore, the majority said, did not involve an establishment of religion.

In *Zorach* the Court declared:

> We are a religious people whose institutions presuppose a Supreme Being. We guarantee the freedom to worship as one chooses. We make room for as wide a variety of beliefs and creeds as the spiritual needs of man deem necessary. We sponsor an attitude on the part of government that shows no partiality to any one group and that lets each flourish according to the zeal of its adherents and the appeal of its dogma. When the state encourages religious instruction or cooperates with religious authorities by adjusting the schedule of public events to sectarian needs, it follows the best of our traditions. For it then respects the religious nature of our people and accommodates the public service to their spiritual needs.

Neither *McCollum* nor *Zorach* gives much help to lower courts and lawyers who practice in them in drawing the line between "aid" that is permissible and that which is not.

The expenditure of tax money and the use of government property are not the only ways to aid religion. This became evident in the case of *Engel v. Vitale*.⁴ This case arose when the New York Board of Regents, which had authority over the state's public school system, recommended that the following prayer be said in all of the classrooms in the state:

> Almighty God, we acknowledge our dependence upon Thee, and we beg Thy blessings upon us, our parents, our teachers and our Country.

A school district in New Hyde Park, New York, directed that this prayer be recited in each class at the beginning of the school day. Steven I. Engel and several others, all taxpayers and parents of children in school, "all [except one nonbeliever] being members of various religious bodies," brought an action against the school district arguing that the "use of this official prayer in the public schools was contrary to the beliefs, religions, or religious practices of themselves and their children." The New York court upheld the use of the Regents' prayer, and that decision was affirmed by the New York Court of Appeals. The Supreme Court reversed. "There can be no doubt," the Court said, "that New York's state prayer program officially establishes the religious beliefs embodied in the Regents' prayer."

After discussing the argument that to prohibit such prayer in school indicated hostility toward religion and prayer, the majority noted:

> It is neither sacrilegious nor antireligious to say that each separate government in this country should stay out of the business of writing or sanctioning official prayers and leave that purely religious function to the people themselves and to those the people choose to look to for religious guidance.

While the *Engel* case has often been cited as prohibiting prayer in school, that case did not say that students could not pray if they wanted to. What was most crucial to the justices was that this was a government sponsored religious exercise, and "it is no part of the business of government to compose official prayers for any group of the American people to recite as a part of a religious program carried on by government."

The required daily reading of verses from the Bible and the recitation of the Lord's Prayer in the public schools, mandated by the laws of Pennsylvania, came under attack in *School District v. Schempp*.⁵

Edward Lewis Schempp, his wife, Sidney, and their children brought suit against the Abington School District to enjoin the reading of the Bible and the recitation of the Lord's Prayer, contending that this religious practice violated the First Amendment. The Schempps were members of the Unitarian Church of Germantown, Pennsylvania.

In opposition to the argument that these requirements constituted a religious exercise, the school district contended that the program really had secular purposes, among which were "the promotion of moral values, the contradiction to the materialistic trends of our times, the perpetuation of our institutions and the teaching of literature."

Justice Tom Clark, writing for the majority, did not accept this argument:

> It certainly may be said that the Bible is worthy of study for its literary and historic qualities. Nothing we have said here indicates that such study of the Bible or of religion, when presented objectively as part of a secular program of education, may not be effected consistently with the First Amendment. But the exercises here do not fall into those categories. They are religious exercises, required by the States in violation of the command of the First Amendment that the Government maintain strict neutrality, neither aiding nor opposing religion.

The opinion in *Schempp* attempts to create a test by which lower courts could determine when government aid had crossed the line and become a First Amendment violation. The test asks the question "What are the purpose and the primary effect of the enactment?"

> If either is the advancement or inhibition of religion then the enactment exceeds the scope of legislative power as circumscribed by the Constitution. That is to say that to withstand the strictures of the Establishment Clause there must be a secular legislative purpose and a primary effect that neither advances nor inhibits religion.

The constitutionality of state tax exemption for real property used by religious organizations came before the Court in 1970 in the case of *Walz v. Tax Commission*.[16] At that time all fifty states provided some form of tax exemption for places of worship. Although this was a difficult case for the Court, it upheld the tax exemption as against a challenge that it violated the Establishment Clause. Only Justice William O. Douglas dissented.

The majority approached a solution to the case by pointing out that:

the course of constitutional neutrality in this area cannot be an absolutely straight line; rigidity could well defeat the basic purpose of these provisions, which is to insure that no religion be sponsored or favored, none commanded, and none inhibited.

The question to be decided was whether granting the tax exemption serves a "secular purpose" and has the "primary effect" of neither advancing nor inhibiting religion.

The justices concluded that the exemption was neither sponsorship nor hostility, and thus the purpose part of the test was satisfied. Although there was some indirect economic benefit to churches, that did not seem to be a "primary effect" of the legislation. Of more concern was whether the implementation of the exemption injected the government into the business of the religious institutions. Granting that there was some involvement here, the Court was of the opinion that there would be much more entanglement were the states to tax the churches.

> The exemption creates only a minimal and remote involvement between church and state and far less than taxation of churches. It restricts the fiscal relationship between church and state, and tends to complement and reinforce the desired separation insulating each from the other.

This concern of government entanglement with religion added a new part to the test. Hereafter, government programs which aid religion not only would have to have a "secular purpose" and a neutral "primary effect," but the program or practice could not create too much government entanglement with the religious organizations being aided. If the aid program failed to meet any part of this three-part test, the program would violate the First Amendment.

Some Government Involvement Is Inevitable

"While some involvement and entanglement are inevitable, lines must be drawn."*

The three-part test for determining whether the Establishment Clause has been violated was confirmed by the Court in the case of *Lemon v. Kurtzman.*[7] The opinion in that case sets forth the facts at issue as follows:

**Lemon v. Kurtzman,* 403 U.S. 602, 625 (1971).

Pennsylvania has adopted a statutory program that provides financial support to nonpublic elementary and secondary schools by way of reimbursement for the cost of teachers' salaries, textbooks, and instructional materials in specified secular subjects. Rhode Island has adopted a statute under which the State pays directly to teachers in nonpublic elementary schools a supplement of 15% of their annual salary.

Considering the issue of the constitutionality of the Pennsylvania and Rhode Island programs, Chief Justice Warren Burger starts the inquiry:

> Every analysis in this area must begin with consideration of the cumulative criteria developed by the Court over many years. Three such tests may be gleaned from our cases. First, the statute must have a secular legislative purpose; second, its principal or primary effect must be one that neither advances nor inhibits religion, ... finally, the statute must not foster "an excessive government entanglement with religion."

In finding that the programs of both states violated the First Amendment, the majority accepted as true the assertion that these programs were not intended to advance religion but rather were adopted to improve the quality of the education received by students attending parochial schools. However, they found that these programs would require a "comprehensive, discriminating and continuing state surveillance" in order to ensure that there was no violation of the First Amendment. This entanglement of religion and government was sufficient to have the programs declared unconstitutional.

In this case, as in others, the Court again points out that "our prior holdings do not call for total separation between church and state; total separation is not possible in an absolute sense. Some relationship between government and religious organizations is inevitable."

For more than forty years states have sought ways to give financial assistancce to nonpublic schools. The reason for this was stated by Justice Lewis F. Powell as follows:

> Parochial schools, quite apart from their sectarian purpose, have provided an educational alternative for millions of young Americans; they often afford wholesome competition with our public schools; and in some States they relieve substantially the tax burden incident to the operation of public schools. The State has, moreover, a legitimate interest in facilitating education of the highest quality for all children within its boundaries, whatever school their parents have chosen for them.[8]

As was true in *Lemon*, when applying the test to monetary aid programs to elementary and secondary schools, the Court has found most of those programs unconstitutional. In so doing, however, the justices have been aware of the difficulty in drawing the line between aid that is permissible and that which violates the command of the Establishment Clause. In discussing the First Amendment's religion clauses in *Committee for Pub. Ed. v. Nyquist*,[9] the Court noted that "James Madison, in his Memorial and Remonstrance Against Religious Assessments, admonished that a 'prudent jealousy' for religious freedoms required that they never become 'entangled . . . in precedents.'" Commenting on Madison's statement, Justice Lewis F. Powell wrote for the majority:

> Yet, despite Madison's admonition and the "sweep of the absolute prohibitions" of the Clauses, the Nation's history has not been one of entirely sanitized separation between Church and State. It has never been thought either possible or desirable to enforce a regime of total separation, and as a consequence cases arising under these Clauses have presented some of the most perplexing questions to come before this Court.

In *Nyquist*, the Court had under consideration three New York aid to school programs. The first program provided money grants to nonpublic schools for "maintenance and repairs" of school facilities and equipment. The second provided for reimbursement of tuition expended by parents who send their children to a nonpublic school, and the third allowed tax relief for those parents not eligible for the tuition reimbursement. Most of the nonpublic schools which benefited from these programs were operated by religious organizations.

Using its previous cases as a guide, the Court noted that all of these programs met the secular purpose part of the test.

> These cases simply recognize that sectarian schools perform secular, educational functions as well as religious functions, and that some forms of aid may be channeled to the secular without providing direct aid to the sectarian. But the channel is a narrow one, as the above cases illustrate.

Whether the primary effect of these programs was impermissibly to aid religion was a more difficult question, particularly with respect to the tuition reimbursement and tax credits, because these were direct benefits to the parents and only an indirect benefit to the schools.

The justices nevertheless concluded that the benefits to the parents were also support for the religious schools and thus violated the primary effect part of the test. Having found that the programs were unconstitutional under one part of the test. The justices saw no need to address the issue of whether the programs constituted an improper entanglement of the state with religion.

A review of the kinds of school aid programs which do not violate the Establishment Clause indicates that the justices are more willing to approve programs that are neutral insofar as religion is concerned and more directly aid students or their parents. For example, a majority has upheld programs which provide students with bus transportation, textbooks, testing and scoring, diagnostic and therapeutic services, and has allowed parents a general tax deduction for the cost of tuition and textbooks at nonpublic schools.

On the other hand, they have struck down money grants for instructional materials; field trips; auxiliary services, including counseling, testing, psychological services, speech and hearing therapy; salaries of employees who provide secular instruction at nonpublic schools; and shared time-release programs of religious instruction conducted on school property. In some of these the justices have concluded that there would be too much entanglement of government with the religious institution, thus violating the third part of the test.

A unanimous decision was issued in *Witters v. Washington Department of Services for the Blind.*[10] Larry Witters of Washington was afflicted with a progressive eye condition that made him eligible for state aid for vocational rehabilitation. "He was at the time attending Inland Empire School of the Bible, a private Christian college in Spokane, . . . in order to equip himself for a career as a pastor, missionary, or youth director." He applied to the Washington Commission for the Blind for aid, which was denied on the grounds that the "Washington State constitution forbids the use of public funds to assist an individual in pursuant of a career or degree in theology or related areas. . . ."

Witters attacked this ruling in a state court, which held in favor of the Commission. He then appealed to the Washington Supreme Court, which agreed that the Commission's decision was correct. It specifically found that a grant to Witters would violate the U.S. Supreme Court's three-part Establishment Clause test, and therefore the state was prohibited from aiding him in his study for the ministry. The U.S. Supreme Court disagreed.

In discussing the Establishment Clause, Justice Thurgood Marshall wrote:

It is well-settled that the Establishment Clause is not violated every time money previously in the possession of a State is conveyed to a religious institution. For example, a State may issue a paycheck to one of its employees, who may then donate all or part of that paycheck to a religious institution, all without constitutional barrier; and the State may do so even knowing that the employee so intends to dispose of his salary.

The issue in the case was stated as follows:

> The question presented is whether, on the facts as they appear in the record before us, extension of aid to ... [Witters] and the use of that aid by ... [him] to support his religious education is a permissible transfer similar to the hypothetical salary donation described above, or is an impermissible "direct subsidy."

The Court answered the question this way:

> On the facts we have set out, it does not seem appropriate to view any aid ultimately flowing to the Inland Empire School of the Bible as resulting from a *state* action sponsoring or subsidizing religion. Nor does the mere circumstance that ... [Witters] has chosen to use neutrally available state aid to help pay for his religious education confer any message of state endorsement of religion.

College Students Are Less Impressionable

*"College students are less impressionable and less susceptible to religious indoctrination."**

Government grants of monetary aid to nonpublic colleges and universities have fared better than aid to primary and secondary schools. A majority of the justices are of the opinion that aid to higher educational institutions does not necessarily translate into aid to religion because college students are less likely to succumb to religious indoctrination.

> There is substance to the contention that college students are less impressionable and less susceptible to religious indoctrination. Common observation would seem to support that view, and Congress may well have entertained it. The skepticism of the college student is not an inconsiderable barrier to any attempt or tendency to subvert the congressional objectives and limitations.[11]

Tilton v. Richardson, 403 U.S. 672, 686 (1971).

Following this line of thought, the Court has upheld federal grants of money to private colleges for construction of buildings as well as general-purpose grants from state government. It has also approved the issuance of state revenue bonds to assist nonpublic colleges in financing construction of buildings.

In approving these kinds of expenditures, the Court again made note of the fact that with a pervasive government such as ours, some government involvement with religion is unavoidable.

> A system of government that makes itself felt as pervasively as ours could hardly be expected to never cross paths with the church. In fact, our State and Federal Governments impose certain burdens upon, and impact certain benefits to, virtually all our activities, and religious activity is not an exception. The Court has enforced a scrupulous neutrality by the State, as among religions, and also as between religions and other activities, but a hermetic separation of the two is an impossibility it has never required.[12]

None of the decisions discussed herein to uphold or strike down a particular aid program to private schools and colleges has been unanimous. The justices are split between those who see the "wall of separation" as an almost impregnable one and those who are willing to uphold aid that does not directly promote sectarian activity.

Is There a Secular Purpose?

"The narrow question is whether there is a secular purpose...."*

The disagreement among the justices is particularly evident in cases dealing with government maintenance and construction of displays that include religious elements. For example, the question of the validity of posting copies of the Ten Commandments in public-school classrooms was the issue in *Stone v. Graham*.[13] A Kentucky statute, which required such posting, also required the posted copy to contain a statement that the Ten Commandments had a secular application because they had been adopted as part of the legal codes of many countries, including the United States. Based on this statement, Kentucky argued that the posting was for a secular and not a religious purpose.

That argument was not accepted by a majority of the justices. They concluded that the reason for displaying the Ten Commandments was

---

*Lynch v. Donnelly, 465 U.S. 668, 681 (1984).

religious and thus violated the secular purpose part of the Establishment Clause test.

> The pre-eminent purpose for posting the Ten Commandments on schoolroom walls is plainly religious in nature. The Ten Commandments are undeniably a sacred text in the Jewish and Christian faiths, and no legislative recitation of a supposed secular purpose can blind us to that fact. The Commandments do not confine themselves to arguably secular matters, such as honoring one's parents, killing or murder, adultery, stealing, false witness, and covetousness. . . . Rather, the first part of the Commandments concerns the religious duties of believers; worshipping the Lord God alone, avoiding idolatry, not using the Lord's name in vain, and observing the Sabbath Day.

Justice William Rehnquist dissented. He argued that "the fact that the asserted secular purpose may overlap with what some may see as a religious objective does not render it unconstitutional."

Many cities and counties participate in the erection of displays as part of the observance of the Christmas holiday season. The validity of the one erected by Pawtucket, Rhode Island, reached the Court in 1984. Its opinion described the city's Christmas display in this way:

> The Pawtucket display comprises many of the figures and decorations traditionally associated with Christmas, including, among other things, a Santa Claus house, reindeer pulling Santa's sleigh, candy-striped poles, a Christmas tree, carolers, cut-out figures representing such characters as a clown, an elephant, and a teddy bear, hundreds of colored lights, a large banner that reads "SEASON'S GREETINGS," and the creche at issue here. All components of this display are owned by the City.[14]

The creche contained the traditional nativity figures of the infant Jesus, Mary, Joseph, angels, shepherds, etc.

At issue was the question of whether the inclusion of the creche violated the three-part Establishment Clause test. A majority of the justices said that it did not. Four justices emphatically disagreed.

What separates the justices is the question of how impregnable the "wall of separation" must be.

Chief Justice Burger argued for the majority:

> The concept of a "wall" of separation is a useful figure of speech probably deriving from views of Thomas Jefferson. The metaphor has served as a reminder that the Establishment Clause forbids an

established church or anything approaching it. But the metaphor itself is not a wholly accurate description of the practical aspects of the relationship that in fact exists between church and state.

The Chief Justice pointed out that throughout our history there have been many official references to religion, including presidential Thanksgiving Day proclamations, the first of which was issued by President George Washington. Further, as noted above, the words *In God We Trust* appear on some of our coins, and we support chaplains in both the Senate and House of Representatives. Referring then to the three-part test, the majority opinion states:

> The narrow question is whether there is a secular purpose for Pawtucket's display of the creche. The display is sponsored by the city to celebrate the Holiday and to depict the origins of that Holiday. These are legitimate secular purposes.

Also:

> To forbid the use of this one passive symbol—the creche—at the very time people are taking note of the season with Christmas hymns and carols in public schools and other public places, and while the Congress and legislatures open sessions with prayers by paid chaplains, would be a stilted overreaction contrary to our history and to our holdings. If the presence of the creche in this display violates the Establishment Clause, a host of other forms of taking official note of Christmas, and of our religious heritage, are equally offensive to the Constitution.

Justice Sandra Day O'Connor joined the decision to allow the display of the creche but took a somewhat different approach. Her principal concern was that government aid or assistance to religion not be seen as government endorsement of religion.

> Endorsement sends a message to nonadherents that they are outsiders, not full members of the political community, and an accompanying message to adherents that they are insiders, favored members of the political community. Disapproval sends the opposite message.

Justice O'Connor found no endorsement of religion in the inclusion of the creche in the Pawtucket Christmas display.

Justice Brennan, writing for the minority, protested vigorously:

The "primary effect" of including a nativity scene in the city's display is, as the District Court found, to place the government's imprimatur of approval on the particular religious beliefs exemplified by the creche. Those who believe in the message of the nativity receive the unique and exclusive benefit of public recognition and approval of their views.

The effect that the display of the creche would have on individuals who hold different religious views was also of concern to the dissenters.

The effect on minority religious groups, as well as those who may reject all religion, is to convey the message that their views are not similarly worthy of public recognition nor entitled to public support. It was precisely this sort of religious chauvinism that the Establishment Clause was intended forever to prohibit.

Pawtucket did not bring an end to the controversy over use of a Nativity scene as part of government observance of the Christmas holiday. For its Christmas display 1986–87, Allegheny County, Pennsylvania, placed a creche on the grand staircase in its courthouse. On the creche was an angel bearing a sign reading *Gloria In Excelsis Deo* ("Glory to God in the Highest").

Outside the city-county building, the county also placed an eighteen-foot Chanukah menorah or candelabrum next to a forty-five-foot fully decorated Christmas tree. Near the tree was a sign with the mayor's name, and text declaring that the display was the city's *salute to liberty*.

The American Civil Liberties Union and several local residents brought an action seeking to enjoin the county from displaying the creche and the menorah on the grounds that to do so violated the Establishment Clause.

Prior to the docketing of this case in the Supreme Court, significant changes in the membership had taken place. Chief Justice Warren E. Burger, who wrote the opinion in *Pawtucket*, and Justice Powell, who joined that opinion, had retired. Justice Rehnquist was the new Chief Justice, and justices Antonin Scalia and Anthony M. Kennedy had recently been appointed.

On the question of the display of the Nativity scene within the courthouse, the justices split 5–4, the majority concluding that such display violated the First Amendment. By a 6–3 majority, however, the display of the menorah was held not to be an Establishment Clause violation.

With regard to the creche, this case saw the majority follow Justice

O'Connor's position in *Pawtucket* that the Establishment Clause prohibits government "endorsement" of religion.

The majority first discussed the fact that ours is a religiously diverse country.

> This Nation is heir to a history and tradition of religious diversity that dates from the settlement of the North American continent. Sectarian differences among various Christian denominations were central to the origins of our Republic. Since then, adherents of religions too numerous to name have made the United States their home, as have those whose beliefs expressly exclude religion.[15]

The opinion then identifies the task before the justices: "Accordingly, our present task is to determine whether the display of the creche and the menorah, in their respective 'particular physical settings,' has the effect of endorsing or disapproving religious beliefs."

In reference to the creche, the opinion concludes:

> In sum, *Lynch* [the *Pawtucket* case] teaches that government may celebrate Christmas in some manner and form, but not in a way that endorses Christian doctrine. Here Allegheny County has transgressed this line. It has chosen to celebrate Christmas in a way that has the effect of endorsing a patently Christian message: Glory to God for the birth of Jesus Christ. Under *Lynch,* and the rest of our cases, nothing more is required to demonstrate a violation of the Establishment Clause. The display of the creche in this context, therefore, must be permanently enjoined.

Justice Kennedy, writing for the minority, would have none of that. To these justices, making Establishment Clause decisions on whether the government appeared to be endorsing religion not only was unworkable but indicated government hostility to religion. It would, according to Justice Kennedy, require the striking down of many traditional practices in effect in our country today.

> Either the endorsement test must invalidate scores of traditional practices recognizing the place religion holds in our culture, or it must be twisted and stretched to avoid inconsistency with practices we know to have been permitted in the past, while condemning similar practices with no greater endorsement effect simply by reason of their lack of historical antecedent. Neither result is acceptable.

The decision with regard to the creche in *Allegheny County* does not necessarily spell the end of the three-part test as discussed above, but it indicates a sharp division among the justices as to the application of that test. The majority now read into the purpose and primary effect parts of the test an examination of whether the particular government action can be viewed as an endorsement of the religious philosophy depicted. If there is no endorsement, then there is no constitutional violation.

The decision to uphold the placing of the menorah near the Christmas tree outside the city-county building follows this approach.

> In the shadow of the tree, the menorah is readily understood as simply a recognition that Christmas is not the only traditional way of observing the winter-holiday season. In these circumstances, then, the combination of the tree and the menorah communicates, not a simultaneous endorsement of both Christian and Jewish faith, but instead, a secular celebration of Christmas coupled with an acknowledgment of Chanukah as a contemporaneous alternative tradition.

Those who dissented from the placement of the creche clearly agreed with this analysis as it applied to the menorah.

Government Should Not Sanction Prayers

*"Each separate government ... should stay out of the business of writing or sanctioning official prayers...."**

As discussed above, during the early years of the development of case law under the Establishment Clause, the Court had struck down released-time religious educational programs on school property, saying a government-composed prayer in school, and reading of a few verses from the Bible at the beginning of each school day.

The validity of another formalized prayer-in-school program found is way to the Court in 1985 in the case of *Wallace v. Jaffree*.[16] The Alabama state legislature had enacted several statutes relating to praying in school. One "authorized a one-minute period of silence in all public schools 'for meditation.'" A second "authorized a period of silence 'for meditation or voluntary prayer.'" And another permitted a teacher to lead willing students in the following prayer:

> Almighty God, You alone are our God. We acknowledge You as our Creator and Supreme Judge of the World. May Your justice,

*Engel v. Vitale, 370 U.S. 421, 435 (1962).

Your truth, and Your peace abound this day in the hearts of our
countrymen, in the counsels of our government, in the sanctity of
our homes and in the classrooms of our schools in the name of our
Lord. Amen.

Ishmael Jaffree, a father with children in a public school, brought
an action seeking a judgment that the Alabama statutes were in con-
travention of the Establishment Clause.

Mr. Jaffree stated that "two of the children had been subjected to
various acts of religious indoctrination 'from the beginning of the
school year in September 1981'; that the ... teachers had 'on a daily
basis' led their classes in saying certain prayers in unison; that the minor
children were exposed to ostracism from their peer group class members
if they did not participate; and that ... [he] had repeatedly but unsuc-
cessfully requested that the devotional services be stopped."

District Judge William Brevard Hand rendered a decision
upholding the statutes, concluding "that 'the establishment clause of
the first amendment ... does not prohibit the state from establishing
a religion.'" He came to that conclusion after extensive research convinced him that the Supreme Court was wrong when it held that the
Fourteenth Amendment made the First Amendment applicable to the
states (see Chapter III).

Judge Hand's decision upholding the one-minute period of silence
for meditation was accepted as correct. The Court of Appeals struck
down both of the other laws as being in conflict with the Establishment
Clause. The state appealed to the Supreme Court, which refused to
reverse the court of appeals concluding that these laws created a government sponsored religious activity and were indeed unconstitutional.

The majority opinion, which deals only with the validity of the law
authorizing "a period of silence 'for meditation and voluntary prayer,'"
was delivered by Justice John P. Stevens. He comments upon Judge
Hand's "remarkable conclusion that the Federal Constitution imposes
no obstacle to Alabama's establishment of a state religion" by noting
that "it is ... appropriate to recall how firmly embedded in our constitutional jurisprudence is the proposition that the several States have
no greater power to restrain the individual freedoms protected by the
First Amendment than does the Congress of the United States."

Turning then to the issue at hand, the validity of the prayer,
Justice Stevens finds that the law does not have a secular purpose but
on the contrary, "the legislature enacted ... [the statute] for the sole
purpose of expressing the State's endorsement of prayer activities for

one minute at the beginning of each schoolday. The addition of 'or voluntary prayer' indicates that the State intended to characterize prayer as a favored practice."

The inclusion in the law of the words *or voluntary prayer* was not enough to invalidate the law, according to Chief Justice Burger. He wrote: "To suggest that a moment-of-silence statute that includes the word 'prayer' unconstitutionally endorses religion, while one that simply provides a moment of silence does not, manifests not neutrality but hostility toward religion."

Justice Rehnquist could see nothing wrong with the legislature endorsing "prayer as a favored practice," and noted that "George Washington himself, at the request of the very Congress which passed the Bill of Rights, proclaimed a day of 'public thanksgiving and prayer, to be observed by acknowledging with grateful hearts the many and signals favors of Almighty God.'"

The teaching of the theory of evolution has found its way into the judicial system in several cases, the most famous being the celebrated *Scopes* trial in Tennessee in 1927. John Scopes was convicted of violating a Tennessee state law that "prohibited the teaching of evolution theory" in the public schools. During his trial he was defended by the well-known lawyer Clarence Darrow. Upon appeal to the Tennessee Supreme Court, Scopes' conviction was affirmed. That court held that the state law did not violate the First Amendment's Establishment Clause.[17]

In 1968 the Supreme Court struck down an Arkansas statute that prohibited the teaching "in its public schools and universities of the theory that man evolved from other species of life." It was clear to the majority that the purpose behind the requirement was that the theory of evolution was contrary to the creation of man according to the teachings of the Bible.

> In the present case, there can be no doubt that Arkansas has sought to prevent its teachers from discussing the theory of evolution because it is contrary to the belief of some that the Book of Genesis must be the exclusive source of doctrine as to the origin of man. No suggestion has been made that Arkansas' law may be justified by considerations of state policy other than the religious views of some of its citizens.[18]

If it is a violation of the First Amendment to prohibit the teaching of evolution, may the state require that such teaching be accompanied by instruction in "creation science"? This was the question in *Edwards v. Aguillard*.[19]

The state of Louisiana required public schools to give equal treatment to both "evolution science" and "creation science" if either theory of the origin of man was to be taught. This requirement was challenged in the federal district court in Louisiana by parents, teachers, and religious leaders. They argued that the statute was designed to promote a religious theory, the biblical story of creation, and that the law had no real secular purpose.

The state, however, asserted that the purpose for the statute was to "protect academic freedom," to be sure that students were not indoctrinated with only one theory of creation.

District Judge Adrian G. Duplantier determined that the purpose of the law was the advancement of a "religious doctrine" and therefore unconstitutional. He was sustained by both the court of appeals and the Supreme Court.

The Court began its search for a solution to the issue by referring to the three-part test discussed above. Even though the state argued that the secular purpose was academic freedom, the majority did not accept that argument.

> The preeminent purpose of the Louisiana Legislature was clearly to advance the religious viewpoint that a supernatural being created humankind. The term "creation science" was defined as embracing this particular religious doctrine by those responsible for the passage of the Creationism Act.

Having concluded that the purpose of the act was a religious one, the court concluded further that it ran afoul of the "secular purpose" part of the test and was thus a violation of the Establishment Clause.

> The Louisiana Creationism Act advances a religious doctrine by requiring either the banishment of the theory of evolution from public classrooms or the presentation of a religious viewpoint that rejects evolution in its entirety. The Act violates the Establishment Clause of the First Amendment because it seeks to employ the symbolic and financial support of government to achieve a religious purpose.

Justice Scalia and Chief Justice Rehnquist strongly disagreed. They were of the opinion that there was a secular purpose for the act because the legislature's goal was to "ensure that students would be free to decide for themselves how life began, based upon a fair and balanced presentation of the scientific evidence."

Underlying the dispute between the majority and the dissenters in this case is the question of whether there is a scientific basis for the theory of creation as set forth in the Bible. The majority seems to be of the opinion that there is not, while the dissenters, without acknowledging that there exists scientific evidence supporting the Bible's theory of creation, argue that the people of Louisiana were entitled to have whatever evidence did exist to support the theory presented to their children.

A religious practice that can be traced back as far as the Continental Congress in 1774 was called into question in *Marsh v. Chambers*. [20] That practice was having each session of the Continental Congress, and later each session of the Congress, opened with a prayer. In *Marsh* it was a similar practice of the Nebraska state legislature. In the Nebraska legislature, as is true in Congress today, chaplains paid with tax funds performed this daily ritual.

Even though the custom is well entrenched in our governmental system, the *Marsh* case, for the first time, focused attention upon whether that custom was a violation of the First Amendment. A majority of the justices said that it was not.

What seemed most conclusive to the majority was that in the same week in 1789 that the Congress voted to employ chaplains to say a prayer in each house they also voted to approve a draft of the First Amendment which, together with the eleven other amendments, were to be submitted to the states for adoption as the Bill of Rights.

> The unique history leads us to accept the interpretation of the First Amendment draftsmen who saw no real threat to the Establishment Clause arising from a practice of prayer similar to that now challenged. We conclude that legislative prayer presents no more potential for establishment than the provision of school transportation, . . . beneficial grants for higher education, . . . or tax exemptions for religious organizations. . . .

Not all of the justices agreed that simply because a religious practice has been in use for a long period of time that it automatically escapes condemnation of the First Amendment. Justice Brennan expressed concern for "the principles of neutrality and separation that are embedded within the Establishment Clause." He was concerned about the effect the custom would have upon the people of Nebraska today:

> It forces all residents of the State to support a religious exercise that may be contrary to their own beliefs. It requires the State to commit itself on fundamental theological issues. It has the potential for

degrading religion by allowing a religious call to worship to be intermeshed with a secular call to order. And it injects religion into the political sphere by creating the potential that each and every selection of a chaplain, or consideration of a particular prayer, or even reconsideration of the practice itself, will provoke a political battle along religious lines and ultimately alienate some religiously identified group of citizens.

Religion and Government Must Harmonize

*"Innumerable civil regulations enforce conduct which harmonizes with religious canons."**

As the Court has said, we are a "religious people." Therefore, as noted herein, throughout our history both federal and state governments have sought to accommodate religion in various ways. The real property tax exemption upheld in *Walz* is one of those accommodations. Others include exemptions from federal income and unemployment compensation taxes, the allowance of personal income tax deductions for contributions to such organizations, and financial aid to nonpublic schools and colleges.

Many states have also enacted Sunday closing laws. These laws have a long history not only in this country but also in England prior to the settlement of America.

The justices considered several cases in 1961 wherein the validity of such laws was affirmed. One of these cases was *McGowan v. Maryland*.[21] Because of a Maryland statute, "all labor, business and other commercial activities" were prohibited on Sunday. The legal question raised in these cases was whether such laws were contrary to the First Amendment. In deciding that they were not, the Court reviewed the history of Sunday closing laws, pointing out that such laws were in existence in England when our country was settled and were brought here during that time. It acknowledged that originally these laws were religiously motivated but concluded that times had changed and that today "the State seeks to set one day apart from all others as a day of rest, repose, recreation and tranquility—a day which all members of the family and community have the opportunity to spend and enjoy together, a day on which there exists relative quiet and disassociation from the everyday intensity of commercial activities, a day on which people may visit friends and relatives who are not available during working days."

McGowan v. Maryland, 366 U.S. 420, 462 (1961).

Therefore, this was a secular and not a religious purpose, even though this one day of rest coincided with the Sabbath.

In light of the evolution of our Sunday Closing Laws through the centuries, and of their more or less recent emphasis upon secular considerations, it is not difficult to discern that as presently written and administered, most of them, at least, are of a secular rather than of a religious character, and that presently they bear no relationship to establishment of religion as those words are used in the Constitution of the United States.

Over the years, in the controversy over civil rights, Congress has enacted many laws prohibiting discrimination in employment because of race, gender, handicap, or religious preference.[22] The prohibition against discrimination on the basis of religious preference is seen as an accommodation to the free exercise of religion which is also protected by the First Amendment and is discussed in Chapter V. However, the law that prohibits such discrimination in employment exempts religious organizations, thus making it possible for them to require their employees to be a member of that organization.

This exemption came under attack in *Corporation of Presiding Bishop v. Amos*.[23] Christine J. Amos and several other women, all of whom worked in a clothing mill owned and operated by the Church of Jesus Christ of Latter-day Saints were discharged "because each of them was unable or refused to satisfy the Mormon Church worthiness requirements for a temple recommend." The women argued that giving religious organizations the right to discriminate in hiring on the basis of religious preference was unconstitutional under the Establishment Clause. The justices unanimously thought differently.

Justice Byron White, who wrote the opinion, noted that "a law is not unconstitutional simply because it *allows* churches to advance religion, which is their very purpose. For a law to have forbidden 'effects' under *Lemon,* it must be fair to say that the *government itself* has advanced religion through its own activities and influence." This was not the situation in this case.

Establishment and Conscientious Objectors

*"Who serves when not all serve?"**

By the Selective Service Act of May 18, 1917, Congress established the Selective Service System. In doing so, it exempted from such service

Gillette v. United States, 401 U.S. 437, 455 (1971).

"regular or duly ordained ministers of religion and theological students." It also relieved "from military service in the strict sense the members of religious sects as enumerated whose tenets excluded the moral right to engage in war...." The latter were, however, required to serve as noncombatants.

When this law was contested before the Supreme Court, it brushed away a claim that granting an exemption from military service because of one's religious beliefs was a First Amendment violation, "because we think ... [the] unsoundness [of such a claim] is too apparent to require us to do more."[24]

A somewhat different Establishment Clause attack was made upon the Selective Service System in *Gillette v. United States*.[25] In this case two individuals, Guy Porter Gillette and Louis A. Negre, sought exemption from participating in the Vietnam War. Gillette stated that he was willing to "participate in a war of national defense or a war sponsored by the United Nations as a peace-keeping measure, but declared his opposition to American military operations in Vietnam, which he characterized as 'unjust.'"

Petitioner Negre, "in line with religious counseling and numerous religious texts, ... [and who was] a devout Catholic, believes that it is his duty as a faithful Catholic to discriminate between 'just' and 'unjust' wars, and to forswear participation in the later." He too thought that the Vietnam War was unjust. Both petitioners had been denied a conscientious objector classification by their local draft boards.

"These cases present the question whether conscientious objection to a particular war, rather than objection to war as such, relieves the objector from responsibilities of military training and service." The petitioners argued that by not granting an exemption for all religious beliefs, including a belief that some wars are just and some unjust, the government was making a choice between religious beliefs, and thus was not being neutral in the treatment of religious views as required under the Establishment Clause.

The Court, in finding no Establishment Clause violation, pointed out:

> The metaphor of a "wall" or an impassable barrier between Church and State, taken too literally, may mislead constitutional analysis ... but the Establishment Clause stands at least for the proposition that when government activities touch on the religious sphere, they must be secular in purpose, evenhanded in operation, and neutral in primary impact.

In this case, exempting only those who objected to all wars fulfilled congressional purposes of not having to convert a sincere conscientious objector into an effective fighting man, and "concern for the hard choice that conscription would impose on conscientious objectors to war. . . ."

> We conclude not only that the affirmative purposes underlying . . . [the conscientious objector classification] are neutral and secular, but also that valid neutral reasons exist for limiting the exemption to objectors to all war, and that the . . . [classification] therefore cannot be said to reflect a religious preference.

Establishment of Religion — 1991 and Beyond

The problem facing the courts in deciding Establishment Clause cases is a difficult one. As our history clearly indicates, there never has been "an impregnable wall" separating church and state. Long before cases relating to the Establishment Clause ever came to the Court, government had extended police and fire protection to religious institutions, chaplains were employed in the Senate and House of Representatives, tax exemptions had been granted, the Nativity scene had become part of many government-sponsored Chirstmas displays, and we printed *In God We Trust* on our coins. We also exempted religious conscientious objectors from service in the armed forces.

At the beginning it was clear that some kind of formula or test was necessary, so that lower courts and lawyers advising government agencies would have some method of evaluating government aid and involvement with religion. As discussed above, many cases were decided before the three-part test came into being in the *Lemon* case. As noted, this test asks, "What is the purpose and primary effect of the government's action?" And, "Will there be too much government entanglement with religion?"

The *Allegheny County* case indicates that this test is not without its problems. Three members of the Court support it, and four do not. Justice O'Connor, while supporting the test generally, would change it somewhat to focus attention on whether the government action indicates an "endorsement" of religion. Justice Souter's views on this issue are unknown at this time.

The four justices who do not fully support the test are of the opinion that the focus of attention should be on whether the government action is coercive. Writing for himself and three others, Justice Kennedy wrote in *Allegheny* that "non-coercive government action within the realm of flexible accommodation or passive acknowledgement of existing symbols does not violate the Establishment Clause unless it benefits religion in a way more direct and more substantial than practices that are accepted in our national heritage."[26]

Neither the three-part test as it originally evolved nor Justice O'Connor's suggested change nor the "coercive" test approved by the minority in *Allegheny* will make the task of deciding Establishment Clause questions any easier for the Court or for lower courts and lawyers. It is clear that we are, and probably always will be, willing to accept some cooperation between government and religion. Difficult Establishment Clause cases, therefore, will always be with us.

V.
THE FREE EXERCISE
OF RELIGION

"If there is any fixed star in our constitutional constellation, it is that no official, high or petty, can prescribe what shall be orthodox in politics, nationalism, religion or other matters of opinion or force citizens to confess by word or act their faith therein."

West Virginia State Bd. of Education v. Barnette, 319 U.S. 624, 642 (1943)

More than three-quarters of a century passed from the time of the adoption of the First Amendment in 1791 before the Court decided the first case involving the Free Exercise Clause. In that case, *Reynolds v. United States,*[1] and in other cases decided prior to 1940, the Court adopted a rather narrow view of free exercise of religion by placing great emphasis upon what it saw as the overriding interests of government and minimizing the religious beliefs protected by the First Amendment.

The *Reynolds* case involved a charge against the defendant, George Reynolds, of violating a federal law making it a crime to have more than one spouse. For his defense, Reynolds proved that he was a member of the Church of Jesus Christ of Latter-day Saints (Mormon Church), part of whose accepted church doctrine included a "duty of male members of said church, circumstances permitting, to practice polygamy . . . and also that the members of the church believed that the practice of polygamy was directly enjoined upon the male members thereof by the Almighty God." The trial judge refused to instruct the jury that they should return a verdict of not guilty because of the defendant's religious beliefs.

The jury found the defendant guilty, and he appealed to the Supreme Court. The question at issue was "whether religious belief can

71

be accepted as a justification of an overt act made criminal by the law of the land." The Court's answer was that a religious belief could not be used to justify the commission of a crime.

The justices placed great weight upon the facts that prior to the settlement of the colonies, polygamy was a crime under the laws of England punishable by death and that the Commonwealth of Virginia in 1788 adopted a law similar to those in effect in England proscribing bigamy.

> Polygamy has always been odious among the Northern and Western Nations of Europe, and until the establishment of the Mormon Church, was almost exclusively a feature of the life of Asiatic and of African people. At common law, the second marriage was always void ... and from the earliest history of England polygamy has been treated as an offense against society.

The Court acknowledged that "Congress cannot pass a law for the government of the Territories which shall prohibit the free exercise of religion." However, they asked and then answered the question:

> Can a man excuse his practices to the contrary because of his religious belief? To permit this would be to make the professed doctrines of religious belief superior to the law of the land, and in effect permit every citizen to become a law unto himself. Government could exist only in name under such circumstances.

Not only did Congress make polygamy a crime, but acts of the Idaho territorial legislature provided that any person who was a bigamist or polygamist could not vote or hold public office. Further, Congress in 1887 repealed the act of incorporation of the Church of Jesus Christ of Latter-day Saints, and directed the seizure of all its properties because of its position on polygamy. These laws were all upheld by the Supreme Court.[2]

The Court in these cases drew a distinction between religious beliefs and conduct motivated by those beliefs. The former were protected by the Free Exercise Clause, but the latter may be subject to reasonable laws prohibiting or regulating such conduct. A person's beliefs are absolute, but those beliefs cannot be relied upon to support any and all physical acts that may be detrimental to the rest of society.

> It was never intended or supposed that the amendment could be invoked as a protection against legislation for the punishment of acts

inimical to the peace, good order and morals of society. With man's relations to his Maker and the obligations he may think they impose, and the manner in which an expression shall be made by him of his belief on those subjects, no interference can be permitted, provided always the laws of society, designed to secure its peace and prosperity, and the morals of its people, are not interfered with.[3]

That the practice of polygamy was the participation in "acts inimical to the peace, good order and morals of society" was reinforced in the case of *Cleveland v. United States.*[4]

Kimball Cleveland and eight other persons were members of a Mormon fundamentalist sect that not only believed in polygamy but practiced it. When it was discovered that they and their wives had traveled throughout the western United States, all were arrested for violating a federal law which made it a crime the transporting "in interstate commerce of 'any woman or girl for the purpose of prostitution or debauchery, or for any other immoral purpose.'" The defendants argued that they did not have a criminal intent because of their religious belief in polygamous marriages. They were convicted, and they appealed. A majority of the Supreme Court turned a deaf ear to their arguments and upheld their convictions.

Justice Douglas wrote for the majority:

> It is also urged that the requisite criminal intent was lacking since petitioners [defendants] were motivated by a religious belief. The defense claims too much. If upheld, it would place beyond the law any act done under claim of religious sanction. But it has long been held that the fact that polygamy is supported by a religious creed affords no defense in a prosecution for bigamy.

Justice Frank Murphy wrote a strong dissent. While the majority had characterized polygamy as "a notorious example of promiscuity," Justice Murphy thought otherwise, noting that the differences between polygamy and monogamy "do not place polygamy in the same category as prostitution or debauchery."

"We must recognize, then," he wrote, "that polygyny [polygamy], like other forms of marriage, is basically a cultural institution rooted deeply in the religious beliefs and social mores of those societies in which it appears."

Preaching the Gospel in the Streets

*"Go ye into all the world, and preach the gospel to every creature."**

By following the exhortation of Jesus Christ to "go . . . into all the world, and preach the gospel to every creature," the Jehovah's Witnesses became very important participants in the development of free exercise of religion and freedom to speak.

Justice Murphy described the faith of the Witnesses:

> And the Jehovah's Witnesses are living proof of the fact that even in this nation concerned as it was in the ideals of freedom, the right to practice religion in unconventional ways is still far from secure. Theirs is a militant and unpopular faith pursued with a fanatical zeal. They have suffered brutal beatings, their property has been destroyed; they have been harassed at every turn by the resurrection and enforcement of little used ordinances and statutes.[5]

In the 1930s, 40s, and 50s the Witnesses were particularly active in their efforts "to preach the gospel to every creature." During this period more than twenty cases were decided by the Supreme Court involving one or more of their members. The Witnesses won sixteen of these cases, and by so doing established some very important First Amendment principles, among which are that (1) laws restricting First Amendment activities, including distribution of literature, canvassing, and solicitation are invalid unless drawn to prevent censorship of the message involved; (2) "a State may not, by statute, wholly deny the right to preach or disseminate religious views"; (3) because "freedom of the press, freedom of speech, freedom of religion are in a preferred position," the government may not require a license for the exercise thereof; and (4) "a State may [however] by general and nondiscriminatory legislation regulate the times, the places, and the manner of soliciting upon its streets, and of holding meetings thereon. . . ."

Justice Robert Jackson details the activities of the Jehovah's Witnesses as follows:

> Each home was visited, a bell was rung or the door knocked upon, and the householder advised that the Witness had important information. If the householder would listen, a record was played on the phonograph. Its subject was "Snare and Racket." The following words are representative of its contents: "Religion is wrong and a snare because it deceives the people, but that does not mean that all

*Bible, Mark 16: 15.

who follow religion are willingly bad. Religion is a racket because it has long been used and is still used to extract money from the people upon the theory and promise that the paying over of money to a priest will serve to relieve the party paying from punishment after death and further insure his salvation." This line of attack is taken by the Witnesses generally upon all denominations, especially the Roman Catholic. The householder was asked to buy a variety of literature for a price or contribution.[6]

These actions came in direct conflict with many state laws and city ordinances regulating the distribution of literature and the solicitation of funds. Such laws, in general, required a permit (1) to distribute "circulars, handbooks, advertising or literature of any kind"; (2) to canvass or solicit "orders for goods, paintings, pictures, wares, or merchandise of any kind"; or (3) to "solicit money, services, subscriptions or any valuable thing for any alleged religious, charitable or philanthropic cause." The application for the permit usually had to be made to the chief of police or other official.

The Witnesses, relying upon the religion, speech, and press clauses of the First Amendment, would proceed with their solicitation and distribution activities, as described by Justice Jackson, without securing the required permit. As a result they were arrested and required to defend their activities in court.

Alma Lovell was one of those who did not apply for a permit to distribute literature "as she regarded herself as sent 'by Jehovah to do His work' and that such an application would have been 'an act of disobedience to His commandment.'"[7] She went door to door in the city of Griffin, Georgia, distributing "a pamphlet and magazine in the nature of religious tracts, setting forth the gospel of the 'Kingdom of Jehovah.'"

Because she had no permit she was arrested and brought to trial. For her defense, Lovell contended that the permit ordinance was a violation of freedom of the press, and of the free exercise of religion. She was convicted and fined $50.00 or in default of the payment thereof, sentenced to imprisonment for fifty days.

When the Supreme Court heard Alma Lovell's appeal, they ordered her conviction set aside. The Court chose to base its decision upon the Freedom of the Press Clause rather than the Free Exercise Clause. It said that "the liberty of the press is not confined to newspapers and periodicals. It necessarily embraces pamphlets and leaflets. These indeed have been historic weapons in the defense of liberty, as the pamphlets of Thomas Paine and others in our history abundantly attest."

The justices were concerned that a government official, in this case the city manager, acting without any standards or guidelines whatsoever, could prohibit a person from exercising her First Amendment rights.

> We think that the ordinance is invalid on its face. Whatever the motive which induced its adoption, its character is such that it strikes at the very foundation of the freedom of the press by subjecting it to license and censorship. The struggle for the freedom of the press was primarily directed against the power of the licensor.

Newton Cantwell and his two sons, Jesse and Russell, all Jehovah's Witnesses, while following the tenets of their faith, also found themselves in violation of an antisolicitation law. They were arrested and charged with violating a Connecticut state law that prohibited the solicitaton of "money, services, subscriptions or any valuable thing for any alleged religious, charitable or philanthropic cause . . . unless such cause shall have been approved by the secretary of the public welfare council."[8] If the secretary of the council found that the cause was not religious, charitable, or philanthropic, he was authorized to disapprove the solicitation.

The Newtons, without having had their "cause" approved, were arrested as they went door to door on Cassius Street in New Haven, Connecticut. They were carrying a bag of books and pamphlets, a phonograph, and records. Cassius Street was "a thickly populated neighborhood, where about ninety per cent of the residents . . . [were] Roman Catholics."

Despite their argument that if the statute were to be applied to them it would violate their right to freedom of speech and the free exercise of their religion, they were convicted, and their convictions were affirmed by the Connecticut Court of Appeals. A unanimous Supreme Court reversed. The justices determined that the statute deprived the Cantwells of the right freely to practice the tenets of their faith.

Justice Owen J. Roberts noted in the Court's opinion that the religion clauses have "a double aspect."

> Freedom of conscience and freedom to adhere to such religious organization or form of worship as the individual may choose cannot be restricted by law. On the other hand, it safeguards the free exercise of the chosen form of religion. Thus the Amendment embraces two concepts, —freedom to believe and freedom to act. The first is absolute but, in the nature of things, the second cannot be. Conduct remains subject to regulation for the protection of society.

But in this case again it was the power of censorship in the hands of the secretary of the public welfare council that the Court found objectionable. "Such a censorship of religion as the means of determining its right to survive is a denial of liberty protected by the First Amendment and included in the liberty which is within the protection of the Fourteenth."

The pamphlets and books the Jehovah's Witnesses distributed were published and sold to the members by the Watch Tower Bible & Tract Society of Brooklyn, New York. By either selling the material or accepting a contribution from the listener in exchange for the publications, it was possible for the members to make a small profit. Much of the material, however, was given away to people who would not make a contribution.

In 1943 Justice Douglas declared that "this form of evangelism is utilized today on large scale by various religious sects whose colporteurs carry the Gospel to thousands upon thousands of homes and seek through personal visitations to win adherents to their faith. It is more than preaching; it is more than distribution of religious literature. It is a combination of both."[9]

This method of evangelism, however, brought Robert Murdock, Jr., and several other Jehovah's Witnesses in conflict with an ordinance of the city of Jeannette, Pennsylvania, which required a licence to canvass or solicit "orders for goods, paintings, pictures, wares, or merchandise of any kind." The license fee for one day was $1.50; for one week, $7.00; and for two weeks, $12.00

Mr. Murdock and his colleagues were convicted of going door to door distributing and offering for sale pamphlets and books of the Watch Tower Society because they had not secured a license as the above ordinance required them to do. When the case reached the Supreme Court, the convictions were set aside. Justice Felix Frankfurter, in a dissenting opinion, said that the issue in the case "is not whether a city may charge for the dissemination of ideas but whether the states have power to require those who need additional facilities to help bear the cost of furnishing such facilities." The additional facilities referred to by Justice Frankfurter would be the public streets, a place that the Witnesses need to spread the Gospel. In addition to using the streets, street hawkers, he argued make demands upon the municipality for maintaining the peace and traffic regulation.

Justice Douglas and the majority clearly saw the matter in a different light. That the literature was for sale did not make it a commercial transaction according to the majority. "Freedom of speech, freedom of the press, freedom of religion are available to all, not merely to those who can pay their own way," Justice Douglas explained. "It is a distortion of the facts of the record to describe their activities as the occupation of selling books and pamphlets."

The majority wanted to be sure that the method of preaching practiced by the Witnesses was not treated any differently than that of more orthodox religions. "This form of religious activity occupies the same high estate under the First Amendment as do worship in the churches and preaching from the pulpits. It has the same claim to protection as the more orthodox and conventional exercises of religion."

Justice Black once said, "I do not believe that it can be too often repeated that the freedoms of speech, press, petition and assembly guaranteed by the First Amendment must be accorded to the ideas we hate or sooner or later they will be denied to the ideas we cherish."[10] The Court applied that principle in the case of *Kunz v. New York.*[11]

Carl Jacob Kunz was a Baptist minister who believed that it was his duty to go out onto the "highways and byways" and preach the gospel. He applied for and received a permit to preach on the streets as required by a New York City ordinance. On one particular day, Kunz made some "scurrilous attacks on Catholics and Jews." He said that "the Catholic Church makes merchandise out of souls," that Catholicism is "a religion of the devil," and that the Pope is "the anti–Christ." The Jews he denounced as "Christ-killers," and he said of them, "All the garbage that didn't believe in Christ should have been burnt in the incinerators. It's a shame they all weren't."

When city officials learned of Kunz's attacks on other religions, they revoked his speaking permit. He then applied for another one, but that was not granted. He took to the streets anyway and began speaking. Shortly thereafter he was arrested and convicted for holding a religious meeting without a permit. Despite his derogatory statements about other religions, the Supreme Court overruled the lower courts and set aside the conviction because the law requiring the permit contained no standards to guide the issuer in granting a permit or in revoking one previously granted. Once again, the justices' major concern was the power of a public official to grant permits to those whose messages he approved and deny a permit to those with whom he disagreed.

> We have here, then, an ordinance which gives an administrative official discretionary power to control in advance the right of citizens to speak on religious matters on the streets of New York. As such, the ordinance is clearly invalid as prior restraint on the exercise of First Amendment rights.

This decision disturbed Justice Jackson.

> The contention which Kunz brings here and which this Court sustains is that such speeches on the streets are within his constitutional freedom and therefore New York City has no power to require a permit. He does not deny that this has been and will continue to be his line of talk.

New York and other cities can of course require a permit to use public streets and parks for the exercise of First Amendment freedoms. They must, however, draw such laws so that the permit issuer has no control over the speaker's message, other than determining the time, place, and manner of the speech.

Many times the issue is not whether a particular law is constitutional but whether a valid law can be applied to the speaker. And sometimes the answer to that question depends upon the *place* where the person is exercising his or her rights to religious freedom. Grace Marsh found herself embroiled in just such a situation when she stood on a sidewalk in Chickasaw, Alabama, in the fall of 1943. She was distributing the *Watchtower* and *Consolation,* both periodicals of the Jehovah's Witnesses.

The whole town of Chickasaw was owned by the Gulf Shipbuilding Corporation. It was a company town with streets, business buildings, homes, a post office, and police officers like any other town. After being detained for a short time by a police officer because she was distributing religious material, Marsh went to see the company's vice president in charge of the town. She told him that she was an "ordained minister" and that "her continuance in this God-given activity . . . meant everlasting 'life or death' at the hand of Almighty God, . . . [she] would have to insist on . . . [her] constitutional right to distribute this printed message of God's Kingdom to the people. . . ."[12]

The vice president told her that because this was a privately owned company town, she could not distribute material without a permit, and he would not give one to her. Further, he warned her not to come on the streets again. Marsh, ignoring the warning, went to the same place a few days later, again distributing pamphlets. She was arrested and charged with a law prohibiting trespassing on private property. She was tried by a judge sitting without a jury, convicted, and fined $50.00. The Alabama Supreme Court affirmed, and Marsh appealed to the U.S. Supreme Court. That Court reversed and held that because this was a town like any other town, Marsh was protected by the First Amendment.

> When we balance the Constitutional rights of owners of property against those of the people to enjoy freedom of press and religion, as we must here, we remain mindful of the fact that the latter occupy a preferred position.[13]

The *Marsh* case does not stand for the proposition that all private property is open and available for the exercise of constitutional rights by everyone. Chickasaw was an unusual situation; it was a town just like any other town, but a privately owned one.

The Court has often written "that the First Amendment does not guarantee the right to communicate one's views at all times and places in any manner that may be desired."[14] Streets and parks, however, have traditionally been places where First Amendment activities can be carried on, but as previously noted, some regulation by government is allowed, provided that such regulation minimizes the chance for censorship of the speaker's message. Streets and parks are not the only pieces of government property that may be available for First Amendment activities. This aspect of the First Amendment will be explored in detail in Chapter VI, Freedom of Speech. However, as the Jehovah's Witnesses cases illustrate, sometimes the speaker's message is a religious one, which brings into play both the Free Exercise and Free Speech clauses.

The International Society for Krishna Conscience (Krishna) found itself involved in such a struggle over the place for proselytizing and distribution of literature at the Minnesota State Fair. The state fair attracts hundreds of exhibitors and thousands of visitors each year. In order to accommodate exhibitors and control visitors, the Fair Board has a rule requiring that distribution or sale of merchandise, including printed or written material, shall be done only from a rented booth. The rule does not prohibit exhibitors from engaging in face-to-face discussions with visitors any place on the fair grounds.

One of the rituals of the Krishna religion is the practice of *Sankirtan* "which enjoins its members to go into public places to distribute or sell religious literature and to solicit donations for the support of the Krishna religion." The Krishnas, in performing *Sankirtan*, often give flowers or American flags to the people they contact. They wanted to do this at the fair without being confined to a booth. When the board refused to allow them to distribute material and seek contributions throughout the grounds, the Krishnas brought an action against the board seeking an injunction against the enforcement of the rule. They argued that forced compliance with the rule was a violation of their rights freely to exercise their religion.

The trial court issued an order allowing the Krishnas to espouse their religious views and distribute literature anyplace on the grounds but prohibiting them from *selling* any literature or items except from a booth. The Minnesota Supreme Court reversed, being of the opinion that the free exercise of the rights of the Krishnas outweighed the state's need to control the orderly movement of the crowd. A majority of the U.S. Supreme Court took a different view. They were of the opinion that "the State's interest in avoiding congestion and maintaining the orderly movement of fair patrons" made the rule valid, and that therefore the Krishnas and the other charitable and religious organizations could be confined to a fixed location.

> None of our cases suggest that the inclusion of peripatetic solicitation as part of a church ritual entitles church members to solicitation rights in a public forum superior to those of members of other religious groups that raise money but do not purport to ritualize the process.

Citizenship and the Conscientious Objector

*"I am willing to do everything that an American citizen has to do except fighting."**

In three cases the Supreme Court has grappled with the question of the admission to citizenship by a person who by reason of religious beliefs could not conscientiously take an oath agreeing to take up arms in defense of the country. In two of the cases, the justices upheld lower court decisions denying citizenship to such persons.[15]

Chief Justice Charles Evans Hughes, however, vigorously defended a person's right to religious beliefs.

> It goes without saying that it was not the intention of the Congress in framing the oath to impose any religious test. When we consider the history of the struggle for religious liberty, the large number of citizens of our country, from the very beginning, who have been unwilling to sacrifice their religious convictions, and in particular, those who have been conscientiously opposed to war and who would not yield what they sincerely believed to their allegiance to the will of God, I find it impossible to conclude that such persons are to be deemed disqualified for public office in this country because of the requirement of the oath which must be taken before they enter upon their duties.

**United States v. Schwimmer,* 279 U.S. 644, 648 (1929).

In 1946, in *Girouard v. United States,*[16] the above decisions were reversed, and the court held that one "who is willing to take the oath of allegiance and to serve in the army as a non-combatant but who, because of religious scruples, is unwilling to bear arms in defense of this country may be admitted to citizenship." In this case, the Court emphasized the importance of religious beliefs in people's lives and pointed out that the Free Exercise Clause was intended to protect those beliefs.

> Throughout the ages, men have suffered death rather than subordinate their allegiance to God to the authority of the State. Freedom of religion guaranteed by the First Amendment is the product of that struggle. As we recently stated, . . . "Freedom of thought, which includes freedom of religious belief, is basic in a society of free men."

Conscientious Objectors and Military Service

"And every citizen owes the reciprocal duty . . . to support and defend government against all enemies."*

Because the defense of our country is a very important public interest, claims of violation of free exercise in the context of service in the armed forces has not met with much success.

The first time the justices addressed the issue of religious beliefs versus military service arose when Albert W. Hamilton and W. Alonzo Reynolds, who were students at the University of California, requested an exemption from a course in military science and tactics given as part of the training in the Reserve Officers Training Corps.

Hamilton and Reynolds were members of the Methodist Church, and their fathers were Methodist ministers. The church had adopted a resolution renouncing "war as an instrument of national policy," and declaring: "We hold that our country is benefited by having as citizens those who unswervingly follow the dictates of their consciences. . . ."[17]

When the students refused to enroll in the military science class, they were suspended but were given permission to reapply for admission upon the condition that they agree to fulfill all school requirements. Instead of reapplying, however, they brought suit against the regents seeking an order readmitting them and exempting them from the military science class. The trial court refused to do so, and that decision was upheld by the Supreme Court.

**Hamilton v. Regents,* 293 U.S. 245, 262–263 (1934).

The Court acknowledged that the students were asserting their position "unquestionably in good faith," but found "untenable" the assertion that the liberty provision of the Fourteenth Amendment "confers the right to be students in the state university free from obligation to take military training as one of the conditions of attendance."

Although the majority did not specifically hold that the Free Exercise Clause might be applicable here, four concurring justices had no doubt that it did. Justice Benjamin N. Cardozo, writing for those justices, noted, "I assume for present purposes that the religious liberty protected by the First Amendment against invasion by the nation is protected by the Fourteenth Amendment against invasion by the states."

Clyde W. Summers fared no better than Hamilton and Reynolds when he applied for admission to the Illinois Bar. Under Illinois law, men were required to serve in the militia in time of war. Summers had completed all of the requirements for admission to the bar, but he conscientiously objected to war and would not agree to serve in the militia if called. Because of his refusal, his application for bar membership was denied. Neither the lower courts nor the Supreme Court gave much weight to his argument that not to admit him to the practice of law burdened his right to the free exercise of religion.

This decision greatly disturbed justices Black, Douglas, Murphy, and Wiley B. Rutledge. Justice Black pointed out that Summers not only possessed all of the educational requirements for the practice of law, but that

> he is honest, moral, and intelligent, has had a college and a law school education. He has been a law professor and fully measures up to the high standards of legal knowledge Illinois has set as a prerequisite to admission to practice law in that State. He has never been convicted for, or charged with, a violation of law. That he would service his clients faithfully and efficiently if admitted to practice is not denied. His ideals of what a lawyer should be indicate that his activities would not reflect discredit upon the bar, that he would strive to make the legal system a more effective instrument of justice.[18]

Because Congress has chosen to exempt conscientious objectors from military service, the justices have never had to face directly the question of whether such exemption is mandated by the Free Exercise Clause. In *Gillette,* discussed in Chapter IV, the petitioners asserted that they were entitled to be classified as conscientious objectors, even though their religious beliefs prohibited them from participating in "unjust" wars but not from "just" wars. As against the argument that the denial of the CO classification was an infringment upon their free exercise rights, Justice Marshall responded in a footnote "that relief for conscientious objectors is not mandated by the Constitution."[19]

Military service versus religious beliefs was brought before the justices again, but in a somewhat different way, in *Johnson v. Robison*.[20] William Robert Robison received CO classification on the condition that he perform two years' alternate service. He agreed and performed the service at Peter Bent Brigham Hospital in Boston.

At the end of the two-year period, Robison applied to the Veteran's Administration for educational benefits available to veterans. He was informed that because he had not been on "active duty," benefits were not available to him. Robison brought suit seeking to force the Veteran's Administration to provide benefits. He was successful in the lower court, but when the government appealed, the Supreme Court reversed. Robison had argued that the refusal to grant him educational benefits because he had not been on "active duty" was in effect a penalty for the exercise of his religous beliefs, but the majority said it was not. "The withholding of educational benefits involves only an incidental burden upon appellee's [Robison's] free exercise of religion—if, indeed, any burden exists at all." Justice Douglas thought otherwise: "Government, as I read the Constitution and the Bill of Rights," he wrote, "may not place a penalty on anyone for asserting his religious scruples. That is the nub of the present case and the reason why the judgment below should be affirmed."

The assertion of one's religious scruples against war does not necessarily always arise in relation to service in the armed forces. For example, when Eddie C. Thomas found himself forced to work in a machinery plant that produced war materials, he resigned.

Thomas, a Jehovah's Witness, had worked in the roll foundry of the plant, but when that department was closed, he was given an assignment working on military tanks. He immediately sought transfer to a department that was not doing military work, being of the opinion that his contribution to the production of arms was a violation of his religious beliefs. Because there was no such department in the plant, he asked to be laid off, and when that was denied, he quit. He then sought unemployment compensation benefits.

Having left his job without good cause, according to state officials, benefits were denied to him. His attempts to seek relief in state courts were to no avail. Upon appeal to the Supreme Court, however, eight members agreed that the denial of benefits was an infringement upon Thomas' First Amendment rights.

Chief Justice Warren Burger set forth the Court's reasoning:

> Where the state conditions receipt of an important benefit upon conduct proscribed by a religious faith, or where it denies such a benefit because of conduct mandated by religious belief, thereby putting substantial pressure on an adherent to modify his behavior and to violate his beliefs, a burden upon religion exists. While the compulsion may be indirect, the infringement upon free exercise is nontheless substantial.[21]

Keep Holy the Sabbath Day

*"But the seventh day is the sabbath of the Lord thy God; in it thou shall not do any work...."**

The sabbath is an important part of the religious lives of many people, even to the extent that the performance of any work on that day becomes a serious matter of conscience. When the government becomes involved in placing a burden upon one's honoring the sabbath, a free exercise problem arises. This question has been before the Court in several cases.

One of those cases involved Adell H. Sherbert, a member of the Seventh-Day Adventists Church, who worked a five-day week at a textile mill. In 1959 the workweek at the mill was changed to six days, including Saturday, for all shifts. Because Saturday was the sabbath for Seventh-Day Adventists like Sherbert, she refused to work that day, and as a result was fired. Shortly thereafter, she applied for unemployment compensation, which was denied because she would not accept other work if that work included working on Saturdays.

In taking the matter to court, Sherbert argued that to deny unemployment benefits because her religious beliefs prevented her from working on her sabbath abridged her First Amendment rights. The state court system did not agree, and upheld the decision of the Unemployment Compensation Commission.

Sherbert's lawyers made the same argument in the Supreme Court and were successful. In reversing the state courts, the Supreme Court first considered whether the refusal of benefits because Sherbert refused to work on Saturday was in any way a burden upon her religious beliefs. In concluding that it was, the majority declared:

*Bible, Deuteronomy 5:12.

> The ruling forces her to choose between following the precepts of her religion and forfeiting benefits, on the one hand, and abandoning one of the precepts of her religion in order to accept work, on the other hand. Governmental imposition of such a choice puts the same kind of burden upon the free exercise of religion as would a fine imposed against appellant [Sherbert] for her Saturday worship.[22]

Having determined that there was a burden upon Sherbert's free exercise of religion, the Court considered whether there were sufficient governmental interests that were so important that they outweighed Sherbert's rights. The state's asserted interest was the "possibility that the filing of fraudulent claims by unscrupulous claimants feigning religious objections to Saturday work might not only dilute the unemployment compensation fund but also hinder the scheduling by employers of necessary Saturday work." This, however, made little impression on the justices. "For even if the possibility of spurious claims did threaten to dilute the fund and disrupt the scheduling of work, it would plainly be incumbent upon the appellees [state] to demonstrate that no alternative forms of regulation would combat such abuses without infringing First Amendment rights."

What the Court did was to weigh Sherbert's free exercise rights against whatever the state declared were the interests which motivated the action it had taken. In order for the state to prevail, however, its interests must be compelling, and the justices will strictly scrutinize those interests to determine whether they are.

Justice Stewart, concurring in the result, discussed what he sees as an anomaly in this decision. Requiring the state to pay benefits in this case was, in effect, the use of public money for the support of religion—Sherbert's religious view that she could not, in good faith, work on Saturdays. Of this anomaly he wrote: "To require South Carolina to so administer its laws as to pay public money to the appellant [Sherbert] under the circumstances of this case is thus clearly to require the State to violate the Establishment Clause as construed by this Court." It was not this decision, however, which disturbed him; rather it was the Court's approach to Establishment Clause cases to which he was opposed.

Both Thomas and Sherbert were members of an established religion. Thomas was a member of the Jehovah's Witnesses; Sherbert, a Seventh-Day Adventist. The situation, however, was different for William A. Frazee, who refused to take a temporary job that would have required him to work on Sunday. Frazee identified himself as a Christian but did not claim to be attached to any organized Christian church. His opposition to working on Sunday, therefore, was not based upon a tenet of faith of a religious body.

His application for unemployment benefits was denied, and, as in *Sherbert* the lower courts agreed with the Department of Employment Security that he did not have "good cause" for not accepting "suitable work," thus making him ineligible for compensation.

The state's rejection of Frazee's application was reversed by the Supreme Court in an unanimous decision. "Our judgments in [previous] cases rested on the fact that each of the claimants had a sincere belief that religion required him or her to refrain from the work in question. Never did we suggest that unless a claimant belongs to a sect that forbids what his job requires, his belief, however sincere, must be deemed a purely personal preference rather than a religous belief."[23]

The state appellate court had attempted to justify the state's refusal of benefits:

> What would Sunday be today if professional football, baseball, basketball and tennis were barred. Today Sunday is not only a day for religion, but for recreation and labor. Today the supermarkets are open, service stations dispense fuel, utilities continue to serve the people and factories continue to belch smoke and tangible products . . . if all Americans were to abstain from working on Sunday, chaos would result.

The justices were not impressed. They doubted "that there [would] be a mass movement away from Sunday employ if William Frazee succeeds in his claim."

As noted in Chapter IV, the Court has upheld Sunday closing laws as against an argument that such laws violate the Establishment Clause. It can be argued, however, that these laws under some circumstances violate the Free Exercise Clause as well. Such was the situation that confronted several members of the Jewish faith in the case of *Braunfeld v. Brown*.[24] Abraham Braunfeld, Isaac Friedman, Alter Diament, S. David Friedmen, and Joseph Friedman were engaged in the business of selling clothing and home furnishings. "Each [was] a member of the Orthodox Jewish faith, which requires the closing of their places of business and a total abstention from all manner of work from nightfall each Friday until nightfall each Saturday." Under the laws of Pennsylvania, they were also required to close on Sunday, a day that they had counted upon somewhat to make up for the business lost by closing on Saturday.

In taking the state to court, these businessmen "contend that the enforcement against them of the Pennsylvania statute will prohibit the free exercise of their religion because, due to the statute's compulsion to close on Sunday [they] will suffer substantial economic loss, to the benefit of their non-Sabbatarian competitiors, if [they] also continue their Sabbath observance by closing their businesses on Saturday."

The courts, including the Supreme Court, turned aside their pleas for an exemption from compliance with the law. The majority reviewed several cases wherein they had been confronted with the question of determining the validity of laws making certain acts criminal, even though those acts were part of a religious belief. "In such cases," the Court wrote, "to make accommodation between the religious action and an exercise of state authority is a particularly delicate task, . . . because resolution in favor of the State results in the choice to the individual of either abandoning his religious principle or facing criminal prosecution."

But, the majority went on to point out, that was not the situation here.

> This is not the case before us because the statute at bar does not make unlawful any religious practices of appellants; the Sunday law simply regulates a secular activity, and as applied to appellants, operates so as to make the practice of their religious beliefs more expensive.

Justice Stewart expressed disagreement with the majority's decision.

> Pennsylvania has passed a law which compels an Orthodox Jew to choose between his religious faith and his economic survival. That is a cruel choice. It is a choice which I think no State can constitutionally demand.

Government Mandates versus Religious Beliefs

"Compulsory unification of opinion achieves only the unanimity of the graveyard."*

Walter Barnette and other members of the Jehovah's Witnesses brought an action against the West Virginia State Board of Education seeking an injunction restraining them from enforcing a flag salute regulation.

**Board of Education v. Barnette,* 319 U.S. 624, 641 (1943).

What is now required is the "stiff-arm" salute, the saluter to keep the right hand raised with palm turned up while the following is repeated: "I pledge allegiance to the Flag of the United States of America and to the Republic for which its stands; one Nation, indivisible, with liberty and justice for all."[25]

Among the religious beliefs of Witnesses is the biblical exhortation in Exodus 20:3–5 that "3. Thou shalt have no other gods before me. 4. Thou shalt not make unto thee any graven image, or any likeness of *anything* that *is* in the heaven above, or that *is* in the earth beneath, or that *is* in the water under the earth: 5. Thou shalt not bow down thyself to them nor serve them. . . ."

The Witnesses' complaint was that to force their children to participate in the flat salute ritual was a denial of their religious liberty under the First Amendment.

Just three years before, a majority of the Court had held that there was no violation of the First Amendment in requiring all children to salute the flag.[26] In that case, the majority seemed to be of the opinion that "the mere possession of religious convictions which contradict the relevant concerns of a political society does not relieve the citizen from the discharge of political responsibilities."

When Barnette's case reached the Supreme Court, a new majority overruled the prior case and upheld the claim that forced participation in the flag salute violated the First Amendment. The Court first acknowledged that the flag was a symbol and that the salute was a form of speech. It then made what has become one of its more notable pronouncements:

> The very purpose of a Bill of Rights was to withdraw certain subjects from the vicissitudes of political controversy, to place them beyond the reach of majorities and officials and to establish them as legal principles to be applied by the courts. One's right to life, liberty, and property, to free speech, a free press, freedom of worship and assembly, and other fundamental rights may not be submitted to vote; they depend on the outcome of no elections.[27]

The justices therefore held that "the action of the local authorities in compelling the flag salute and pledge transcends constitutional limitations on their power and invades the sphere of intellect and spirit which it is the purpose of the First Amendment to our Constitution to reserve from all official control."

The majority opinion in the earlier flag salute case was written by Justice Frankfurter, who dissented in this case. Justice Frankfurter, a Jew, started his dissenting opinion by stating that "one who belongs to the most vilified and persecuted minority in history is not likely to be insensible to the freedoms guaranteed by our Constitution." And he went on to point out that he would join the majority opinion if his "personal attitude" were relevant, but of course it was not. "It can never be emphasized too much that one's own opinion about the wisdom or evil of a law should be excluded altogether when one is doing one's duty on the bench." His concern was that the other justices were using their personal feelings to usurp the power of the state legislature in its effort to promote good citizenship by the flag salute requirement.

As pointed out in Chapter I, many of those who came to settle our country came to escape religious persecution. Among their concerns was the requirement of having to take a religious test oath. That concern formed the basis for the inclusion in Article VI of the Constitution that "no religious Test shall ever be required as a Qualification to any Office or public Trust under the United States." It also played a part in the inclusion of the Free Exercise Clause in the First Amendment.

In order to become a notary public in the state of Maryland, the applicant was required to take the following oath: "I, _____, do declare that I believe in the existence of God."[28] Roy R. Torcaso was appointed as a notary by the governor of Maryland, but when he was asked to take the oath, he declined to declare an existence of God. As a result, the county clerk refused to deliver the commission which validated his appointment. Torcaso sought relief in the state courts.

In upholding the oath, however, the Maryland Court of Appeals was of the opinion that Mr. Torcaso was not being compelled to believe anything because he was not compelled to be a notary. This argument did not convince the justices of the Supreme Court, who all agreed that Maryland's oath requirement violated Torcaso's right to believe whatever he wanted to.

> This Maryland religious test for public office unconstitutionally invades the appellant's freedom of belief and religion and therefore cannot be enforced against him.[29]

The Old Order Amish believe in a simple Christian life that emphasizes spiritual values and renounces material things. They do not use modern conveniences such as automobiles, telephones, radios, or television sets, and their dress is different and simple.

> Amish society emphasizes informal learning-through-doing; a life of "goodness," rather than a life of intellect; wisdom, rather than technical knowledge; community welfare, rather than competition; and separation from rather than integration with, contemporary worldly society.[30]

Because this lifestyle is an integral part of the Amish religious beliefs, they firmly object to public education for their children beyond the eighth grade. Education to that point is acceptable to them "because they agree that their children must have basic skills in the 'three R's' in order to read the Bible, to be good farmers and citizens, and to be able to deal with non–Amish people when necessary in the course of daily affairs."

But education in high school exposes their children to worldy values and takes them away from home at a period in their lives when they should be learning the skills "needed to perform the adult role of an Amish farmer or housewife." During this time the children "must learn to enjoy physical labor."

Amish members Jonas Yoder and Wallace Miller had sent their children to the public schools in Green County, Wisconsin, until the children graduated from the eighth grade. Although the children had not reached age 16, their parents refused to allow them to continue in school. This brought the parents in conflict with the state compulsory school attendance law which required attendance until 16. They were charged, tried, and convicted of violating the law and fined $5.00.

Upon appeal to the Wisconsin Supreme Court, the convictions were reversed because forced schooling beyond the eighth grade violated Amish religious beliefs. The state appealed to the U.S. Supreme Court, which agreed with the Wisconsin court and affirmed its decision.

The justices recognized that a state has a "high responsibility for education of its citizen" but declared that no matter how high that interest is ranked, it "is not totally free from a balancing process when it impinges on fundamental rights and interests, such as those specifically protected by the Free Exercise Clause . . . and the traditional interest of parents with respect to the religious upbringing of their children. . . ."

Before balancing the state's interest against the Amish assertion of their First Amendment claim, the Court needed to determine whether "the Amish religious faith and their mode of life are, as they claim, inseparable and interdependent."

After reviewing the evidence with regard to the Amish beliefs and method of living, the Court found:

> The conclusion is inescapable that secondary schooling, by exposing Amish children to worldly influences in terms of attitudes, goals, and values contrary to beliefs, and by substantially interfering with the religious development of the Amish child and his integration into the way of life of the Amish faith community at the crucial adolescent stage of development, contravenes the basic religious tenets and practice of the Amish faith, both as to the parent and the child.

Having concluded that forcing the Amish children to attend school beyond the eighth grade would burden the religious rights of the parents and the child, the justices inquired whether there were any state interests which were of sufficient weight to override the rights of the Amish.

Two interests were asserted by the state: (1) "some degree of education is necessary to prepare citizens to participate effectively and intelligently in our open political system if we are to preserve freedom and independence"; (2) "education prepares individuals to be self-reliant and self-sufficient participants in society."

While a majority of the justices accepted these as valid and important governmental interests, they were of the opinion that additional education for Amish children "would do little to serve those interests" because these children were not being educated "for life in a modern society as the majority live," but education in this case is "the preparation of the child for life in the separated agrarian community that is the keystone of the Amish faith." Therefore, in the balancing equation, the religious rights of the Amish were more important than the state's interest, and the Amish need not send their children to school beyond the eighth grade.

But what about the rights of the Amish children? This question concerned Justice Douglas, and he therefore filed a dissenting opinion.

> On this important and vital matter of education, I think the children should be entitled to be heard. While the parents, absent dissent, normally speak for the entire family, the education of the child is a matter on which the child will often have decided views. He may want to be a pianist or an astronaut or an oceanographer. To do so he will have to break from the Amish tradition.
>
> It is the future of the student, not the future of the parents, that is imperiled by today's decision.

Although the Court has acknowledged that the values of the Amish faith "are worthy of preservation," sometimes such values must give way to what a majority of the justices see as the greater interests of government.

For example, "The Amish believe that there is a religiously based obligation to provide for their fellow members the kind of assistance contemplated by the social security system."[31] Because of that belief, Amish member Edwin D. Lee, a self-employed farmer and carpenter, being of the opinion that it would be a violation of this tenet of his faith, paid his share of social security taxes in protest and sued the government for reimbursement.

In denying reimbursement, the Supreme Court willingly accepted the assertion that the payment of such taxes and receipt of benefits from the social security program were forbidden by Lee's faith. Nevertheless, the Court held that "to maintain an organized society that guarantees religious freedom to a great variety of faiths requires that some religious practices yield to the common good."

Another religious practice which was required to "yield to the common good," was the use of "peyote for sacramental purposes at a ceremony of the Native American Church. . . ."[32]

Alfred Smith and Galen Black, who worked for a drug rehabilitation organization and were members of the Church in Oregon, were discharged for using peyote during a church ceremony. Their application for unemployment compensation was thereafter denied because "they had been discharged for work-related 'mis-conduct,'" The misconduct being the use of a "controlled substance" [peyote], which was a felony under Oregon law.

Smith and Black appealed to the Oregon Court of Appeals, which reversed the decision of the Employment Division because "the denial of benefits violated [Smith's and Black's] free exercise rights under the First Amendment." The Supreme Court of Oregon agreed. Although that court held that the law "'makes no exception for the sacramental use' of the drug," it also held that for the state to deny unemployment compensation in this case would be a violation of free exercise of religion. Six justices of the U.S. Supreme Court reversed and in an opinion written by Justice Scalia held that "because [the] ingestion of peyote was prohibited under Oregon Law, and because that prohibition is constitutional, Oregon may, consistent with the Free Exercise Clause, deny [Smith and Black] unemployment compensation when their dismissal results from use of the drug."

The majority relied upon cases similar to that of farmer Lee, wherein the Court had held that the Amish faith did not protect him from paying his share of social security taxes. Our "decisions," Justice Scalia explained, "have consistently held that the right of free exercise does not relieve an individual of the obligation to comply with a 'valid and neutral law of general applicability on the ground that the law proscribes (or prescribes) conduct that his religion prescribes (or proscribes).'"

When confronted with the argument that the Court had used a "balancing test" in cases such as that of Adell H. Sherbert and Eddie C. Thomas, Justice Scalia responded that those decisions "have nothing to do with an across-the-board criminal prohibition on a particular form of conduct." And further, "we conclude today that the sounder approach, and the approach in accord with the vast majority of our precedents, is to hold the test inapplicable to such challenges."

Justice O'Connor concurred only in the result. "In my view," she insisted, "today's holding dramatically departs from well-settled First Amendment jurisprudence, appears unnecessary to resolve the question presented, and is incompatible with our Nation's fundamental commitment to individual religious liberty." "To reach this sweeping result," she continued, "...the Court must not only give a strained reading of the First Amendment but must also disregard our consistent application of free exercise doctrine to cases involving generally applicable regulations that burden religious conduct."

Justice O'Connor, turning to the issue in this case, concluded that the proper inquiry was whether Oregon had a compelling interest in the enforcement of its drug laws so as to outweigh the religious rights of Smith and Black. She held that the state did have such an interest. "There is . . . no dispute," she declared, "that Oregon has a significant interest in enforcing laws that control the possession and use of controlled substances by its citizens" and that "in view of the societal interest in preventing trafficking in controlled substances, uniform application of the criminal prohibition at issue is essential to the effectiveness of Oregon's stated interest in preventing any possession of peyote."

Dissenters Blackmun, Brennan, and Marshall were also of the opinion that the majority was departing from long-established free exercise jurisprudence. Justice Blackmun described that policy as follows:

> This Court over the years painstakingly has developed a consistent and exacting standard to test the constitutionality of a state statute that burdens the free exercise of religion. Such a statute may stand

only if the law in general, and the State's refusal to allow a religious exemption in particular, are justified by a compelling interest that cannot be served by less restrictive means.

Applying that approach, the dissenters found that Oregon did not have a compelling reason for enforcing its drug laws against the Native American Church. There was absolutely "no evidence that the religious use of peyote has ever harmed anyone." Furthermore, Justice Blackmun noted, "the Native American Church's internal restrictions on, and supervision of its members' use of peyote substantially obviate the State's health and safety concerns." This led the dissenters to the conclusion "that Oregon's interest in enforcing its drug laws against religious use of peyote is not sufficiently compelling to outweigh [Smith and Black's] right to the free exercise of their religion."

The Right Not to Speak

"The right of freedom of thought ... includes both the right to speak freely and the right to refrain from speaking at all." *

Sometimes what the government declares as the "common good" may be quite elusive, especially when such declaration collides with free exercise rights. Such was the situation that George and Maxine Maynard found themselves in when they received their license plates from the state of New Hampshire. Embossed on the plates was the state motto, Live Free or Die.[33] The Maynards, who were Jehovah's Witnesses, found the motto "repugnant to their moral, religious, and political beliefs...." Following their conscience, they therefore covered the words with tape in violation of a state law prohibiting the covering of any of the letters or numbers.

On two occasions, Mr. Maynard was given citations for violating the law. He was found guilty of both offenses and fined $25 for each conviction. He refused to pay the fines and was sentenced to jail for fifteen days.

In reversing Maynard's convictions, the Supreme Court declared that "the right to speak and the right to refrain from speaking are complementary components of the broader concept of 'individual freedom of mind.'" And further, "the First Amendment protects the right of individuals to hold a point of view different from the majority and to

---

*Wooley v. Maynard, 430 U.S. 705, 714 (1977).

refuse to foster, in the way New Hampshire commands, an idea they find morally objectionable."

But having decided that the Maynards were protected by the First Amendment does not end the inquiry. Still to be resolved is whether the benefit the state gains was sufficient to outweigh free exercise values. The values sought to be gained by New Hampshire were that the "display of the motto (1) facilitates the identification of passenger vehicles, and (2) promotes appreciation of history, individualism, and state pride."

The majority found that the obliteration of the motto in no way advanced the first goal of the law because the letters and numbers on the plate clearly identified the vehicle without reference to the motto. Regarding the second interest, although the majority found it legitimate, it held that "no matter how acceptable to some, such interest cannot outweigh the individual's First Amendment right to avoid becoming the courier" for the state's message.

Justice Rehnquist, writing for himself and Justice Blackmun, dissented. "The state has not forced [the Maynards] to 'say' anything. . . . The State has simply required that *all* non-commercial automobiles bear license tags with the state motto, 'Live Free or Die.' . . . [The Maynards] have not been forced to affirm or reject that motto. . . ."

Freedom to Believe the Unbelievable

*"Men may believe what they cannot prove."**

The very essence of faith is a belief in matters that are beyond proof. And the very heart of the First Amendment is the protection of just such beliefs.

This truism was put to the test in the case of *United States v. Ballard*.[34] Edna W. Ballard, Donald Ballard, and others were indicted for using the mails to defraud. They were part of a religious movement referred to as I Am. They claimed to be divine messengers and teachers with the power to heal and cure disease, including some considered to be incurable. In carrying out this mission, they produced and distributed literature relating to the I Am movement. This material was sold, and funds and memberships were solicited through the postal system. The government, being of the opinion that the declarations

United States v. Ballard, 322 U.S. 78, 86 (1944).

made by the Ballards were false, had them indicted by a grand jury for using the mail to defraud.

At the trial, Judge J.F.T. O'Connor allowed the jury to consider whether defendants sincerely believed that which they represented but would not permit them to consider whether the representations were true or false. The defendants were found guilty and appealed to the court of appeals. That court reversed on the grounds that in order to prove that the defendants acted fraudulently, it was necessary for the government to prove that the beliefs were false.

The Supreme Court disagreed, reversed the court of appeals, and remanded the case for further consideration in light of its opinion.

> Man's relation to his God was made no concern of the state. He was granted the right to worship as he pleased and to answer to no man for the verity of his religious views. The religious views espoused by respondents might seem incredible, if not preposterous, to most people. But if those doctrines are subject to trial before a jury charged with finding their truth or falsity, then the same can be done with the religious beliefs of any sect. When the triers of fact undertake that task, they enter a forbidden domain.

The decision then focused on whether the defendants truly believed that their message was true rather than on the truth or falsity of those beliefs. If the jury found that the Ballards believed that which they proclaimed, then of course there was no fraud. Although Justice Jackson thought the defendants' "teachings nothing but humbug," he found the decision very troubling and would have dismissed the case entirely. He could "not see how we can separate an issue as to what is believed from considerations as to what is believable." He recognized that the promotion of the "unbelievable" causes many "believers" to part with their money, but he did not think that such "individual payments [were] ruinous."

> But the real harm is on the mental and spiritual plane. There are those who hunger and thirst after higher values which they feel wanting in their humdrum lives. . . . When they are deluded and then disillusioned, cynicism and confusion follow. The wrong of these things, as I see it, is not in the money the victims part with half so much as in the mental and spiritual poison they get. But that is precisely the thing the Constitution put beyond the reach of the prosecutor, for the price of freedom of religion or of speech or of the press is that we must put up with, and even pay for, a good deal of rubbish.

Upon remand, the court of appeals affirmed the conviction, but upon a second appeal to the Supreme Court that decision was set aside because women had been excluded from the grand jury that had indicted the defendants in the first place.

Freedom to Be Different

*"The guarantee of free exercise is not limited to beliefs which are shared by all of the members of a religious sect."**

The court of appeals applied the above principle in an unusual case that arose in the state of Nebraska when Frances J. Quaring applied for a driver's license. Quaring was denied a license because she refused to have her picture taken and affixed to the license as required by state law. She was not a member of any organized religion but did attend a Pentecostal Church and participated in a nondenominational Bible study group.

Quaring based her rejection of the picture requirement on the Second Commandment:

> Thou shalt not make unto thee any graven image or likeness of anything that is in heaven above, or that is in the earth beneath, or that is in the water under the earth.

Her interpretation of this commandment is described by the court of appeals:

> She believes the Second Commandment forbids her from possessing any image having a likeness of anything in creation. She possesses no photographs of her wedding or family, does not own a television set, and refuses to allow decorations in her home that depict flowers, animals, or other creations in nature. When she purchases foodstuffs displaying pictures on their labels, she either removes the label or obliterates the picture with a black marking pen.[35]

The Pentecostal Church did not interpret the Second Commandment as prohibiting the making of photographs or images.

Quaring needed a license to assist her husband in operating a large farming and livestock business as well as to drive to a nearby community where she worked as a bookkeeper.

*Thomas v. Review Bd., Ind. Empl. Sec. Div., 450 U.S. 707, 715–716 (1981).

Based upon this information, the court of appeals determined that "a burden upon Quaring's free exercise of her religion exists in this case." And when such a burden exists, the state must come forth with some compelling reasons why that burden should be sustained. Nebraska offered several reasons. First it argued that "only drivers' licenses containing a photograph of the licensee can provide police officials with an accurate and instantaneous means of identifying a motorist." Judge Myron Bright, writing for the court of appeals, agreed that this was a valid interest but pointed out that the state granted exemptions from the photograph requirement to learners, for school permits issued to farm children, to persons with restricted or minimal driving ability, and for temporary permits. He also took note of the fact that some states do not require photographs on drivers' licenses.

The second reason advanced related to "an important state interest in facilitating the identification of persons writing checks or using credit cards. . . ." Judge Bright responded that many people do not drive at all and therefore have no license, and that to exempt Quaring would simply put her in the same position as those people.

Finally, the state contended that granting exemptions would create an administrative burden upon the licensing system, and that alone should be sufficient to outweigh Quaring's free exercise rights. This did not convince the court of appeals because it was of the opinion that "persons seeking an exemption from the photograph requirement on religious grounds are likely to be few in number."

This led the judges to conclude that "none of the interests the Nebraska officials advance are sufficient to justify the burden upon Quaring's religious liberty." She was therefore entitled to a license without her picture on it.

Nebraska appealed the case to the Supreme Court where, with one justice not participating, the court of appeals decision was affirmed by an equally divided Court.[36]

Government Must Be Accommodated

"The Free Exercise Clause is written in terms of what the government cannot do to the individual, not in terms of what the individual can extract from the government."*

Shortly after *Quaring,* the Court heard another case in which government requirements collided with religious beliefs.

**Sherbert v. Verner,* 374 U.S. 398, 412 (1963).

The question presented is whether the Free Exercise Clause of the First Amendment compels the Government to accommodate a religiously based objection to the statutory requirements that a Social Security number be provided by an applicant seeking to receive certain welfare benefits and that the States use these numbers in administering the benefit programs.[37]

Stephen J. Roy, a Native American of the Abenaki tribe, and Karen Miller applied for benefits under the Aid to Families with Dependent Children (AFDC) and food stamp programs administered by the Pennsylvania Department of Public Welfare. When asked for the social security number of their daughter, Little Bird of the Snow, they refused to supply one, contending that it "would violate their Native American religious beliefs." AFDC benefits were then denied.

Roy and Miller filed an action against the department seeking to be relieved from the social security number requirement, claiming that the Free Exercise Clause entitled them to such exemption. Roy testified that he

is a Native American descended from the Abenaki tribe, and he asserts a religious belief that control over one's life is essential to spiritual purity and indispensable to "becoming a holy person." Based on recent conversations with an Abenaki chief, Roy believes that technology is "robbing the spirit of man." In order to prepare his daughter for greater spiritual power, therefore, Roy testified to his belief that he must keep her person and spirit unique and that the uniqueness of the Social Security number . . . over which she has no control, will serve to "rob the spirit" of his daughter and prevent her from attaining greater spiritual power.

Although a social security number had been issued for Little Bird of the Snow, Roy explained that it was the *use* of the number that would rob his daughter of her spirit.

District Judge Malcolm Muir agreed with the parents and "permanently restrained (the Secretary of Health and Human Services) from making any use of the social security number which was issued in the name of Little Bird of the Snow Roy and from disseminating the number to any agency, individual, business entity, or any other third party." Judge Muir was of the opinion that the possibility of fraud occurring because Little Bird did not have a number was very remote.

The Supreme Court reversed, not because of disagreement with Judge Muir on the fraud issue but because a majority did not believe that the Free Exercise Clause was even involved by the facts.

Never to our knowledge has the Court interpreted the First Amendment to require the Government *itself* to behave in ways that the individual believes will further his or her spiritual development or that of his or her family.

The majority could see no difference between the parents' demands in this case than if they voiced "a sincere religious objection to the size or color of the Government's filing cabinets." And further, "the Free Exercise Clause affords an individual protection from certain forms of governmental compulsion; it does not afford an individual a right to dictate the conduct of the Government's internal procedures."

Justice White dissented and cited the cases of *Thomas v. Review Board* and *Sherbert v. Verner,* discussed above, in which the Court had previously required payment of unemployment benefits to one whose religious beliefs prohibited him from working in an arms factory and for another who could not work on Saturday because it was the Sabbath for her. Justice White apparently found the decision not to allow benefits to Little Snow's parents inconsistent with the decisions to allow unemployment compensation benefits in those cases.

Military Rules versus the Free Exercise Clause

"Review of military regulations challenged on First Amendment grounds is far more deferential than constitutional review of similar laws or regulations designed for civilian society."*

S. Simicha Goldman was an Orthodox Jew and ordained Rabbi. He entered an armed forces scholarship program and studied clinical psychology. After obtaining his degree, he was assigned to active service in the air force and sent to March Air Force Base, California. During this time he wore a yarmulke, the traditional headgear worn by male members of Orthodox Judaism.

After Goldman appeared as a witness in a court-martial, a complaint was lodged that the wearing of the yarmulke was a violation of AF Reg 35-10-"Headgear will not be worn . . . while indoors except by armed security police in the performance of their duties."[38]

No complaint had been made that the yarmulke in any way hindered Goldman from the performance of his duties or that it was offensive to anyone with whom he came in contact.

**Goldman v. Weinberger,* 475 U.S. 503, 507 (1986).

Upon being threatened with a court-martial if he did not cease wearing the headpiece, Goldman brought an action in the federal district court asserting that the application of AFR 35–10 to him violated his free exercise rights. Judge Aubrey E. Robinson, Jr., agreed. The secretary of defense appealed to the court of appeals, which reversed and held that there was no denial of First Amendment rights by the application of the regulation in this case. Upon appeal to the Supreme Court, five justices reached the same conclusion.

The majority followed a line of cases wherein the Court had previously held "that 'the military is, by necessity, a specialized society separate from civilian society.'" It also placed great emphasis upon the need of the military for uniformity and discipline. "The First Amendment therefore does not prohibit [the regulations] from being applied to petitioner, even though their effect is to restrict the wearing of the headgear required by his religious beliefs."

Justice Stevens wrote a concurring opinion in which justices White and Powell concurred. These justices found the application of the regulation sustainable because "it was not motivated by hostility against, or any special respect for, any religious faith. An exception for yarmulkes would represent a fundamental departure from the true principle of uniformity that supports the rule."

But Justice Brennan thought the justices were not fulfilling their obligation to protect fundamental rights to the fullest extent.

> The Court's response to Goldman's request is to abdicate its role as principal expositor of the Constitution and protector of individual liberties in favor of credulous deference to unsupported assertions of military necessity.

Religious Freedom in Prison

*"Prison walls do not form a barrier separating prison inmates from the protections of the Constitution."**

Ahmad Ulhman Shabazz and Sadr-Ud-Din Mateen, inmates at the New Jersey State Prison, sued prison officials claiming a violation of their free exercise rights when the officials adopted regulations making it impossible for the plaintiffs to participate in a weekly Muslim congregational service referred to as Jumu'ah.[39] Jumu'ah, "commanded

*Turner v. Safley, 482 U.S. 78, 84 (1987).

by the Koran . . . must be held every Friday after the sun reaches its zenith and before the Asr, or afternoon prayer."

These services were held regularly in the main prison building. Some inmates, however, were assigned to work details outside. "Because details of inmates were supervised by only one guard, the whole detail was forced to return to the main gate when one prisoner desired to return to the facility." This caused security and administrative problems, and prompted officials to adopt a policy requiring all persons working on outside details to stay there through the entire day. Any Muslim inmate on an outside detail was therefore prohibited from attending Jumu'ah on Friday.

With this exception, however, attempts were made by prison officials to accommodate the demands of the Muslim prisoners. Whenever pork was being served, those of the Islamic faith were given a different meal, and during the month-long period of Ramadan, arrangements were made to allow the inmates time for fasting and prayer.

Not being able to participate in Jumu'ah was a serious impediment to the practice of faith of Shabazz and Mateen. Nevertheless, the Supreme Court, in a 5–4 decision, upheld the regulations as "reasonable."

> To ensure that courts afford appropriate deference to prison officials, we have determined that prison regulations alleged to infringe constitutional rights are judged under a "reasonableness" test less restrictive than that ordinarily applied to alleged infringements of fundamental constitutional rights.

Although a majority recognized the heavy burden this placed upon the Muslim inmates' free exercise rights, that burden was constitutionally permissible, considering the security and administrative needs, and the "ability on the part of the [inmates] to participate in other religious observances of their faith. . . ."

The justices in the minority were not happy with the majority's use of a "reasonable test" to decide the outcome of this case rather than the more restrictive "balancing" test generally used to evaluate "infringements of fundamental constitutional rights" that arise outisde the penal system. "Prisoners," wrote Justice Brennan, "are persons whom most of us would rather not think about. Banished from everyday sight, they exist in a shadow world that only dimly enters our awareness." Acknowledging that inmates do retain some measure of their constitutional rights, the dissenters argued that when prison regulations place a heavy burden on the exercise of fundamental rights, courts ought to scrutinize very carefully the need for such a burden. Such scrutiny is necessary in this case when one considers that "Jumu'ah is the central religious ceremony of Muslims, 'comparable to the Saturday service of the Jewish faith and the Sunday service of the various Christian sects.'" And further, "the State has neither demonstrated that the restriction is necessary to further an important objective nor proved that less extreme measures may not serve its purpose."

Government Should Stay Out of Church Disputes

*"The First Amendment severely circumscribes the role that civil courts may play in resolving church property disputes."**

More than a hundred years ago, the Court adopted a hands-off policy with regard to disputes arising within a religious organization.

> We think the rule of action which should govern the civil courts, founded in a broad and sound view of the relations of church and state under our system of laws . . . is, that, whenever the questions of discipline, or of faith, or ecclesiastical rule, custom, or law have been decided by the highest of . . . [the] church judicatories to which the matter has been carried, the legal tribunals must accept such decisions as final, and as binding on them, in their application to the case before them.[40]

That policy has not prevented resort to the judicial system by church members seeking resolution of disputes within the religious organization to which they belong. But the Court has been adamant that lower courts not become involved in ecclesiastical matters while attempting to resolve such disputes.

One such controversy was the central issue in the case of *Jones v. Wolf*[41] in 1979. A majority of the members of the Vineville Presbyterian Church of Macon, Georgia, voted to separate from the Presbyterian Church of the United States (PCUS) to which it had belonged since 1904. In an effort to resolve the schism within the church, a commission was appointed by the Presbyterian Church to investigate the matter. At the conclusion of its investigation, the commission "issued a written ruling declaring that the minority faction constituted 'the true congregation of Vineville Presbyterian Church. . . .'"

*Presbyterian Church v. Hull Church, 393 U.S. 440, 449 (1969).

Based upon this ruling, the minority faction sought a declaration from a local court that it had the right to possession and use of church property. The majority faction, however, argued that because the title of the property was in the name of the Vineville Presbyterian Church and that they were in control of that church, they were entitled to the property.

The Georgia court, adopting what it said were "neutral principles of law," simply examined the title to the property, a typical legal procedure. Finding that the title was as indicated above and noting that a majority of the members had voted to break away from the PCUS, the court held that the majority faction were entitled to the property. The Georgia Supreme Court affirmed, as did the U.S. Supreme Court.

Justice Blackmun delivered the opinion for the Court's majority by acknowledging that "the First Amendment prohibits civil courts from resolving church property disputes on the basis of religious doctrine and practice." And further, "as a corollary to this commandment, the Amendment requires that civil courts defer to the resolution of issues of religious doctrine or polity by the highest court of a hierarchical church organization."

But in this case, even though "a hierarchical church organization," the PCUS commission, had determined that the minority faction constituted the real Vineville Presbyterian Church, Justice Blackmun and the majority were of the opinion that the "neutral principles" approach taken by the Georgia courts was the correct one.

> The primary advantages of the neutral-principles approach are that it is completely secular in operation, and yet flexible enough to accommodate all forms of religious organization and polity. The method relies exclusively on objective, well-established concepts of trust and property law familiar to lawyers and judges. It thereby promises to free civil courts completely from entanglement in questions of religious doctrine, polity, and practice.

Having said all of this, the Court sent the case back to the Georgia courts because they had not fully explained how they had reached the conclusion that a "majority faction" necessarily constituted the body of the church.

A dissenting opinion written by Justice Powell for himself and three other justices criticized the majority for departing from earlier decisions "that civil courts defer to the resolution of issues of religious doctrine or polity by the highest court of a hierarchical church organization." Pointing out that church disputes should be decided "not to interfere with the free exercise of religion in accordance with church polity and doctrine," Justice Powell declared that "the only course that achieves this constitutional requirement is acceptance by civil courts of the decisions reached within the polity chosen by the church members themselves." In this case that was the Presbyterian Church of the United States to which the Vineville Church belonged.

> It is undisputed that under the established government of the Presbyterian Church—accepted by the members of the church before the schism—the use and control of the church property have been determined authoritatively to be in the petitioners.

Free Exercise of Religion—1991 and Beyond

As the quotation at the beginning of this chapter states, the First Amendment requires that "no official, high or petty can prescribe what shall be orthodox in politics, nationalism, religion, or other matters of opinion." This means that our freedom to believe whatever we wish is absolute. However, sometimes religious beliefs or actions taken based upon those beliefs collide with valid governmental interests.

The Court solved the collision between the beliefs of the Jehovah's Witness and local government by requiring that laws regulating pro-selytizing and solicitation on streets and in parks be narrowly drawn to regulate the time, place, and manner of such activities and leave the government very little power to censor the message of the proselytizers. This method of solving that kind of a case is so well established that it is doubtful that the Court will make any change, certainly not in the near future.

In other cases where there is a direct conflict between a religious belief and valid governmental interests, the Court has used a "balancing of interests" approach to determine whether the right to religious freedom is outweighed by those interests. It scrutinizes the case very carefully and requires the government to cite compelling reasons why the balance ought to be in its favor. The Sabbatarian cases and cases such as the compulsory school attendance, the driver's license, and the unemployment compensation cases fall into this category.

This approach was changed somewhat with the Oregon "peyote case." There are now five justices who have abandoned the balancing of interests test in those cases where a "valid and netural law of general applicability" is being applied to a religious practice. These justices would leave to the state the determination of whether its laws should be applied or not.

If this also means a majority will no longer require a state to prove a compelling interest to sustain its infringement upon religious freedoms, then, in Justice O'Connor's words, this "dramatically departs from well-settled First Amendment Jurisprudence" and does not bode well for free exercise of religion.

VI.
FREEDOM OF SPEECH

"The maintenance of the opportunity for free political discussion to the end that government may be responsive to the will of the people and that changes may be obtained by lawful means, an opportunity essential to the security of the Republic, is a fundamental principle of our constitutional system."
Stromberg v. California, 283, U.S. 359, 369 (1931)

The above quotation contains the very essence of the First Amendment—that free speech is essential to the preservation of a free society. But the Court's recognition thereof did not come until 1931 in the *Stromberg* case when the justices for the first time (140 years after the adoption of the Bill of Rights) upheld the right to speak by overturning the conviction of a person found guilty of displaying a red flag.

Yetta Stromberg, a member of the Young Communist League, was a supervisor in a children's summer camp organized by Communists "for children of the so-called 'working class.'" She taught classes in history and economics, and "'among other things, . . . taught class consciousness, the solidarity of the workers, and the theory that the workers of the world are of one blood and brothers all.'" She also supervised a morning flag-raising ceremony during which the children stood "by their cots and saluted a red flag on which was a device of sickle and hammer. . ." and repeated the following pledge:

> I pledge allegiance to the workers' red flag, and to the cause for which it stands, one aim throughout our lives, freedom for the working class.

Stromberg was found guilty of violating the following California law:

> Any person who displays a red flag, . . . or any flag, . . . of any color or form whatever in any public place . . . as a sign, symbol or

108

emblem of opposition to organized government or as an invitation
or stimulus to anarchistic action or as an aid to propaganda that is
of a seditious character is guilty of a felony.[1]

At the end of Stromberg's trial, the judge instructed the jury that
they could find Stromberg guilty if she displayed the flag for any one
or more of the following purposes: (1) "as a sign, symbol or emblem
of opposition to organized government," (2) if the flag "was an invitation or stimulus to anarchistic action" or (3) "was in aid to propaganda
that is of a seditious character...."

The jury convicted Stromberg but did not specify whether they
found her guilty of one or all of the possibilities given them by the
judge's instructions. In affirming the verdict, the California appellate
courts accepted the instructions as a correct interpretation of the law.
That in effect gave approval to the possibility that Stromberg might
have been convicted for doing nothing more than displaying a red flag
in "opposition to organized government."

A majority of the Supreme Court voted to reverse, being of the
opinion that to make it a crime just to display a flag "as a sign, symbol,
or emblem of opposition to organized government" would be inconsistent with the intent of the First Amendment.

Freedom to Advocate the Unpopular

*"The best test of truth is the power of the thought to get itself accepted
in the competition of the market...."**

Sometimes the problem is not that a speaker's views are not accepted in the marketplace but whether a speaker can be punished for
his or her opinions, accepted or not. A number of speakers found
themselves in this kind of predicament during World War I—Charles
T. Schenck and Clinton H. Pierce, who advocated opposition to conscription; a Mr. Abrams, who printed and circulated a pamphlet urging
resistance to the war effort; and Joseph Gilbert, accused of discouraging
enlistment in the military or naval forces of the United States. These
individuals, and some others who spoke out against the war, found that
they could be sent to jail for expressing their views, even though they
claimed protection of the First Amendment.

In what is generally recognized as the Supreme Court's first case

---

**Abrams v. United States,* 250 U.S. 616, 630 (1919).

involving free speech, the Court upheld the conviction of Charles T. Schenck for "causing and attempting to cause insubordination . . . in the military forces of the United States, and to obstruct the recruiting and enlistment service of the United States, when the United States was at war with the German Empire. . . ."[2]

Schenck was general secretary of the Socialist party. As such, he printed and distributed a pamphlet that quoted the Thirteenth Amendment to the effect that "neither slavery nor involuntary servitude . . . shall exist within the United States. . . ." The pamphlet connected the prohibition of slavery to the Conscription Act and stated that "a conscript is little better than a convict." Further, "in impassioned language it intimated that conscription was despotism in its worst form and a monstrous wrong against humanity in the interest of Wall Street's chosen few." The document then urged opposition to the draft.

Schenck was arrested and charged with violating the Espionage Act by conspiring to obstruct recruiting for, and causing insubordination in, the armed forces. He was found guilty and appealed to the Supreme Court, which unanimously upheld the verdict.

The Court's opinion in *Schenck* was written by Justice Holmes and is one of those remembered for such rhetorical statements as

> The most stringent protection of free speech would not protect a man in falsely shouting fire in a theatre and causing a panic.

Further:

> The question in every case is whether the words used are used in such circumstances and are of such a nature as to create a clear and present danger that they will bring about the substantive evils that Congress has a right to prevent.

For Schenck's cause, however, the most telling statement was Justice Holmes' admonition that "when a nation is at war many things that might be said in time of peace are such a hindrance to its effort that their utterance will not be endured so long as men fight and that no Court could regard them as protected by any constitutional right." That justified the conviciton, even though the Court admitted "that in many places and in ordinary times [Schenck] in saying all that was said in the circular would have been within [his] constitutional rights."

Schenck was decided on March 3, 1919. Before the end of that year, Justice Holmes found himself on the opposite side of a very similar case, *Abrams v. United States.*[3] Abrams and four others, all of whom were born in Russia and still citizens thereof, published a number of circulars criticizing our involvement in the war and "denouncing President Wilson as a hypocrite and a coward because troops were sent into Russia...."

One of the circulars contained such statements as

> His [the President's] shameful, cowardly silence about the intervention in Russia, reveals the hypocrisy of the plutocratic gang in Washington and vicinity.

> The Russian Revolution cries: Workers of the World! Awake! Rise! Put down your enemy and mine!
> Yes! friends, there is only one enemy of the workers of the world and that is CAPITALISM.

A second circular, which was printed in Yiddish, read: "Workers, Russian emigrants, you who had the least belief in the honesty of *our* Government, ... must now throw away all confidence, must spit in the face the false, hypocritic, military propaganda which has fooled you so relentlessly, calling forth your sympathy, your help, to the prosecution of the war."

Abrams and his colleagues were found guilty of violating the Espionage Act, and a majority of the Supreme Court, justices Holmes and Brandeis dissenting, affirmed that decision. The majority were of the opinion that the defendants hoped "to persuade persons of character such as those whom they regarded themselves as addressing, not to aid government loans and not to work in ammunition factories, where their work would produce 'bullets, bayonets, cannon' and other munitions of war, the use of which would cause the 'murder' of Germans and Russians." "The plain purpose of their propaganda was to excite, at the supreme crisis of the war, disaffection, sedition, riots, and, as they hoped, revolution, in this country for the purpose of embarrassing and if possible defeating the military plans of the Government in Europe."

Justices Holmes and Brandeis not only disagreed with the majority about the intent of Abrams and other defendants but also whether there was as much of a "clear and present danger" to the government here as in *Schenck*. Holmes wrote: "It is only the present danger of immediate evil or an intent to bring it about that warrants Congress in setting a limit to the expression of opinion where private rights are not concerned. Congress certainly cannot forbid all effort to change the mind of the country."

To the dissenters, the defendants were being persecuted for

expressing their opposition to the war, which expression was speech protected by the First Amendment. Justice Holmes pointed out that our constitutional protection for free expression was "an experiment, as all life is an experiment," and "while that experiment is part of our system I think that we should be eternally vigilant against attempts to check the expression of opinions that we loathe and believe to be fraught with death, unless they so imminently threaten immediate interference with the lawful and pressing purposes of the law that an immediate check is required to save the country."

Following *Abrams,* the Court upheld convictions under the Espionage Act of Clinton H. Pierce, Angelo Crero, Charles Z. Zeilman, and Charles Nelson, justices Holmes and Brandeis dissenting.[4] It also affirmed a guilty verdict for Joseph Gilbert's violating a Minnesota law making it unlawful "to interfere with or discourage the enlistment of men in the military or naval forces of the United States or of the State of Minnesota."[5]

As pointed out in Chapter III, justices Holmes and Brandeis were on the losing side in *Gitlow v. New York,* a case in which Benjamin Gitlow was found guilty of violating a state criminal anarchy statute. In that case Justice Holmes planted a seed for what was eventually to become the Court's approach to "advocacy" cases when he discussed the lack of imminent danger to the government from Gitlow's expression of his views. "If the publication of this document," he wrote, "had been laid as an attempt to induce an uprising against the government at once and not at some indefinite time in the future it would have presented a different question."[6]

The late 1940s and early 1950s were turbulent years in our history, an era during which the country was engaged in a prolonged witch-hunt for subversives. Public employees, and especially teachers, were required to take a loyalty oath pledging that they did not advocate the overthrow of the government and were not members of any organization that did so advocate; members of the Communist party were prosecuted for allegedly advocating the overthrow of the government; some teachers were required to list *every* organization to which they belonged during the previous five years, and the House of Representatives created the House Un-American Activities Committee, which conducted an ongoing investigation of subversive activities in the country. Even the writers and producers of motion pictures came under scrutiny during an investigation to see if there were Communists in Hollywood.

Of this period, Elwyn Brooks White wrote:

The most alarming spectacle today is not the spectacle of the
atomic bomb in an unfederated world, it is the spectacle of the
Americans beginning to accept the device of loyalty oaths and witch-
hunts, beginning to call anybody they don't like a Communist.[7]

During these times when the country was obsessed with ferreting
out subversives, the rights protected by the First Amendment—the
right openly to advocate one's views, no matter how unpopular, and to
associate with whomever one chose, no matter how unacceptable they
might be—took a severe beating. During a period commencing in the
late 1940s and extending into the early 1960s, of thirty cases that came
before the Court dealing with communism, or allegedly subversive
organizations, in only twelve was the assertion of constitutional rights
by the individual upheld. And of course there were many other cases,
federal and state, that never reached the Supreme Court.

The most notorious of the "subversive" cases that came to the
Court was *Dennis v. United States,*[8] which involved the prosecution of
eleven officers of the Communist party in the United States. Those
eleven persons—Eugene Dennis, Robert G. Thompson, Gus Hall,
Gilbert Green, John B. Willamson, Henry Winston, Irving Potash,
John Gates, Carl Winter, Jacob Stachel, and Benjamin J. Davis, Jr.—
were charged with violating a federal law commonly referred to as the
Smith Act. Section 2 of that act reads as follows:

Sec. 2. (a) It shall be unlawful for any person—(1) to knowingly
or willfully advocate, abet, advise, or teach the duty, necessity,
desirability, or propriety of overthrowing or destroying any government in the United States by force or violence...;

(2) with intent to cause the overthrow or destruction of any
government in the United States, to print, publish, edit, issue, circulate, sell, distribute, or publicly display any written or printed
matter advocating, advising, or teaching the duty, necessity,
desirability, or propriety of overthrowing or destroying any government in the United States by force or violence;

(3) to organize or help to organize any society, group, or assembly
of persons who teach, advocate, or encourage the overthrow or
destruction of any government in the United States by force or
violence; or to be or become a member of, or affiliate with, any such
society, group, or assembly of persons, knowing the purposes
thereof.[9]

During the trial, which lasted for nine months, there were public
demonstrations outside of the courthouse and much controversy in the
courtroom. Federal District Judge Harold Medina was the trial judge.

"The record discloses a judge, sorely tried for many months of turmoil, constantly provoked by useless bickering, exposed to offensive slights and insults, harried with interminable repetition, who, if at times he did not conduct himself with the imperturbability of a Rhadamanthus, showed considerably greater self-control and forebearance than it is given to most judges to possess."[10]

After hearing testimony sufficient to fill 16,000 pages of the record, the jury convicted all of the defendants, and the court of appeals affirmed. Six justices of the Supreme Court voted to sustain the judgment, two dissented, and one did not participate.

The majority first discussed the Smith Act by noting that "the obvious purpose of the statute is to protect existing Government, not from change by peaceable, lawful and constitutional means, but from change by violence, revolution and terrorism." They agreed with Judge Medina's instructions to the jury, that "they could not convict if they found that [defendants] did 'no more than pursue peaceful studies and discussions or teaching and advocacy in the realm of ideas.'" The majority acknowledged that "the basis of the First Amendment is the hypothesis that speech can rebut speech, propaganda will answer propaganda, free debate of ideas will result in the wisest governmental policies." But the question was whether the activities of these men constituted advocacy of ideas concerning change in government or constituted advocating that the government be overthrown by force and violence in the future. The way to answer this question was, according to the Court, to examine the evidence to see if the endeavors of Dennis and his colleagues "created a clear and present danger" of overthrow of the government.

> Obviously, the words cannot mean that before the Government may act, it must wait until the *putsch* is about to be executed, the plans have been laid and the signal is awaited. If Government is aware that a group aiming at its overthrow is attempting to indoctrinate its members and to commit them to a course whereby they will strike when the leaders feel the circumstances permit, action by the Government is required.[11]

The majority concluded that there was a "clear and present danger" to the country from the activities of the defendants and that their convictions should therefore be affirmed.

Justice Frankfurter, a strong believer that courts should give great deference to legislative judgments, thought that that ought to be done in this case.

Can we then say that the judgment Congress exercised was denied it by the Constitution? Can we establish a constitutional doctrine which forbids the elected representatives of the people to make this choice? Can we hold that the First Amendment deprives Congress of what it deemed necessary for the Government's protection?

But justices Black and Douglas did not see that as the question in this case and dissented. To them, the government did not need protection from what the defendants had done or were doing. Justice Black described the case this way:

These petitioners were not charged with an attempt to overthrow the Government. They were not charged with overt acts of any kind designed to overthrow the Government. They were not even charged with saying anything or writing anything designed to overthrow the Government. The charge was that they agreed to assemble and to talk and publish certain ideas at a later date....

And he went on to note that "public opinion being what it now is, few will protest the conviction of these Communist petitioners. There is hope, however, that in calmer times, when present pressures, passions and fears subside, this or some later Court will restore the First Amendment liberties to the high preferred place where they belong in a free society."

What Dennis and his friends had done, according to Justice Douglas, "was to organize people to teach and themselves teach the Marxist-Leninist doctrine contained chiefly in four books...." "Those books," he went on, "are to Soviet Communism what Mein Kampf was to Nazism." And "[the defendants] are fervent Communists to whom these volumes are gospel. They preached the creed with the hope that some day it would be acted upon." He did not believe, however, that there was any "clear and present danger" to the United States; therefore, First Amendment values ought to prevail.

Some nations less resilient than the United States, where illiteracy is high and where democratic traditions are only budding, might have to take drastic steps and jail these men for merely speaking their creed. But in America they are miserable merchants of unwanted ideas; their wares remain unsold. The fact that their ideas are abhorrent does not make them powerful.

In upholding the convictions of Dennis and his associates, the majority recognized that the First Amendment does protect advocacy, even advocacy of the overthrow of the government by force and violence as long as there is no "present danger" of the accomplishment of that goal. In so doing, however, they left clouded the line of demarcation between protected advocacy on the one hand and punishable advocacy on the other.

The justices attempted to solve this dilemma in *Yates v. United States*,[12] another case involving leaders of the Communist party. In this case, Oleta O'Conner Yates and thirteen others, leaders of the party in California, were also accused of violating the Smith Act.

> The indictment charged that in carrying out the conspiracy the defendants and their co-conspirators would (a) become members and officers of the Communist Party, with knowledge of its unlawful purposes, and assume leadership in carrying out its policies and activities; (b) cause to be organized units of the Party in California and elsewhere; (c) write and publish, in the "Daily Worker" and other Party organs, articles on the proscribed advocacy and teaching; (d) conduct schools for the indoctrination of Party members in such advocacy and teaching, and (e) recruit new Party members, particularly from among persons employed in the key industries of the nation.

At the close of the trial, Judge William C. Mathes instructed the jury to the effect "that in its view the illegal advocacy was made out simply by showing that what was said dealt with forcible overthrow and that it was uttered with a specific intent to accomplish that purpose, insisting that all such advocacy was punishable 'whether it is language of incitement or not.'" Yates and the other defendants were convicted, and their convictions were sustained by the court of appeals.

In the words of the Supreme Court when it reviewed the case, it was "thus faced with the question whether the Smith Act prohibits advocacy and teaching of forcible overthrow as an abstract principle, divorced from any effort to instigate action to that end, so long as such advocacy or teaching is engaged in with evil intent."

A majority, after closely examining the instructions to the jury, concluded that the convictions must be reversed because "the jury was never told that the Smith Act does not denounce advocacy in the sense of preaching abstractly the forcible overthrow of the Government."

That free speech protects advocacy of abstract doctrine not an incitement to imminent lawless action was considered again in a case involving the conviction of a Ku Klux Klan leader. Just prior to a Klan rally in Hamilton County, Ohio, a Mr. Brandenburg (first name not available) called a television reporter in Cincinnati and invited him to attend. The reporter, together with a cameraman, attended the meeting and filmed the events, some of which were later shown on a local station and on a national network.

> One film showed 12 hooded figures, some of whom carried firearms. They were gathered around a large wooden cross, which they burned. No one was present other than the participants and the newsmen who made the film. Most of the words uttered during the scene were incomprehensible when the film was projected, but scattered phrases could be understood that were derogatory of Negroes and, in one instance, of Jews.[13]

One of the speakers, who was identified as Brandenburg, stated: "Personally, I believe the nigger should be returned to Africa, the Jew returned to Israel."

Following the rally, Brandenburg was arrested and charged with the crime of "advocat[ing] ... the duty, necessity, or propriety of crime, sabotage, violence, or unlawful methods of terrorism as a means of accomplishing industrial or political reform" and for "voluntarily assembl[ing] with any society, group, or assemblage of persons formed to teach or advocate the doctrines of criminal syndicalism." He was found guilty, and his appeal to the Ohio Supreme Court was dismissed without an opinion.

The Supreme Court, in an opinion concurred in by all justices, reversed.

The opinion first discusses several previous cases dealing with freedom to advocate and points out that "these later decision have fashioned the principle that the constitutional guarantees of free speech and free press do not permit a State to forbid or proscribe advocacy of the use of force or of law violation except where such advocacy is directed to inciting or producing imminent lawless action and is likely to incite or produce such action." In testing the Ohio law under this principle, the justices found it wanting. "We are here confronted with a statute which, by its own words and as applied, purports to punish mere advocacy and to forbid, on pain of criminal punishment, assembly with others merely to advocate the described type of action. Such a statute falls within the condemnation of the First and Fourteenth Amendments."

Streets Are Proper Places for Speech

*"The streets are natural and proper places for the dissemination of information and opinion...."**

Frequently the right of a person to speak depends upon the place where the speech is to be given. The "use of the streets and public places, [however], has, from ancient times, been a part of the privileges, immunities, rights, and liberties of citizens."[14] But that does not mean that one has the right to speak in any public place at any time he or she wishes to do so. As was pointed out in Chapter V and will be more fully discussed hereafter, "a State constitutionally may by general and non-discriminatory legislation regulate the time, place, and manner of soliciting upon its streets, and of holding meetings thereon...."[15] Time, place, and manner regulations must be reasonable, and a total ban on such activity, even for a justifiable reason, may still violate the First Amendment. For example, the cities of Los Angeles, Milwaukee, and Worcester, Massachusetts, attempted to control litter on the streets by enacting ordinances that absolutely prohibited the distribution of literature. Recognizing that keeping streets clean was a valid governmental interest, the Court nevertheless struck down convictions of persons who, although not themselves actually littering, were handing out literature. "We are of the opinion that the purpose to keep the streets clean and of good appearance is insufficient to justify an ordinance which prohibits a person rightfully on a street from handing literature to one willing to receive it."[16]

Sometimes, however, government does have interests that are so important that it may totally prohibit the exercise of free speech rights at certain locations. One of those locations is near a courthouse, a place the state of Louisiana, by law, declared to be off limits for parading or picketing.[17] This law was tested during a civil rights demonstration in downtown Baton Rouge in December 1961. On December 14, twenty-three college students were arrested for picketing stores that maintained segregated lunch counters. The next day about two thousand students met in the center of the city in preparation for a march to the courthouse to protest the arrest and detention of the twenty-three picketers. The Reverend B. Elton Cox joined the demonstrators. Captain Font of the city police and Chief Kling of the sheriff's office, who had learned of the rally earlier, approached Cox and requested that the meeting be disbanded. "Cox did not acquiesce in this request but told

Schneider v. State, 308 U.S. 147, 163 (1939).

the officers that they would march by the courthouse, say prayers, sing hymns, and conduct a peaceful program of protest."[18] When the students reached an area near the courthouse, Cox, after consultation with the officers, assembled the group on the west sidewalk about 101 feet from the courthouse steps.

> They were lined up on this sidewalk about five deep and spread almost the entire length of the block. The group did not obstruct the street. It was close to noon and, being lunch time, a small crowd of 100 to 300 curious white people, mostly courthouse personnel, gathered on the east sidewalk and courthouse steps, about 100 feet from the demonstrators. Seventy-five to eighty policemen, including city and state patrolmen and members of the Sheriff's staff, as well as members of the fire department and a fire truck were stationed in the street between the two groups. Rain fell throughout the demonstration.

Cox addressed the demonstrators, telling them that it was lunchtime and they should go the lunch counters, even though those counters would not serve them because they were black. About this time, several tear-gas bombs exploded, and the students quickly dispersed. Cox was arrested the next day and charged with several offenses, including "picketing near a courthouse" for which he was convicted and sentenced to one year in jail and ordered to pay a $5,000 fine. His conviction was upheld by the Louisiana Supreme Court.

When the case was reviewed by the U.S. Supreme Court, Justice Arthur J. Goldberg was assigned to write the majority opinion, which overturned the decision of the Louisiana courts. Holding in Cox's favor, the majority concluded from its examination of the trial record that the demonstrators had received permission from the chief of police, who was on the scene, to congregate on the west sidewalk facing the courthouse. "In effect, appellant [Cox] was advised that a demonstration at the place it was held would not be one 'near' the courthouse within the terms of the statute." Arresting him under those circumstances was an entrapment and a violation of due process of law.

With regard to the validity of the law prohibiting the picketing or parading near the courthouse, however, the justices unanimously upheld its constitutionality.

> There can be no question that a State has a legitimate interest in protecting its judicial system from the pressures which picketing near a courthouse might create. Since we are committed to a government of laws and not of men, it is of the utmost importance that administration of justice be absolutely fair and orderly.[19]

In balancing this important governmental interest against free speech rights of picketers and paraders, the Court found the scales to tip in favor of the law. Even Justice Black, who as pointed out above was a strong supporter of First Amendment rights, agreed that protection of the administration of justice was more important than picketing near a courthouse.

> This statute . . . was enacted to protect courts and court officials from the intimidation and dangers that inhere in huge gatherings at courthouse doors and jail doors to protect arrests and to influence court officials in performing their duties. The very purpose of a court system is to adjudicate controversies, both criminal and civil, in the calmness and solemnity of the courtroom according to legal procedures.

Justice Black was also of the opinion that the demonstrators had violated the law, and therefore Cox's conviction for picketing "near" the courthouse should have been affirmed. Justices Clark, White, and Harlan agreed.

If the administration of justice is such a substantial governmental interest as to outweigh the free speech interests in picketing near a courthouse, can the same be said of the exercise of free speech rights near a school? The justices answered the question in the affirmative in the case of *Grayned v. City of Rockford.*[20] This case involved a demonstration near West Senior High School, Rockford, Illinois, in which the defendant in the case, Richard Grayned, participated. Negro students at the school had presented some grievances to school authorities, but when no action was forthcoming, a public demonstration was planned. On the day assigned, "approximately 200 people — students, their family members, and friends — gathered next to the school grounds. [Grayned], whose brother and twin sisters were attending the school, was part of this group."

> The demonstrators marched around on a sidewalk about 100 feet from the school building, which was set back from the street. Many carried signs which summarized the grievances: "Black cheerleaders to cheer too"; "Black history with black teachers"; "Equal rights, Negro counselors." Others without placards, made the "power to the people" sign with their upraised and clenched fists.

Shortly after the demonstration began, the police arrested forty of the demonstrators, including Grayned, and charged them with violating an "antinoise" ordinance that provided that "no person, while on public or private grounds adjacent to any buiding in which a school or any class thereof is in session, shall willfully make or assist in the making of any noise or diversion which disturbs or tends to disturb the peace or good order of such school session or class thereof. ..."

Whether those arrested made any "noise" was the subject of dispute at their trial. "Government witnesses reported that the demonstrators repeatedly cheered, chanted, baited policemen, and made other noise that was audible in the school. ..." "Defense witnesses claimed that the demonstrators were at all times quiet and orderly ... [and] that the only noise was made by policemen using loudspeakers. ..." In any event, Grayned was found guilty and fined $25.00. On appeal he argued "that the Rockford ordinance unduly interferes with First and Fourteenth Amendment rights to picket on a public sidewalk near a school." With only Justice Douglas dissenting, the Supreme Court disagreed. While the Court agreed that the "government has no power to restrict such activity because of its message," it pointed out "that reasonable 'time, place and manner' regulations may be necessary to further significant governmental interests, and are permitted." This, the majority believed, was just such a regulation.

> We would be ignoring reality if we did not recognize that the public schools in a community are important institutions, and are often the focus of significant grievances. Without interfering with normal school activities, daytime picketing and handbilling on public grounds near a school can effectively publicize those grievances to pedestrians, school visitors, and deliverymen, as well as to teachers, administrators, and students.
>
> . . .
>
> On the other hand, schools could hardly tolerate boisterous demonstrators who drown out classroom conversation, make studying impossible, block entrances, or incite children to leave the schoolhouse.

This law "is narrowly tailored to further Rockford's compelling interest in having an undisrupted school session conducive to the students' learning, and does not unnecessarily interfere with First Amendment rights."

Justice Douglas' disagreement with the majority focused attention upon the evidence. As he read the record, "there was no evidence that appellant [Grayned] was noisy or boisterous or rowdy. He walked quietly and in an orderly manner."

By approving reasonable time, place, and manner regulations of speech on public streets, the Court has not given specific guidelines to government about just what is reasonable. Drafters of legislation, therefore, must speculate on what may or may not be constitutional. The officials of Brookfield, Wisconsin, found themselves in just such a dilemma when a group of antiabortionists began picketing on the street in front of the home of a doctor who allegedly performed abortions.

> The picketing was generally orderly and peaceful; the town never had occasion to invoke any of its various ordinances prohibiting obstruction of streets, loud and unnecessary noises, or disorderly conduct. Nevertheless, the picketing generated substantial controversy and numerous complaints.[21]

In order to alleviate the problem, the town enacted an ordinance that placed a total ban on all residential picketing.

> It is unlawful for any person to engage in picketing before or about the residence or dwelling of any individual in the Town of Brookfield.

When Sandra C. Schultz and Robert C. Braun learned of the new law, they ceased picketing the doctor's residence and brought an action in the federal district court seeking an injunction prohibiting the town from enforcement of the ordinance. Judge John W. Reynolds interpreted the ordinance as placing a ban on all residential picketing and therefore found it an infringement on First Amendment rights. But the Supreme Court took a different view. By accepting representations of counsel for the town that "picketing must be directed at a single residence" and that "general marching through residential neighborhoods, or even walking a route in front of an entire block, is not prohibited," a majority determined that the law did not violate free speech rights.

In balancing the right of the protestors to picket against the privacy rights of persons in the residence, the majority opted in favor of the residents' privacy. "Our prior decisions," wrote Justice O'Connor for the majority, "have often remarked on the unique nature of the home, 'the last citadel of the tired, the weary, and the sick,' . . . and have recognized that 'preserving the sanctity of the home, the one retreat to which men and women can repair to escape from the tribulations of their daily pursuits, is surely an important value.'"

Justice Stevens, however, was concerned about the potential reach of the ordinance and began his dissenting opinion as follows:

"GET WELL CHARLIE—OUR TEAM NEEDS YOU."
In Brookfield, Wisconsin, it is unlawful for a fifth grader to carry such a sign in front of a residence for the period of time necessary to convey its friendly message to its intended audience.

What concerned Justice Stevens was the possibility that this law could be applied to the fifth grader in his illustration. He conceded "that the picketers have a right to communicate their strong opposition to abortion to the doctor, but after they have had a fair opportunity to communicate that message, [there is] little justification for allowing them to remain in front of his home and repeat it over and over again simply to harm the doctor and his family."

The solution he proposed was for the town to amend the ordinance "to limit the ban to conduct that unreasonably interferes with the privacy of the home and does not serve a reasonable communicative purpose." Thus the fifth grader would be allowed to get his message to his fellow teammate.

As will be more fully developed hereafter, the Court has been very concerned about the possibility of officials censoring a speaker's message. Most often the power to do so arises when laws requiring a permit to speak, parade, picket, solicit, or demonstrate give the permit issuer too much discretion in issuing permits. Too much discretion allows the official to grant permits to the "good guys," as he or she sees them, and to deny permits to the "bad guys." (See Jehovah's Witness cases in Chapter V.)

Sometimes a legislative body—city council, county board, state legislature, or Congress—may adopt a law that is aimed at a specific kind of message and therefore is not content-neutral. This too is censorship and is generally disapproved by the Court. District of Columbia Code Section 22-1115 is such a law:

> It shall be unlawful to display any flag, banner, placard ... designed ... to intimidate, coerce, or bring into public odium any foreign government, party, or organization, ... or to bring into public disrepute political, social, or economic acts, views, or purposes of any foreign government, party or organization ... within 500 feet of any building or premises ... used or occupied by any foreign government or its representative ... as an embassy, legation, consulate, or for other official purposes....[22]

Michael Boos and Bridget M. Brooker desired to display signs "stating 'RELEASE SAKHAROV' and 'SOLIDARITY' in front of the Soviet Embassy." "J. Michael Waller wishe[d] to display a sign reading 'STOP

THE KILLING' within 500 feet of the Nicaraguan Embassy." Being aware of the existence of Section 22-1115, they joined in an action against the mayor of the District of Columbia and others, challenging the validity the law. Judge Oliver Gasch sustained the law, as did the court of appeals. In reversing, the Supreme Court described three important features of Section 22-1115:

> First, the display clause operates at the core of the First Amendment by prohibiting petitioners from engaging in classically political speech.
>
> . . .
>
> Second, the display clause bars such speech on public streets and sidewalks, traditional public fora that "time out of mind, have been used for purposes of assembly, communicating thoughts between citizens, and discussing public questions."
>
> . . .
>
> Third, Section 22-1115 is content-based. Whether individuals may picket in front of a foreign embassy depends entirely upon whether their picket signs are critical of the foreign government or not.

The government argued "that the statute [was] not content-based because the government is not itself selecting between viewpoints; the permissible message on a picket sign is determined solely by the policies of a foreign government." A majority rejected this argument. "Here the government has determined that an entire category of speech — signs or displays critical of foreign governments — is not to be permitted."

Having determined that the law was not content-neutral, the Court then turned to the question of whether the "regulation is necessary to serve a compelling state interest and that it is narrowly drawn to achieve that end."

The government asserted that the law was necessary to protect the dignity of foreign officials and to isolate them from insulting or outrageous speech. But the Court noted: "We have indicated that in public debate our own citizens must tolerate insulting, and even outrageous, speech in order to provide 'adequate 'breathing space' to the freedoms protected by the First Amendment.'" Therefore, "we are not persuaded that the differences between foreign officials and American citizens require us to deviate from these principles here." Chief Justice Rehnquist and justices White and Blackmun would have upheld Section 22-1115.

Forums Must Be Open to All

"A State ... [cannot] enforce ... exclusions from a forum ... open to the public, even if it was not required to create the forum in the first place."*

In addition to streets and parks, federal, state, and municipal governments own much other property. The extent to which this property is open and available for the exercise of First Amendment rights has been the subject of much litigation. Some government property, such as the grounds around a capitol building, are open for public speaking as are streets and parks. Other property, such as military bases, courthouses, and grounds around a jail, are considered nonpublic forums in which the public's right to speak may be severely restricted and in some cases totally prohibited. When a government opens property and allows it to be used by some speakers, it may have opened that property for all speakers. John Thomas Flower found that to be the case when he went upon a street that passes through Fort Sam Houston in San Antonio, Texas, to distribute leaflets. The street, although actually on the grounds of the fort, was open for use by civilian and military traffic twenty-four hours a day.

Flower was the peace education secretary of the American Friends Service Committee for Texas, Oklahoma, and Arkansas. He had previously distributed leaflets on the street and had been warned by the deputy commander of the fort that he would be arrested if he returned. He did return and was distributing a leaflet advertising a meeting on the Vietnam War when he was arrested for reentering a military post "after having been ... ordered not to reenter by an officer ... in command or charge thereof."[23]

District Judge Adrian A. Spears found Flower guilty and sentenced him to six months in prison. The court of appeals voted 2–1 to affirm. The Supreme Court reversed and issued a per curiam opinion. (A per curiam opinion is one in which a majority of the justices agree, but no justice is identified as the author. These opinions are usually very short, and that was true in this case.) Taking note of the facts concerning the street upon which Flower was arrested, the justices declared:

> Under such circumstances the military has abandoned any claim
> that it has special interests in who walks, talks or distributes leaflets on

*Widmar v. Vincent, 454 U.S. 263, 268 (1981).

the avenue. The base commandant can no more order petitioner off this public street because he was distributing leaflets than could the city police order any leafleteer off any public street.

Not all justices agreed with this result. Justice Rehnquist, in an opinion in which Chief Justice Burger joined, explained that "simply because some activities and individuals are allowed on government property does not require the abandonment of otherwise allowable restrictions on its use."

When a public university makes its facilities available to some for First Amendment activities but excludes others, it too may find itself in conflict with the Constitution. The University of Missouri at Kansas City (UMKC) found itself in this situation when it refused to allow Cornerstone, a student religious organization, use of its buildings for meetings. The university encouraged formation of student organizations and at one time recognized ninety of them, including Cornerstone. For four years Cornerstone had been allowed to hold on-campus meetings, but that practice was terminated when the board of curators adopted new rules regulating use of university buildings. The new rules prohibited "religious worship or religious teaching" on the campus. When Cornerstone requested permission to continue meeting on the campus, the dean of students requested more details about the content of their meetings. Cornerstone's attorney supplied the following information:

> Typical Cornerstone meetings in the University facilities usually include the following:
> 1. The offering of prayer;
> 2. The singing of hymns in praise and thanksgiving;
> 3. The public reading of scripture;
> 4. The sharing of personal views and experiences (in relation to God) by various persons;
> 5. An exposition of, and commentary on, passages of the Bible by one or more persons for the purpose of teaching practical biblical principles; and
> 6. An invitation to the interested to meet for a personal discussion.[24]

Based upon this information, the university denied the group permission to meet in any of its buildings.

Florian Frederick Chess with eleven other students sought a declaratory judgment and an order of the federal district court allowing them use of the university's facilities. District Judge William R.

Collinson denied the request and ordered the case dismissed. The students appealed to the court of appeals, which reversed on the grounds that the primary effect of the university's policies was to inhibit religion and was therefore a violation of the Establishment Clause. As pointed out in Chapter IV, the Establishment Clause is violated when the government either inhibits or promotes religion.

The university appealed to the Supreme Court, which agreed with the court of appeals that Cornerstone should be allowed to meet at the university. But the justices did not agree that the Establishment Clause required that result. Justice Powell wrote for the majority that "cases hold that a policy will not offend the Establishment Clause if it can pass a three-pronged test: 'First, the [governmental policy] must have a secular legislative purpose; second, its principal or primary effect must be one that neither advances nor inhibits religion ...; finally, the [policy] must not foster 'an excesive government entanglement with religion.'"[25] Because the university's open-forum policy was secular in nature, it clearly passed the first and third prongs of the test. Further, the majority was of the opinion that that policy would have only an "incidental" effect on religion and thus also satisfied the second requirement.

Having disposed of the Establishment Clause problem, Justice Powell turned to the question of a possible burden on free speech, because the university, having created a forum for other student organizations, had excluded Cornerstone from that forum. The constitutional rule, Justice Powell wrote, "forbids a State ... [from] enforc[ing] certain exclusions from a forum generally open to the public, even if it was not required to create the forum in the first place." The only justification given for excluding Cornerstone was the possible conflict with the Establishment Clause. Having concluded that that was not a valid reason, the majority held that these students must be allowed to use the facilities as were other approved organizations.

> Having created a forum generally open to student groups, the University seeks to enforce a content-based exclusion of religious speech. Its exclusionary policy violates the fundamental principle that a state regulation of speech should be content-neutral, and the University is unable to justify this violation under applicable constitutional standards.

This does not, of course, prevent the university from establishing "reasonable time, place and manner regulations."

The only dissenter was Justice White. He took issue with the idea "that because religious worship uses speech, it is protected by the Free Speech Clause of the First Amendment." He was of the opinion that that approach was "plainly wrong" and that religious speech should be analyzed under the religious clauses of the First Amendment, as discussed in Chapters IV and V, above.

Almost everyone who travels by air has been contacted while passing through the airport terminal by persons distributing literature or soliciting contributions. Most airports are operated by some governmental organization, thus making them public property. The extent to which such solicitations or distributions can be regulated or prohibited was considered by the Court when a Los Angeles Board of Airport Commissioners resolution banning *all* First Amendment activities in the airport's central terminal was brought on appeal.

Justice O'Connor described the basis for the case:

> On July 6, 1984, Alan Howard Snyder, a minister of the Gospel for Jews for Jesus, was stopped by a Department of Airports peace officer while distributing free religious literature on a pedestrian walkway in the Central Terminal Area at LAX. The officer showed Snyder a copy of the resolution, explained that Snyder's activities violated the resolution, and requested that Snyder leave LAX. The officer warned Snyder that the city would take legal action against him if he refused to leave as requested. ... Snyder stopped distributing the leaflets and left the airport terminal.[26]

Snyder and Jews for Jesus filed an action against the board of airport comissioners contending that the regulation was unconstitutional under the First Amendment "because it bans all speech in a public forum." Judge Edward Rafeedie agreed and declared that because the airport terminal was a traditional public forum, Snyder and Jews for Jesus had a right to distribute literature there. The court of appeals also found that the "airport complex is a traditional public forum" and affirmed.

A unanimous Supreme Court reached the same conclusion, but took a different route to get there. It did not agree that Snyder's right to distribute literature depended upon a finding that the airport was a "traditional public forum," and it refused to make that determination. What concerned the justices was that "the resolution at issue in this case reaches the universe of expressive activity, and, by prohibiting *all* protected expression, purports to create a virtual 'First Amendment Free Zone' at LAX." And further, the resolution "prohibits even talking and reading, or the wearing of campaign buttons or symbolic clothing." "Such a ban," Justice O'Connor declared, "cannot be justified even if LAX were a nonpublic forum because no conceivable governmental interest would justify such an absolute prohibition of speech."

This decision leaves airports free to adopt reasonable time, place, and manner regulations for their terminals, as universities are for their buildings and municipalities for streets and parks.

Some Places Are Closed for Speech

*"The United States Constitution does not forbid a State to control the use of its own property for its own lawful nondiscriminatory purpose."**

Because most government-owned property has the same characteristics as privately owned property, it is not available to the public for the exercise of First Amendment rights. Harriett Louise Adderley and thirty-one other persons learned this lesson the hard way. Adderley, together with approximately two hundred other students from Florida A & M University, Tallahassee, Florida, went to the county jail to protest the arrest of other protesting students the previous day and to protest segregation generally.

They arrived at the jail singing and clapping, and went to the entrance where they were met by a deputy sheriff. At his request, they moved away from the door and continued singing and clapping. When the sheriff arrived, he told the group leaders that they were trespassing and that if they did not leave, they would be arrested. Because the crowd was not dispersing, the sheriff loudly announced "that he was the legal custodian of the jail and its premises, that they were trespassing on county property in violation of the law, that they should all leave forthwith or he would arrest them. . . ."[27] Some of the demonstrators did leave, most stayed, and 107 of those were placed under arrest, including Adderley. She and 31 others were convicted by a jury of "trespass with a malicious and mischievous intent." Their convictions were upheld by two Florida appellate courts.

By a 5–4 vote the Supreme Court sustained the judgment of the Florida courts. Justice Black delivered the opinion. Among the important questions the justices needed to answer was to what extent, if any, were the jailhouse grounds available for free speech purposes. Justice

Adderley v. Florida, 385 U.S. 39, 48 (1966).

Black's answer for the majority was short and concise. "Traditionally, state capitol grounds are open to the public. Jails, built for security purposes, are not." And he explained that "this particular jail entrance and driveway were not normally used by the public, but by the sheriff's department for transporting prisoners to the courts . . . and by commercial concerns for servicing the jail." That justified the application of the trespass law to the protestors because "nothing in the Constitution of the United States prevents Florida from even-handed enforcement of its general trespass statute against those refusing to obey the sheriff's order to remove themselves from what amounted to the curtilage of the jailhouse."

Chief Justice Warren and justices Douglas, Brennan, and Fortas did not agree. They thought "the jailhouse, like an executive mansion, a legislative chamber, a courthouse, or the statehouse . . . is one of the seats of government, whether it be the Tower of London, the Bastille, or a small county jail. And when it houses political prisoners or those who many think are unjustly held, it is an obvious center for protest."

The minority pointed out that "the right to petition for redress of grievances has an ancient history," but in today's world the more conventional methods of protest have been denied to many people. Requests for legislative action get lost in "bureaucratic maze," and radio, television, and newspaper advertising are beyond protestors' means. "We do violence to the First Amendment," Justice Douglas explained, "when we permit this 'petition for redress of grievances' to be turned into a trespass action." Demonstrating, therefore, even on the jailhouse grounds, "should not be condemned . . . as long as the assembly and petition are peaceable, as these were."

Although John Flower's right to distribute literature on the street that ran through Fort Sam Houston was upheld, Benjamin Spock and Julius Hobson, presidential and vice-presidential candidates of the People's Party, and Linda Jenness and Andrew Pulley, presidential and vice-presidential candidates of the Socialist Workers Party were not allowed to do the same at Fort Dix, New Jersey. In September 1972, the latter group wrote a letter to the commanding general at Fort Dix indicating that they intended to distribute campaign leaflets and hold a meeting on the reservation. The general refused the request and by letter referred to regulations relating to speech activities at Fort Dix. These regulations provided that "demonstrations, picketing, . . . political speeches and similar activities are prohibited . . ." on the base, and that literature could not be distributed "without prior written approval of the Adjutant General. . . ."[28]

Spock and the others sought a court order prohibiting the enforcement of the regulations, believing that they were an infringement on their constitutional rights. Judge Clarkson S. Fisher refused to grant a preliminary injunction, but that decision was reversed by the court of appeals. Spock then conducted a rally on a parking lot within the fort.

Judge Fisher eventually granted a permanent injunction against enforcement of the rules, which was sustained by the court of appeals on the grounds that the base's regulations did infringe upon Spock's First Amendment rights. In so doing, the appeals court relied upon the *Flower* case, being of the opinion that there was little difference between Fort Sam Houston and Fort Dix, and therefore Fort Dix also ought to be open to the public for free speech activities.

Writing for himself, and five other members of the Supreme Court, Justice Stewart came to a different conclusion and reversed. Justice Stewart first describes Fort Dix by noting that it is in a rural area and contains fifty-five square miles, and some state and county roads run through it.

> Civilian vehicular traffic is permitted on paved roads within the reservation, and civilian pedestrian traffic is permitted on both roads and footpaths. Military police regularly patrol the roads within the reservation, and they occasionally stop civilians and ask them the reason for their presence. Signs posted on the roads leading into the reservation state: "All vehicles are subject to search while on the Fort Dix Military Reservation" and "Soliciting prohibited unless approved by the commanding general." The main entrances to Fort Dix are not normally guarded, and a sign at one of the entrances says "Visitors Welcome." Civilians are freely permitted to visit unrestricted areas of the reservation.

The justice distinguished the situation at Fort Sam Houston from that at Fort Dix by recounting that the authorities at Fort Sam Houston had literally "abandoned any claim [of] special interests in who walks, talks, or distributes leaflets on the avenue," but that was not true at Fort Dix.

> What the record shows, therefore, is a considered Fort Dix policy, objectively and evenhandedly applied, of keeping official military activities there wholly free of entanglement with partisan political campaigns of any kind.

This policy was in line with what the "Court over the years has on countless occasions recognized [as] the special constitutional function of the military in our national life, a function both explicit and in-dispensable."

Chief Justice Burger concurred. He had no difficulty with pro-hibiting political campaigning on the base. "Permitting political cam-paigning on military bases," he said, "cuts against a 200-year tradition of keeping the military separate from political affairs...." He also agreed that the rule requiring prior consent from the commander before distributing literature was all right, but "the hard question for [him was] whether the Constitution requires a ban on all distributions in order to preserve the separation of the military from politics." He concluded that it did not, and in so doing approved the "prior consent" leafleting rule.

Justice Brennan found the majority's conclusions faulty and dissented. He was particularly disturbed by how easily the majority per-mitted infringement upon personal rights by deferring to alleged governmental interests. "If the recent lessons of history mean any-thing," he argued, "it is that the First Amendment does not evaporate with the mere intonation of interests such as national defense, military necessity, or domestic security." And further, "in all cases where such interests have been advanced, the inquiry has been whether the exercise of First Amendment rights necessarily must be circumscribed in order to secure those interests."

In this case he did not agree that distributing leaflets on the streets or permitting some political rallies would be too disruptive of military activities on the base. Even if some disruption were to occur, "this Court has recognized that some quite disruptive forms of expression are protected by the First Amendment."

Adult Theaters Can't Be Just Anyplace

*"But few of us would march our sons and daughters off to war to preserve the citizen's right to see 'Specified Sexual Activities' exhibited in the theaters of our choice."**

The sentiment expressed in the quotation above underlies the Court's willingness to allow cities to enact zoning laws that exclude adult motion picture theaters from certain neighborhoods, even though the Court recognizes that such theaters are protected by the First Amendment.

*Young v. American Mini Theatres, Inc., 427 U.S. 50, 70 (1976).

The city of Renton, Washington, enacted a zoning law that "prohibited any 'adult motion picture theater' from locating within 1,000 feet of any residential zone, single- or multiple-family dwelling, church, or park, and within one mile of any school."[29] In a lawsuit brought by Playtime Theatres, Inc., the district court upheld the city's right to enact such a law, but the court of appeals reversed because "the Renton ordinance constituted a substantial restriction on First Amendment interests." The Supreme Court thought otherwise and reversed.

In 1915 the Court for the first time was confronted with the question of whether the exhibition of films was speech. It held that it was not.[30] That decision, however, was overruled in 1952, and since that time, motion pictures have been protected by the First Amendment.

In concluding that Renton's zoning law did not violate the Constitution, Justice Rehnquist, who delivered the opinion, said that the ordinance was a "time, place and manner regulation." The question that needed to be answered, however, was whether it was "content-neutral." He acknowledged that "the ordinance treats theaters that specialize in adult films differently from other kinds of theaters"[31] but did not believe that that was necessarily decisive of the issue. He explained that "the Renton ordinance is aimed not at the *content* of the films shown at 'adult motion picture theatres,' but rather at the *secondary* effect of such theaters on the surrounding community."

The city made no showing of the "secondary" effects of having adult theaters in residential areas; it chose instead to rely upon studies made by Seattle, which had adopted a similar ordinance. Seattle asserted two goals to sustain its requirement that adult theaters should be concentrated in the business area of the city. The goals were "to preserve the character and quality of residential life in its neighborhoods," and "to protect neighborhood children from increased safety hazards, and offensive and dehumanizing influence created by . . . adult movie theaters."[32]

The justices accepted these goals as legitimate and concluded that "the Renton ordinance is 'narrowly tailored' to affect only that category of theaters shown to produce the unwanted secondary effects. . . ."[33] They also found that "more than five percent of the entire land area of Renton [was] open to use as adult theater sites"; thus the ordinance allowed for reasonable alternative avenues of communication.

The majority's decision did not go unchallenged. Justices Brennan and Marshall did not accept the view that the law was "content-neutral." They were of the opinion that "the ordinance imposes special restrictions on certain kinds of speech on the basis of *content*, [and therefore they could not] accept, as the Court does, Renton's claim that the ordinance was not designed to suppress the content of adult movies."

Speech That Causes a Clear and Present Danger

"Speech ... is ... protected ... unless shown to ... produce a clear and present danger of a ... substantive evil that rises far above public inconvenience, annoyance or unrest."*

Justice Douglas once declared that "a function of free speech under our system of government is to invite dispute."[34] Even though inviting dispute is an acceptable objective of speech, when speech passes beyond dispute and creates danger of a breach of the peace, it is no longer protected and can be punished. Determining when a speaker has passed the bounds of acceptable speech and crossed into the area of punishable speech is sometimes very difficult.

Generally, before speech can be punished, there must be some rule, regulation, or law that defines the kind of utterances that are prohibited. Such laws, regulations, or rules must be carefully drafted so that maximum protection is given to the right of free speech. The case of *Terminiello v. Chicago*[35] illustrates the importance of careful draftsmanship.

Arthur W. Terminiello was a Catholic priest under suspension by his bishop, who was brought from Alabama to Chicago to speak under the auspices of the Christian Veterans of America. The year was 1946. The conditions under which the meeting was held were described by Justice Jackson.

> The crowd [estimated to be 1,500] constituted "a surging, howling mob hurling epithets" at those who would enter and "tried to tear their clothes off." One young woman's coat was torn off and she had to be assisted into the meeting by policemen. Those inside the hall could hear the loud noises and hear those on the outside yell, "Facists," "Hitlers" and curse words like "damn Fascists." Bricks were thrown through the windowpanes before and during the speaking. ... The street was black with people on both sides for at least a block either way; bottles, stink bombs and brickbats were thrown. Police were unable to control the mob, which kept breaking the windows at the meeting hall, drowning out the speaker's voice at times and

**Terminiello v. Chicago*, 337 U.S. 1, 4 (1949).

breaking in through the back door of the auditorium. About 17 of the group outside were arrested by the police.

In spite of the disturbance outside, Terminiello made a speech critical of Russia, communism, Jews, and the government under President Franklin D. Roosevelt. He referred to Eleanor Roosevelt as Queen Eleanor and to Secretary of Agriculture Henry Wallace as Henry Adolph Wallace.

Terminiello was arrested for disorderly conduct, which was described by a city ordinance as making "any improper noise, riot, disturbance, (or) breach of peace...." At the trial, the testimony with regard to the reaction of those inside the hall was contradictory. One witness testified that "the people were disturbed and angry." Another said that "when [Terminiello] said there was no crime too great for the Jews to commit, the woman next to her said, 'Yes the Jews are all killers, murderers. If we don't kill them first, they will kill us....'"[36]

A witness for the defendant testified that the audience was quiet and attentive at all times.

The trial judge charged the jury that "misbehavior may constitute a breach of the peace if it stirs the public to anger, invites dispute, brings about a condition of unrest, or creates a disturbance...."[37]

Following his conviction, Terminiello appealed to the Illinois Supreme Court, which sustained the jury's decision. The U.S. Supreme Court granted review "because of the importance of the question presented." The question presented was whether it was a violation of the First Amendment to convict someone whose speech "stirs the public to anger, invites dispute, brings about a condition of unrest, or creates a disturbance...."

Six justices held that such a conviction was an infringement on freedom of speech and voted to reverse Terminiello's conviction. Justice Douglas, after noting that "a function of free speech under our system of government is to invite dispute," continued, "it may indeed best serve its high purpose when it induces a condition of unrest, creates dissatisfaction with conditions as they are, or even stirs people to anger. Speech is often provocative and challenging. It may strike at prejudices and preconceptions and have profound unsettling effect as it presses for acceptance of an idea." Only when speech is "shown likely to produce a clear and present danger of a serious substantive evil that rises far above public inconvenience, annoyance or unrest..." can it be punished.

While the situation surrounding Terminiello's speech could reasonably have been considered to have produced a "clear and present danger," the possibility that the jury may have convicted him only for "inviting dispute" was enough to require the conviction to be set aside. Allowing Terminiello to go free did not sit well with justices Jackson and Harold H. Burton. Rather than focus on the judge's instructions, Justice Jackson discussed at length the volatile situation that existed outside and inside the hall, and argued that in "the long run, maintenance of free speech will be more endangered if the population can have no protection from the abuses which lead to violence."

Whether a speaker has created a "clear and present danger" by his or her speech is a question upon which people may differ. And this is true whether the person called upon to make the decision serves as a juror, judge, or justice of the Supreme Court.

In *Feiner v. New York*,[38] the trial judge, after hearing testimony about a speech by Irving Feiner on a street in Syracuse, New York, decided the police were justified in arresting him to "prevent a breach of the peace." There wasn't much dispute over whether Feiner's statements were controversial. For example, he said: "Mayor Costello (of Syracuse) is a champagne-sipping bum; he does not speak for the Negro people." "President Truman is a bum." "Mayor O'Dwyer is a bum." "The American Legion is a Nazi Gestapo." "The Negroes don't have equal rights; they should rise up in arms and fight for their rights."

Nor was there much disagreement over what happened as Feiner was speaking. The police officers who were on the scene testified that the gathering had spilled over into the street. They moved the people back to the sidewalk. The crowd was "restless and there was some pushing, shoving and milling around," and "some of the onlookers made remarks to the police about their inability to handle the crowd, and at least one threatened violence if the police did not act. There were others who appeared to be favoring the [speaker's] arguments."

After observing the situation for a while, the police stepped in and requested Feiner to stop, but he refused. After waiting a short while and again asking him to stop, a request which Feiner ignored, the officers arrested him. The speaker's final words were "The law has arrived, and I suppose they will take over now."

Feiner was charged with "ignoring and refusing to heed and obey reasonable police orders issued at the time and place mentioned in the Information to regulate and control said crowd and to prevent a breach or breaches of the peace and to prevent injury to pedestrians attempting to use said walk, and being forced into the highway adjacent to the place in question, and prevent injury to the public generally."

The speaker was tried before a judge who agreed that there was danger of a breach of the peace from the listeners reacting to the speech and therefore found Feiner guilty. This decision was upheld by two New York appellate courts and by the Supreme Court.

The majority's opinion acknowledges "that the ordinary murmurings and objections of a hostile audience cannot be allowed to silence a speaker...."

> But we are not faced with such a situation. It is one thing to say that the police cannot be used as an instrument for the suppression of unpopular views, and another to say that, when as here the speaker passes the bounds of argument or persuasion and undertakes incitement to riot, they are powerless to prevent a breach of the peace.

Justice Black's view of this case was substantially different. "The record before us," he explained, "convinces me that petitioner, a young college student, has been sentenced to the penitentiary for the unpopular views he expressed on matters of public interest while lawfully making a street-corner speech in Syracuse, New York." Justice Black was joined in dissent by Justice Douglas, who declared that "one high function of the police is to protect these lawful gatherings so that speakers may exercise their constitutional rights." He saw no danger of a riot or breach of the peace in the record of the case. "It shows an unsympathetic audience and the threat of one man to haul the speaker from the stage. It is against that kind of threat that speakers need police protection."

In *Feiner,* it should be noted, no breach of the peace occurred. Feiner did not breach the peace, nor did the grumbling, pushing, and threats by one man constitute such a breach. His conviction was upheld because the majority agreed that there was a clear and present danger that a riot or disturbance would break out.

The principle that speech that creates a danger of disorderly conduct may be punished applies even though the audience is only one person. That lesson was brought home to Walter Chaplinsky, a Jehovah's Witness, while he was distributing literature on the streets of Rochester, New Hampshire. Some of the people on the streets did not like what he was doing and complained to the city marshal, who "told them that Chaplinsky was lawfully engaged and that he must be left alone."[39] The marshal then warned Chaplinsky, but "some hours later, the crowd got out of hand and treated Chaplinsky with some violence. He was then led towards the police station, though apparently more for his protection than for arrest...." On the way to the station, Chaplinsky said to the marshal, "You are a God damned racketeer" and "a damned Fascist and the whole government of Rochester are Fascists or agents of Fascists...."[40] He was charged with violating the following New Hampshire statute:

> No person shall address any offensive, derisive or annoying word to any other person who is lawfully in any street ... nor call him by any offensive or derisive name....

Chaplinsky's version of the incident is somewhat different than the marshal's. He claimed that "when he met Bowering [the marshal], he asked him to arrest the ones responsible for the disturbance. In reply, Bowering cursed him and told him to come along." Chaplinsky also denied that he had used the "name of the Deity." He was found guilty, and the conviction was affirmed by the New Hampshire Supreme Court.

In discussing the meaning of the statute, that court explained that "the statute's purpose was to preserve the public peace, no words being 'forbidden except such as have a direct tendency to cause acts of violence by the persons to whom, individually, the remark is addressed.'" Further, the court said, "the word 'offensive' [as used in the statute] is not to be defined in terms of what a particular addressee thinks.... The test is what men of common intelligence would understand would be words likely to cause an average addressee to fight." In other words, what the statute condemned was speech, in this case Chaplinsky's, directed at an individual, the marshal, "likely to cause an average addressee to fight."

When the case reached the Supreme Court, Chaplinsky's conviction was sustained because "there are certain well-defined and narrowly limited classes of speech, the prevention and punishment of which has never thought to raise any Constitutional problem. These include the lewd and obscene, the profane, the libelous, and the insulting or 'fighting' words—those which by their very utterance inflict injury or tend to incite an immediate breach of the peace."

The New Hampshire statute did no more than punish "fighting words," according to the majority, and the only question that remained was whether Chaplinsky's words were within the statute. The justices said they were. "Argument is unnecessary to demonstrate that the appellations 'damn racketeer' and 'damned Facist' are epithets likely to provoke the average person to retaliation, and thereby cause a breach of the peace."

Here again, no breach of the peace occurred. But that was not the question before the Court. The question to be decided was "what men of common intelligence would understand would be words likely to cause an average addressee to fight." In the early 1940s, "men of common intelligence" might agree that "damn racketeer" and "damned Facist" would "likely" cause a fight.

As the *Terminiello* and *Chaplinsky* cases illustrate, the laws under which a speaker is arrested must be drawn with precision so that there is no infringement of speech protected by the First Amendment. These cases stand for the proposition that speech that presents a "clear and present danger" and speech that includes "fighting words" may be punished without violating the First Amendment.

Section 49-7 of the ordinances of the city of New Orleans is an example of an attempt to draft a valid "fighting words" law but which was not drawn carefully enough to accomplish that result. Section 49-7 reads as follows:

> It shall be unlawful and a breach of the peace for any person wantonly to curse or revile or to use obscene or opprobrious language toward or with reference to any member of the city police while in the actual performance of his duty.[41]

Mallie Lewis was arrested for violating Section 49-7, but the evidence concerning the arrest was conflicting. Lewis and her husband were following a police car in which their son, who had been arrested, was being taken to the police station. Officer Berner, who was driving another police car, stopped the Lewis truck, and "words were exchanged between Berner and [Lewis], and Berner arrested" her.

> The parties' respective versions of the words exchanged were in sharp contradiction. Berner testified that [Lewis] left the truck and "started yelling and screaming that I had her son or did something to her son and she wanted to know where he was.... She said, "you god damn m.f. police—I am going to [the superintendent of police] about this." ... [Lewis'] husband testified that Berner's first words were "let me see your god damned license. I'll show you that you can't follow the police all over the streets...." After ... [Lewis] got out and said "Officer I want to find out about my son." He said "you get in the car woman. Get your black ass in the god damned car or I will show you something...." [Lewis] denied that she used "any profanity toward the officer."

The municipal judge who heard the case believed the officer and found Lewis guilty of violating Section 49-7. If the officer's testimony is taken as true, then certainly Lewis did "wantonly . . . curse or revile or use obscene . . . language toward . . . a member of the city police while in the actual performance of his duty." Believing that to be the case, the Louisiana Supreme Court upheld the conviction. Without being concerned with the facts, the Supreme Court reversed. A majority of the justices found the ordinance not to be a narrowly drawn "fighting words" law. "At least," Justice Brennan wrote, "the proscription of the use of 'opprobrious language,' embraces words that do not 'by their very utterance inflict injury or tend to incite an immediate breach of the peace.'" Because the law embraced more than "fighting words," it was unconstitutional as an infringement on free speech.

Although Justice Powell did not agree with all that the majority said, he did agree that the conviction should be overturned. His concern was that the law conferred upon the police almost "unrestrained power to arrest and charge persons with a violation." "Many arrests are made," he noted, "in 'one-on-one' situations where the only witnesses are the arresting officer and the person charged." That makes it too easy to convict.

One Person's Vulgarity Is Another's Lyric

*"To shut off discourse solely to protect others from hearing it is . . . dependent upon a showing that substantial privacy interests are being invaded in an essentially intolerable manner."**

> On April 26, 1968, . . . [Paul Robert Cohen] was observed in the Los Angeles County Courthouse in the corridor outside of division 20 of the municipal court wearing a jacket bearing the words "Fuck the Draft" which were plainly visible. There were women and children present in the corridor. [Cohen] testified that he wore the jacket knowing that the words were on the jacket as a means of informing the public of the depth of his feelings against the Vietnam War and the draft.
>
> [Cohen] did not engage in, nor threaten to engage in, nor did anyone as the result of his conduct in fact commit or threaten to commit any act of violence.[42]

Cohen was charged with violating California Penal Code Seciton 415 "which prohibits 'maliciously and willfully disturb[ing] the peace

*Cohen v. California, 403 U.S. 15, 21 (1971).

or quiet of any neighborhood or person ... by ... offensive conduct...."' He was found guilty in Los Angeles Municipal Court and was sentenced to thirty days' imprisonment. His conviction was affirmed by the California Court of Appeal. The Supreme Court reversed in a 5–4 decision, the majority holding that the application of the California law to Cohen was a denial of his right to freedom of speech.

In order to bring the issue into proper focus, Justice Harlan states that "the only 'conduct' which the State sought to punish is the fact of communication. Thus, we deal here with a conviction resting solely upon 'speech'...." He then distinguishes this case from the *Chaplinsky, Feiner,* and *Terminiello* cases. This case is not a "fighting words" case like *Chaplinsky* because the message was not directed at any one person. "Nor do we have here an instance of the exercise of the State's police power to prevent a speaker from intentionally provoking a given group to hostile reaction," as in *Feiner* and *Terminiello.*

In response to the argument that the state was justified in punishing Cohen "to protect the sensitive from otherwise unavoidable exposure to ... [his] crude form of protest," Justice Harlan stated that while "government may properly act in many situations to prohibit intrusion into the privacy of the home of unwelcome views and ideas which cannot be totally banned from the public dialogue, ... we have at the same time consistently stressed that "we are often 'captives' outside the sanctuary of the home and subject to objectionable speech.'"

What this case is really all about, then, "is whether California can excise, as 'offensive conduct' one particular scurrilous epithet from the public discourse, either upon the theory of the court below that its use is inherently likely to cause violent reaction or upon a more general assertion that the States, acting as guardians of public morality, may properly remove this offensive word from the public vocabulary."

The majority's answer was that the state could not "excise, as 'offensive conduct' [this] one particular scurrilous epithet from the public discourse." Realizing that because of this decision people may be subjected to language that they find offensive, Justice Harlan declared:

> To many, the immediate consequence of this freedom may often appear to be only verbal tumult, discord, and even offensive utterance. These are, however, within established limits, in truth necessary side effects of the broader enduring values which the process of open debate permits us to achieve. That the air may at times seem filled with verbal cacophony is, in this sense not a sign of weakness but of strength.

He concluded: "While the particular four-letter word being litigated here is perhaps more distasteful than most others in its genre, it is nevertheless often true that one man's vulgarity is another's lyric."

It is surely understandable that at least in 1971, the use of this four-letter word in public was offensive to many people. Justice Blackmun, writing for himself, Chief Justice Burger, and Justice Black, thought it was. He wrote that "Cohen's absurd and immature antic, in my view, was mainly conduct and little speech."

Government's attempt to cleanse the public discourse is fraught with difficulties, not the least of which is choosing the language that is to be expunged. Humorist George Carlin compiled a list of seven words that were unacceptable in public conversation, and he admitted that the list "was open to amendment." Carlin included his list of seven words in a twelve-minute monologue. These were "words you couldn't say on the public, ah, airwaves, um, the ones you definitely wouldn't say, ever."[43]

A New York radio station operated by Pacifica Foundation aired the monologue at two P.M. October 30, 1973. Shortly thereafter, the Federal Communications Commission (FCC) received a letter of complaint from a man who heard the broadcast while driving with his young son. "He stated that, although he could perhaps understand the 'record's being sold for private use, I certainly cannot understand the broadcast of same over the air that, supposedly, you control.'"

The FCC sent the complaint to Pacifica, which responded "that the monologue had been played during a program about contemporary society's attitude toward language and that, immediately before its broadcast, listeners had been advised that it included 'sensitive language which might be regarded as offensive to some.'"

In reply, the FCC reprimanded the station, noting that it "could have been the subject of administrative sanctions." Further, it told Pacifica that if other complaints were forthcoming, it would consider using the sanctions authorized by Congress. Authority for its power to apply sanctions, it explained, came from 18 United States Code, Section 1464, which reads as follows: "Whoever utters any obscene, indecent, or profane language by means of radio communication shall be fined not more than $10,000 or imprisoned not more than two years, or both."

The commission did not think that the monologue was obscene but held that it was indecent. "The concept of 'indecent' is intimately connected with the exposure of children to language that describes, in terms patently offensive as measured by contemporary community standards for the broadcast medium, sexual or excretory activities and organs, at times of the day when there is a reasonable risk that children may be in the audience."

Pacifica, concerned that the commission's order might adversely affect the renewal of its license, turned to the courts for help. The case eventually reached the Supreme Court where five justices supported the FCC's position but could not agree on the reasoning for doing so.

Justice Stevens, writing for himself and two others, said that "when the issue is narrowed to the facts of this case, the question is whether the First Amendment denies government any power to restrict the public broadcast of indecent language in any circumstances." The radio station, however, argued that only "obscene" material, as defined by the justices, may be prohibited.

Acknowledging that obscene materials have been denied First Amendment protection "because their content is so offensive to contemporary moral standards," Stevens justifies the prohibition of Carlin's language, although not obscene, because "these words offend for the same reasons that obscenity offends." "In this case," he argued, "it is undisputed that the content of Pacifica's broadcast was 'vulgar,' 'offensive,' and 'shocking.'" He is, however, careful to point out that if the commission were objecting to the monologue's underlying message which he says it is not, that would be censorship and violate the First Amendment. The monologue's message was "to show that the words it uses are 'harmless' and that our attitudes toward them are 'essentially silly.'"

Justice Stevens turns to a discussion of broadcast media:

> The broadcast media have established a uniquely pervasive presence in the lives of all Americans. Patently offensive, indecent material presented over the airwaves confronts the citizen, not only in public, but also in the privacy of the home, where the individual's right to be left alone plainly outweighs the First Amendment rights of an intruder.

He concludes: "We simply hold that when the Commission finds that a pig has entered the parlor, the exercise of its regulatory power does not depend on proof that the pig is obscene."

The two concurring justices, Powell and Blackmun, voted to sustain the commission's decision because "the unique characteristics of the broadcast media, combined with society's right to protect its children from speech generally agreed to be inappropriate for their years, and with the interest of unwilling adults in not being assaulted by such offensive speech in their homes," justified that result.

For dissenting justices Stewart, Brennan, and Marshall, this was not a very difficult case. They thought that the word "indecent" in Section 1464 "should properly be read as meaning no more than 'obscene,'" and "since Carlin's monologue concededly was not 'obscene,'" the commission had no power to ban it.

The result in this case greatly disturbed justices Brennan and Marshall. Writing for both, Justice Brennan declared: "I find the Court's misapplication of fundamental First Amendment principles so patent, and its attempt to impose *its* notions of propriety on the whole of the American people so misguided, that I am unable to remain silent." Brennan criticized both the Stevens and Powell opinions in which "both stress the time-honored right of a parent to raise his child as he sees fit—a right this Court has consistently been vigilant to protect." "This principle," he asserted, "supports a result directly contrary to that reached by the Court." The Court's prior cases, he argued "hold that parents, *not* the government, have the right to make certain decisions regarding the upbringing of their children." Therefore, whether children listen to the broadcast is a decision that parents, not the government, should make.

The problem with the *FCC* decision is that it does not provide assistance to legislatures, courts, or lawyers in determining which words are "vulgar," "offensive," or "shocking." Carlin thought "the list . . . [was] open to amendment," and said, "I found three more words you could never say on television, and they were fart, turd, and twat, those three."

When the "pig has entered the parlor" voluntarily, the government bears a heavier burden in justifying its exclusion. Such was the case when the government sought approval of legislation regulating "dial-a-porn" messages in the case of *Sable Communications of California, Inc. v. F.C.C.*[44] In 1988, Congress, "imposed a blanket prohibition on indecent as well as obscene interstate commercial telephone messages." Because Sable Communications was providing sexually oriented telephone messages, it brought an action against the FCC seeking a declaration that the law was unconstitutional under the First Amendment, and an order prohibiting the FCC from enforcing it. Federal District Judge A. Wallace Tashima upheld the statutory ban on obscene telephone calls but struck down the "indecent speech" provision. The Supreme Court reached the same conclusion. Its analysis with respect to the question of the validity of the prohibition of obscenity will be discussed in Chapter IX, Freedom of the Press.

The Court acknowledges that "sexual expression which is indecent but not obscene is protected by the First Amendment," but "government may . . . regulate [such speech] in order to promote a compelling interest if it chooses the least restrictive means to further the articulated interest." One compelling interest is "protecting the physical and psychological well-being of minors." This interest, the government argued, is sufficient to sustain the restriction on indecent calls that may be heard by minors and cited the Court's decision in the "seven dirty words" case. But the majority held that that case was inapplicable here.

> The context of dial-in services, where the caller seeks and is willing to pay for the communication, is manifestly different from a situation in which a listener does not want the received message. Placing a telephone call is not the same as turning on a radio and being taken by surprise by an indecent message.

Noting that the FCC had previously determined that "its credit card, access code, and scrambling rules were a satisfactory solution to the problem of keeping indecent dial-a-porn messages out of the reach of minors," the justices said that "these rules represented a 'feasible and effective' way to serve the Government's compelling interest in protecting children."

The citizens of the borough of Mount Ephraim, New Jersey, had no difficulty in determining that one kind of expression that they did not want in their community was nude dancing. When Schad (first name not available) and others, operators of an adult bookstore, installed a coin-operated viewing machine through which a viewer could watch a live nude dancer, a complaint was filed against them for violating the zoning ordinance. That ordinance contained an extensive list of permitted commercial uses, but live entertainment was not included. Schad and the others were found guilty, and fines were imposed. They appealed through three levels of New Jersey appellate courts asserting that live nude dancing was speech within the meaning of the First Amendment and that prohibiting them from offering that kind of entertainment was a violation of their rights. They were unsuccessful.

The Supreme Court set aside the convictions and took the opportunity to explain the relationship of entertainment to the First Amendment.

> By excluding live entertainment throughout the Borough, the Mount Ephraim ordinance prohibits a wide range of expression that has long been held to be within the protections of the First and

Fourteenth Amendments. Entertainment, as well as political and ideological speech, is protected; motion pictures, programs broadcast by radio and television, and live entertainment, such as musical and dramatic works, fall within the First Amendment guarantee.[45]

Turning its attention to the ordinance, the majority took notice that nude dancing was prohibited throughout the borough. "No property . . . may be principally used for the commercial production of plays, concerts, musicals, dance, or any other form of live entertainment." It would be all right, however, to sing Christmas carols at an office party and for a high school to perform a play as long as it did not charge for the performance.

In searching the record to find the basis for the exclusion of live entertainment, the justices could find none. Some reasons were advanced during presentation of the case to the Court. Among those were that "problems that may be associated with live entertainment such as parking, trash, police protection, and medical facilities" were avoided by the ordinance. This argument did not impress the justices because at no time throughout the litigation was evidence presented that these problems existed in Mount Ephraim.

The borough next tried to justify the law as a "reasonable time, place and manner" restriction. But here again, no evidence was presented that it was reasonable to exclude all such entertainment, and even if there were reasons, the First Amendment required that "adequate alternative channels of communication" be available. Such was not the case here.

Justice Stevens concurred in the result but wanted it understood that in some cases he would approve "a carefully drawn ordinance, [that] regulate[s] or ban[s] public entertainment within" municipal boundries. "Surely," he stated, "a municipality zoned entirely for residential use need not create a special commercial zone solely to accommodate purveyors of entertainment."

Chief Justice Burger and Justice Rehnquist dissented because they thought that a small mostly residential community such as Mount Ephraim should have the right to regulate its environment. "The residents of this small enclave chose to maintain their town as a placid, 'bedroom' community of a few thousand people. To that end, they passed an admittedly broad regulation prohibiting certain forms of entertainment. Because I believe that a community of people are—within limits—masters of their own environment, I would hold that, as applied, the ordinance is valid."

Flags and the First Amendment

*"What is known of all, that to every free American the flag is the symbol of the Nation's power, the emblem of freedom in its truest, best sense."**

Even before the First Amendment was made applicable to the states, the Supreme Court recognized that "flags" conveyed messages.

> From the earliest periods in the history of the human race, banners, standards and ensigns have been adopted as symbols of the power and history of the peoples who bore them.[46]

And for our flag, particularly, "every true American has not simply an appreciation but a deep affection." Because of this "deep affection" and to prevent "indignities" being put upon it, state governments have enacted laws punishing improper uses of the flag. Nebraska had such a law. It punished the sale or "possession for sale, any article of merchandise, upon which shall have been printed or placed, for purposes of *advertisement,* a representation of the flag of the United States."

Sometime prior to 1907, Halter and others were charged with "having . . . unlawfully exposed to public view, sold, exposed for sale, and had in their possession for sale, a bottle of beer, upon which, for purposes of advertisement, was printed and painted a representation of the flag of the United States." When charged with violating the law, Halter and his friends pleaded not guilty and argued that the "statute . . . was null and void, as infringing their personal liberty guaranteed by the Fourteenth Amendment." They did not specify just what "liberty" the flag law violated. They were found guilty and ordered to pay a fine of $50 plus costs of prosecution. The Nebraska Supreme Court agreed with the jury, let the judgment stand, and the U.S. Supreme Court affirmed.

> We cannot hold that any privilege of American citizenship or that any right of personal liberty is violated by a state enactment forbidding the flag to be used as an advertisement on a bottle of beer.

The *Halter* case upholds the power of government to punish desecration of the American flag. The First Amendment, however, played no part in that decision, even though it might have been argued that in using the picture of the flag on the beer bottle, Halter and the other were saying something, although it's not clear just what.

*Halter v. Nebraska, 205 U.S. 34, 43 (1907).

More than sixty years later, the Court considered a situation in which a flag, with a symbol attached to it, was used to convey a message. The facts of the case are given by the Court as follows:

> On May 10, 1970, [Harold Omand Spence,] a college student, hung his United States flag from the window of his apartment on private property in Seattle, Washington. The flag was upside down, and attached to the front and back was a peace symbol made of removable black tape. The window was above the ground. The flag measured approximately three by five feet and was plainly visible to passersby. The peace symbol occupied roughly half of the surface of the flag. Three Seattle police officers observed the flag and entered the apartment house. They were met at the main door by [Spence], who said: 'I suppose you are here about the flag. I didn't know there was anything wrong with it. I will take it down.' [Spence] permitted the officers to enter his apartment, where they seized the flag and arrested him. [He] cooperated with the officers. There was no disruption or altercation.[47]

Spence was charged with having placed or caused "to be placed ... [a] word, figure, mark, picture, design, drawing or advertisement ... upon ... [a] flag, ... of the United States" and for having exposed such a flag to public view. He testified that he "displayed [the flag] as a protest against the invasion of Cambodia and the killings at Kent State University" and "that his purpose was to associate the American flag with peace instead of war and violence."

Spence was convicted, and the Washington Supreme Court "sustained the conviction, rejecting [his] contention, *inter alia,* that the improper use statute, on its face and as applied, contravened the First and Fourteenth Amendments."

A majority of the U.S. Supreme Court accepted Spence's arguments and held that the "statute, as applied to [his] activity, impermissibly infringed a form of protected expression." The justices noted several factors about the case: (1) This was Spence's flag, not public property. (2) The display was on private property—there was no trespass nor disorderly conduct. (3) There was no evidence of a breach of peace, no crowd gathered. (4)"[Spence] was engaged in a form of communication."

The justices recognized that there was speech here and that the upside-down flag with the peace symbol on it did convey a "message [that] would be understood by those who viewed it." That being the case, the question focused on the state's justification for punishing Spence. The state argued that it was justified because a purpose of the law was the prevention of breaches of the peace. The Court rejected this argument because "it is totally without support in the record," as no one who saw the flag was upset. Nor could the conviction be sustained "on the ground that the State may have desired to protect the sensibilities of passersby." Passersby, who might have been offended, "could easily have avoided the display." Finally the majority turned to the argument that the state had "an interest in preserving the national flag as an unalloyed symbol of our government."

"But we need not decide in this case," the opinion states, "whether the interest advanced by the court below is valid. We assume, *arguendo,* that it is. The statute is nevertheless unconstitutional as applied to [Spence's] activities."

> Given the protected character of his expression and in light of the fact no interest of the State may have in preserving the physical integrity of a privately owned flag was significantly impaired on these facts, the conviction must be invalidated.

Proceeding on the theory that "the right of free speech is not absolute at all times and under all circumstances," Justice Rehnquist, Chief Justice Burger, and Justice White dissented. Justice Rehnquist argued that "even protected speech may be subject to reasonable limitation when important countervailing interests are involved." The "countervailing interest" sought to be protected here was "'the physical integrity of the flag,' but also one of preserving the flag as 'an important symbol of nationhood and unity.'" In support of these goals, this law does nothing more than "simply [withdraw] a unique national symbol from the roster of materials that may be used as a background for communications. Since I do not believe the Constitution prohibits Washington from making that decision, I dissent."

The difference between the majority and the dissenters focuses upon whether the governmental interest in preserving the flag as a national symbol is compelling enough to outweigh a speaker's right to express his or her views. If the speaker's actions, whether it be the use of the flag as in *Halter* or placing a symbol on it as Spence did, created a clear and present danger of a breach of peace, there is little doubt that a majority would have approved punishment for the speaker.

A few months before *Spence,* the same majority that upheld Spence's right to express his views by placing a peace symbol on a flag agreed with a federal district court that a staute making it a crime to "publicly . . . treat contemptuously the flag of the United States," violated the Due Process Clause. The district court had before it a case involving the prosecution of Valarie Goguen for wearing a small U.S. flag on the seat of his pants.[48] It held that the words *treat contemptuously* were so vague that the statute did not provide adequate warning of the conduct which was forbidden. A majority of the Supreme Court agreed.

As was pointed out in the *Feiner* case, if a speaker's speech creates a clear and present danger of a breach of the peace, he or she can be punished. This would also be true if the danger is created by desecrating a flag as a means of expressing a point of view. If no such disturbance appears likely, the speech is protected by the First Amendment, even though the government asserts an interest "in preserving the national flag as an unalloyed symbol of the country." That was the decision of a majority of the justices in *Texas v. Johnson*,[49] a case involving the burning of an American flag as a protest against certain policies of the Reagan administration. Gregory Lee Johnson, in concert with a number of others, gathered outside the Dallas, Texas, City Hall during the 1984 Republican National Convention. They engaged in anti-Reagan chants, "die-ins," and the burning of an American flag.

> While the flag burned, the protestors chanted, "America, the red, white, and blue, we spit on you." After the demonstrators dispersed, a witness to the flag-burning collected the flag's remains and buried them in his backyard.

There were no injuries or threatened injuries, although some of the witnesses were offended. Johnson was charged under the following state law:

> Section 42.09. Desecration of Venerated Object
> (a) A person commits an offense if he intentionally or knowingly desecrates:
> . . . .
> (3) a state or national flag.

Johnson was convicted by a jury, sentenced to one year in jail, and fined $2,000. The Dallas Court of Appeals affirmed, but the Court of Criminal Appeals reversed, holding that the statute violated the First Amendment. The Supreme Court sustained the court of appeals 5–4.

Justice Brennan, delivering the majority opinion, dismisses the state's asserted interest that a prosecution for a breach of peace justifies the conviction by pointing out that no disturbance or threatened disturbance occurred. Nor could the conviction be sustained on the grounds that "an audience that takes serious offense at particular expression is necessarily likely to disturb the peace and that the expression may be prohibited on this basis." As was said in *Terminiello,* one of the "functions of free speech under our system of government is to invite dispute."

Finally, "Johnson's expressive conduct [does not] fall within that small class of 'fighting words' that are 'likely to provoke the average person to retaliation, and thereby cause a breach of the peace,'" because the speech here was not a face-to-face confrontation with any person.

This brought the majority to a discussion of the question whether the "State's interest in preserving the flag as a symbol of nationhood and national unity justifies Johnson's conviction." Justice Brennan pointed out that the Texas law was "not aimed at protecting the physical integrity of the flag in all circumstances, but is designed instead to protect it only against impairments that would cause serious offense to others." But speech cannot be punished just because it is offensive to some people. "If there is a bedrock principle underlying the First Amendment, it is that the Government may not prohibit the expression of an idea simply because society finds the idea itself offensive or disagreeable."

The justices summed up their holding:

> Johnson was convicted for engaging in expressive conduct. The State's interest in preventing breaches of the peace does not support his conviction because Johnson's conduct did not threaten to disturb the peace. Nor does the State's interest in preserving the flag as a symbol of nationhood and national unity justify his criminal conviction for engaging in political expression.

Justice Kennedy concurred, noting that Justice Brennan "says with power all that is necessary to explain our ruling." And he added an insight into the mental struggle that justices go through with tough cases like this one.

> The case before us illustrates better than most that the judicial power is often difficult in its exercise. We cannot here ask another branch to share responsibility, as when the argument is made that a statute is flawed or incomplete. For we are presented with a clear and simple statute to be judged against a pure command of the Constitution. The outcome can be laid to no door but ours.

Chief Justice Rehnquist, in a dissenting opinion joined by justices White and O'Connor, discussed the place of the American flag in our history, pointing out that prior to the Revolutionary War

> there were many colonial and regimental flags, adorned with such symbols as pine trees, beavers, anchors, and rattle snakes, bearing slogans as 'Liberty or Death,' 'Hope,' 'An Appeal to Heaven,' and 'Don't Tread on Me.'

He concluded:

> Surely one of the high purposes of a democratic society is to legislate against conduct that is regarded as evil and profoundly offensive to the majority of people—whether it be murder, embezzlement, pollution, or flag burning.

The *Johnson* decision loosed a storm of protest across the nation. There were editorials condemning and approving the decision, as well as hundreds of letters to editors, both for and against. President George Bush and many members of Congress called for a constitutional amendment to make it a crime to descrate the flag under any circumstances. In response to the furor, Congress passed and the President signed the Flag Protection Act of 1989.

> The Act criminalizes the conduct of anyone who 'knowingly mutilates, defaces, physically defiles, burns, maintains on the floor or ground, or tramples upon' a United States flag, except conduct related to the disposal of a 'worn or soiled' flag.[50]

Shortly thereafter, a number of individuals, including Shawn D. Eichman, Mark John Haggerty, and others "were prosecuted in the District Courts for violating the Act: some for knowingly burning several flags while protesting various aspects of the Government's policies, and others, in a separate incident, for knowingly burning a flag while protesting the Act's passage." In separate cases, District Judge June L. Green of the District of Columbia and District Judge Barbara J. Rothstein of the Western District of Washington held the act unconstitutional and dismissed the charges.

Both cases were immediately appealed to the Supreme Court, which affirmed both decisions, with the same five justices—Brennan, Marshall, Blackmun, Scalia, and Kennedy—voting to strike down the act and Chief Justice Rehnquist with justices Stevens, White, and O'Connor voting to uphold it.

The government contended that the Flag Protection Act was constitutional because it "does not target expressive conduct on the basis of the content of its message" and the government's interest is "in 'protect[ing] the physical integrity of the flag under all circumstances' in order to safeguard the flag's identity 'as the unique and unalloyed symbol of the Nation.'"

The majority did not accept the government's argument that the act was not intended to punish expression. Justice Brennan, who authored the majority opinion, declared, "It is nevertheless clear that the Government's asserted *interest* is related 'to the suppression of free expression,' . . . and concerned with the content of such expression." Insofar as safeguarding the flag's identity was concerned, Justice Brennan wrote:

> The Government's interest in protecting the "physical integrity" of a privately owned flag rests upon a perceived need to preserve the flag's status as a symbol of our Nation and certain national ideals. But the mere destruction or disfigurement of a particular physical manifestation of the symbol, without more, does not diminish or otherwise affect the symbol itself in any way.

The majority then concluded that "punishing desecration of the flag dilutes the very freedom that makes this emblem so revered, and worth revering."

Justice Stevens, writing for the dissenters, first pointed out that "it is now conceded that the Federal Government has a legitimate interest in protecting the symbolic value of the American flag." And he acknowledged that there is an "important interest in allowing every speaker to choose the method of expressing his or her ideas." But, he insisted,

> to us, the flag is a reminder both that the struggle for liberty and equality is unceasing, and that our obligation of tolerance and respect for all of our fellow citizens encompasses those who disagree with us—indeed, even those whose ideas are disagreeable, or offensive.
>
> Thus, the Government may—indeed, it should—protect the symbolic value of the flag without regard to the specific content of the flag burners' speech.

The Power to Censor

*"An ordinance which . . . makes the peaceful enjoyment of freedoms
. . . contingent upon the uncontrolled will of an official — is an
unconstitutional censorship . . . upon the enjoyment of those freedoms."**

As discussed in Chapter V, the Court for many years has condemned attempts to punish religious solicitation upon streets and from
door to door. One of the concerns has been laws that give some government official the uncontrolled authority to grant or deny permits. The
concern is not just for religious solicitation but extends to the use of
streets and parks for other First Amendment activities, such as speech,
press, and assembly. Laws requiring permits to engage in these freedoms must also be narrowly drawn so that the permit issuer cannot
choose between messages she is willing to hear and those she dislikes.

The justices affirmed this principle when they struck down the
conviction of Rose Staub for soliciting workers in Baxley, Georgia, to
join a union. Staub and one Mamie Merritt, employees of the International Ladies' Garment Workers Union, were going door to door in Baxley seeking to organize women factory workers. When questioned by
the chief of police and telling him that they were "going around talking
to some of the women to organize the factory workers . . . and [were]
hold[ing] meetings with them for that purpose," the chief had a summons issued against Staub. She was charged with violating a city ordinance requiring solicitors to "make application in writing to Mayor
and Council of the city of Baxley for the issuance of a permit to solicit
members . . . from among the citizens of Baxley." The mayor's court
found her guilty, sentenced her to thirty days' imprisonment and a fine
of $300. This decision was affirmed by two appellate courts, and the
Georgia Supreme Court refused to hear the case. The U.S. Supreme
Court, reversing the conviction, accepted Staub's "contention . . . that
the ordinance is invalid on its face because it makes enjoyment of the
constitutionally guaranteed freedom of speech contingent upon the
will of the Mayor and Council . . . and thereby constitutes a prior
restraint upon, and abridges, that freedom."[51]

Picketing, parading, and demonstrating are types of conduct that
are protected by the Free Speech Clause because they generally convey
a message. Therefore, laws requiring permits for engaging in these activities that do not contain guidelines controlling the discretion of the

*Staub v. City of Baxley, 355 U.S. 313, 322 (1958).

permit issuer are also unconstitutional. This was confirmed by the Court in *Shuttlesworth v. Birmingham.*[52]

> On the afternoon of April 12, Good Friday, 1963, 52 people, all Negroes, were led out of a Birmingham church by three Negro ministers, one of whom was . . . Fred L. Shuttlesworth. They walked in orderly fashion, two abreast for the most part, for four blocks. The purpose of their march was to protest the alleged denial of civil rights to Negroes in the City of Birmingham. The marchers stayed on the sidewalks . . . and they did not interfere with other pedestrians. . . . As the marchers moved along, a crowd of spectators fell in behind them at a distance. The spectators at some points spilled out into the street, but the street was not blocked and vehicles were not obstructed.

After having marched for about four blocks, they were stopped and arrested because they had not obtained a permit required by a local law that made it "unlawful to organize or hold, . . . or to take part . . . in, any parade or procession . . . on the streets . . . unless a permit therefore has been secured from the commission."

Shuttlesworth was convicted and sentenced to 138 days at hard labor. After his conviction was sustained by the Alabama Court of Appeals, the Supreme Court reversed without a dissenting vote. Justice Stewart, delivering the opinion for the Court, took the opportunity to set the record straight on what the constitutional rule is with regard to permit laws.

> There can be no doubt that the Birmingham ordinance, as it was written, conferred upon the City Commission virtually unbridled and absolute power to prohibit any 'parade,' 'procession,' or 'demonstration' on the city's streets or public ways. For in deciding whether or not to withhold a permit the members of the Commission were to be guided only by their own ideas of 'public welfare, peace, safety, health, decency, good order, morals or convenience.' This ordinance as it was written, therefore, fell squarely within the ambit of the many decisions of this Court over the last 30 years holding that a law subjecting the exercise of First Amendment freedoms to the prior restraint of a license, without narrow, objective and definite standards to guide the licensing authority, is unconstitutional.

Local governments have tried other methods of placing restrictions on the First Amendment right of solicitation. For example, the village of Schaumburg, Illinois, enacted a very comprehensive ordinance regulating solicitation for charitable organizations. Such organizations desiring to solicit within the village were required to obtain a permit, which would be issued only after the organization furnished proof that "at least seventy-five percent of the proceeds of such solicitation [would] be used directly for the charitable purpose of the organization."[53]

The Citizens for a Better Environment (CBE) applied for a permit, which was denied because it could not meet the 75 percent requirement. CBE was organized to protect and maintain the environment. In so doing, its members went door to door distributing environmental literature, answering questions, and soliciting contributions for support of their cause. More than 60 percent of their funds went for salaries, and none was used for any charitable purposes.

Having been denied a permit, CBE turned to the federal district court for relief. Judge Prentice H. Marshall declared the 75 percent requirement unconstitutional as in effect "a form of censorship." The court of appeals agreed, as did the Supreme Court, with only Justice Rehnquist dissenting.

Relying upon former cases, some of which have been discussed in Chapter V, Justice White, writing for the majority, declared:

> Prior authorities, therefore, clearly establish that charitable appeals for funds, on the street or door to door, involve a variety of speech interests — communication of information, the dissemination and propagation of views and ideas, and the advocacy of causes — that are within the protection of the First Amendment.

The issue, therefore, "is whether the Village has exercised its power to regulate solicitation in such a manner as not to unduly intrude upon the rights of free speech." The majority accepted the village's position that the 75 percent requirement "related to substantial governmental interests 'in protecting the public from fraud and undue annoyance,'" but noted that some "organizations . . . are primarily engaged in research, advocacy, or public education" and that "the village consistently with the First Amendment, cannot label such groups 'fraudulent' and bar them from canvassing on the streets and house to house." Nor was the law justified as protecting public safety or residential privacy, because there was no proof "that organizations devoting more than one-quarter of their funds [for] expenses are any more likely to . . . be a threat to public safety than are other charitable organizations."

This led the majority to conclude that "the 75-percent requirement in the Village ordinance plainly is insufficiently related to the governmental interests asserted in support to justify its interference with protected speech."

Justice Rehnquist considered that because the ordinance here relates to the solicitation of money, the Court's prior cases were not applicable. "I would uphold Schaumburg's ordinance as applied to CBE because that ordinance, while perhaps too strict to suit some tastes, affects only door-to-door solicitation for financial contributions, leaves little or no discretion in the hands of municipal authorities to 'censor' unpopular speech, and is rationally related to the community's collective desire to bestow largesse upon organizations that are truly 'charitable.'"

Campaign Spending and Free Speech

*"Competition in ideas and governmental policies is at the core of our electoral process and of the First Amendment freedoms."**

The concern over political campaign contributions and expenditures goes back to the nineteenth century when many states enacted laws requiring disclosure of such contributions and expenditures. The concern at the time was the influence the wealthy, especially corporations, had upon the political process.

President Theodore Roosevelt, in his annual message to Congress on December 5, 1905, recommended that

> all contributions by corporations to any political committee or for any political purpose should be forbidden by law; directors should not be permitted to use stockholders' money for such purposes; and, moreover, a prohibition of this kind would be, as far as it went, an effective method of stopping the evils aimed at in corrupt practice acts.[54]

Congress responded in 1907 by enacting a law making it "unlawful for any national bank, or any corporation . . . to make a money contribution in connection with any election to public office."

Preventing subversion of the political process was not the only goal of these laws. Their "underlying philosophy was to sustain the active, alert responsibility of the individual citizen in a democracy for the wise conduct of government."

In 1971 Congress passed a comprehensive campaign-financing law,

Williams v. Rhodes, 393 U.S. 23, 32 (1968).

The Federal Election Campaign Act of 1971.[55] Among the act's many provisions was a limitation on expenditures by individuals or groups "relative to a clearly identified candidate." Persons wishing to spend money "advocating the election or defeat of [a] candidate" were limited to spending no more than $1,000. Expenditures made by a candidate from personal funds were limited depending upon the office sought. The ceiling for the office of president or vice president was $50,000; for senatorial candidates, $35,000; and $25,000 for candidates for the House of Representatives. The law also placed a spending limit of $10 million on campaigns for presidential nominations and an additional $20 million for the general election campaign.

James L. Buckley, senator from New York, together with several others and five organizations, brought an action seeking to have certain provisions of the law, including the expenditure limitations, declared unconstitutional as a violation of the First Amendment. By the time Buckley's case reached the Supreme Court, these limitations had been upheld by lower courts.

In a per curiam opinion, the justices struck down all sections of the act that placed limits on the sums that individuals could spend on campaigns. In so doing, the majority first pointed out that "the Act's expenditure ceilings impose direct and substantial restraints on the quantity of political speech."[56]

Equating campaign expenditures with speech gave rise to the question of whether asserted governmental interests for the limitations were sufficient to sustain the burden on speech. With regard to the ceiling on expenditures for or against a candidate, the majority said the government's interests were not sufficient and declared them invalid. "We find that the governmental interest in preventing corruption and the appearance of corruption inadequate to justify [the] ceiling on independent expenditures." They could see little danger in this kind of spending, and explained that "the independent advocacy restricted by the provision does not presently appear to pose dangers of real or apparent corruption comparable to those identified with large campaign contributions." Therefore, "while the independent expenditure ceiling thus fails to serve any substantial governmental interest in stemming the reality or appearance of corruption in the electoral process, it heavily burdens core First Amendment expression. . . . . Advocacy of the election or defeat of candidates for federal office is no less entitled to protection under the First Amendment than the discussion of political policy generally or advocacy of the passage or defeat of legislation."

Furthermore,

the candidate, no less than any other person, has a First Amendment right to engage in the discussion of public issues and vigorously and tirelessly to advocate his own election and the election of other candidates. Indeed, it is of particular importance that candidates have the unfettered opportunity to make their views known so that the electorate may intelligently evaluate the candidates' personal qualities and their positions on vital public issues before choosing among them on election day.

The attempt to limit total campaign expenditures in presidential nominations and campaigns was also held to be unconstitutional. The two justifications urged for these limits—to reduce dependency upon large contributions and equalizing the financial resources of candidates—found little support from the justices.

Justice White dissented. He did not see either "the limitations on contributions nor those on expenditures [as] directly or indirectly [controlling] the content of political speech by candidates or by their supporters or detractors."

The *Buckley* case dealt generally with political expenditures by candidates and their individual supporters. In *F.E.C. v. National Conservative PAC* (NCPAC)[57], the question at issue was the validity of a law that "makes it a criminal offense for independent 'political committees' . . . to expend more than $1,000 to further [the] election" of presidential or vice presidential candidates who have elected to accept public funds for their campaigns.

The NCPAC was a "political committee" that solicited and expended funds for the election of Ronald Reagan as president during the 1980 presidential campaign. It was not, however, a part of Reagan's official organization. In an action brought by the Democratic party and Edward Mezvinsky seeking to have the law upheld and enforced, NCPAC was joined as a defendant. Circuit Judge Edward R. Becker held that "[the law] abridges First Amendment freedoms of speech and association," and a majority of the Supreme Court agreed. The justices acknowledged that "PACs . . . are not lone pamphleteers or street corner orators in the Tom Paine mold; they spend substantial amounts of money in order to communicate their political ideas through sophisticated media advertisements." Nevertheless, "for purposes of presenting political views in connection with a nationwide Presidential election, allowing the presentation of views while forbidding the expenditure of more than $1,000 to present them is much like allowing a speaker in a public hall to express his views while denying him the use of an amplifying system."

The majority therefore held that the government's interest of preventing corruption or appearance of corruption is not furthered by the law's restrictions. "The hallmark of corruption is the financial *quid pro quo:* dollars for political favors. But here the conduct proscribed is not contributions to the candidate, but independent expenditures in support of a candidate."

It was argued by those supporting the limitation "that candidates may take notice of and reward those responsible for PAC expenditures by giving official favors to the latter in exchange for the supporting messages." The justices thought "such an exchange of political favors for uncoordinated expenditures remains a hypothetical possibility and nothing more."

Because he continued to believe that the "First Amendment protects the right to speak, not the right to spend, and limitations on the amount of money that can be spent are not the same as restrictions on speaking," Justice White dissented.

When the Court in *Buckley* upheld limits on *contributions* to candidates, it acknowledged that such limitations affected the contributor's freedom of political association directly but impacted free speech rights only incidentally. However, it found that these limitations did not violate either constitutional freedom. The effect of contribution limits on associational rights will be discussed in Chapter VIII.

Although restrictions upon contributions to political candidates only minimally affected free speech rights, the justices saw a different problem in regulations that placed a ceiling on contributions to campaigns for or against a ballot measure. Berkeley, California, had an ordinance that placed "a limitation of $250 on contributions to committees formed to support or oppose ballot measures...."[58]

Berkeley urged two interests in support of the law: (1) "a prophylactic measure to make known the identity of supporters and opponents of ballot measures"; (2) "to preserve voters' confidence in the ballot measure process."

With only Justice White dissenting, the justices found the limitation an unconstitutional burden upon both speech and associational rights. Writing for the majority, Chief Justice Burger said: "Apart from the impermissible restraint on freedom of association, [the law] imposes a significant restraint on freedom of expression of groups and those individuals who wish to express their views through committees." And "the integrity of the political system will be adequately protected if contributors are identified in a public filing revealing the amounts contributed," which the law requires.

As more fully discussed hereafter, corporations are entitled to the protection of the First Amendment. But when the Court considered the validity of direct corporate expenditures for political purposes, it upheld a state prohibition on such spending even though it was admitted that such a ban was an infringement on the corporation's freedom to speak. The precise question arose when the Michigan Chamber of Commerce brought an action against Richard H. Austin, Michigan Secretary of State, challenging a Michigan law that prohibits "corporations from using corporate treasury funds for independent expenditures in support of or in opposition to candidates in elections for state office."[59] Judge Douglas W. Hillman, of the federal district court, upheld the law, but the court of appeals reversed, reasoning that the law was a burden upon corporations' right to speak. By a 6–3 vote, the Supreme Court determined the law constitutional.

This is one of those cases in which the majority straightforwardly acknowledges that "the mere fact that the Chamber is a corporation does not remove its speech from the ambit of the First Amendment." But it then finds that the "State has articulated a sufficiently compelling rationale to support its restriction on independent expenditures by corporations" and that the act "is precisely targeted to eliminate the distortion caused by corporate spending while also allowing corporations to express their political views."

In order to sustain its position, the majority had to distinguish it from another case involving corporate spending, which it had decided in 1986. The former case involved the question of whether part of the Federal Election Campaign Act, which prohibited a corporation from using its funds to support candidates, could be applied to a nonprofit, nonstock corporation organized to "foster human life." Under the act, corporations could spend money for political purposes, but only through a special segregated fund.

The Massachusetts Citizens for Life (MCFL) was formed "to foster respect for human life and to defend the right to life for all human beings, born and unborn." Its funds came from voluntary contributions by its members and from "fund-raising activities such as garage sales, bake sales, dances, raffles, and picnics."[60] It did not accept donations from either corporations or unions.

Although there was no majority opinion, five justices agreed that the act could not be applied to a corporation like MCFL because "groups such as MCFL . . . do not pose [a] danger of corruption" as do other corporations. Furthermore, to require a small nonprofit corporation to form a special fund for campaign purposes would place a heavy administrative burden on it and infringe upon its First Amendment rights. But the Michigan law was entirely different according to the majority. There, the ability of corporations to amass huge amounts of money gives them an advantage in the political arena.

> Corporate wealth can unfairly influence elections when it is deployed in the form of independent expenditures, just as it can when it assumes the guise of political contributions. We therefore hold that the State has articulated a sufficiently compelling rationale to support its restriction on independent expenditures by corporations.[61]

The majority also pointed out that the Michigan act "does not impose an *absolute* ban on all forms of corporate political spending but permits corporations to make independent political expenditures through segregated funds. Because persons contributing to such funds understand that their money will be used solely for political purposes, the speech generated accurately reflects contributors' support for the corporation's political views."

Justice Scalia, in a forceful dissent, wrote that "the Court today endorses the principle that too much speech is an evil that the democratic majority can proscribe. I dissent because that principle is contrary to our case law and incompatible with the absolutely central truth of the First Amendment: that governnment cannot be trusted to assure, through censorship, the 'fairness' of political debate."

The majority's holding that the Michigan law could be applied to the Chamber of Commerce caused Justice Kennedy to write: "With the imprimatur of this Court, it is now a felony in Michigan for the Sierra Club, or the American Civil Liberties Union, or the Michigan State Chamber of Commerce, to advise the public how a candidate voted on issues of urgent concern to their members. In both practice and theory, the prohibition aims at the heart of political debate."

A quite different kind of restriction on political activities was considered by the courts in *Meyer v. Grant*,[62] an action brought in the Federal District Court for Colorado by Paul K. Grant, Edward Haskins, Nancy P. Bigbee, Lori A. Massie, Ralph R. Harrison, and Coloradians for Free Enterprise, Inc. They challenged the constitutionality of a Colorado statute that made it unlawful to pay individuals for circulating a ballot petition. Judge John P. Moore upheld the law, but the court of appeals reversed, and a unanimous Supreme Court agreed that the law was unconstitutional.

> The circulation of an initiative petition of necessity involves both the expression of a desire for political change and a discussion of the

merits of the proposed change. . . . Thus, the circulation of a petition involves the type of interactive communication concerning political change that is appropriately described as "core political speech."

Colorado attempted to support the law by arguing that "the prohibition is justified by its interest in making sure that an initiative has sufficient grass roots support to be placed on the ballot, [and] by its interests in protecting the integrity of the initiative process." But the justices responded that initiatives could not be put on the ballot unless a required number of persons signed and that the integrity of the process was protected by other Colorado statutes making it a crime "to make false or misleading statements relating to a petition . . . or to pay someone to sign a petition."

Public Employees Have the Right to Speak

*"I have not been able to accept the recent doctrine that a citizen who enters the public service can be forced to sacrifice his civil rights."**

Restraint upon actions of public employees goes back to 1789 when the first Congress made it "unlawful for certain officers of the Treasury Department to engage in the business of trade or commerce, or to own a sea vessel, or to purchase public lands or other public property, or to be concerned in the purchase or disposal of the public securities of a State, or of the United States."[63]

Many similar laws were enacted thereafter, including one in 1876 that prohibited "certain officers of the United States from requesting, giving to, or receiving from, any other officer money or property or other thing of value for political purposes. . . ."

A man named Curtis was convicted of violating this law "for receiving money for political purposes from other employees of the government." He was convicted, fined, and taken into custody until the fine was paid. Curtis attempted to gain release by a writ of habeas corpus, which was denied by the Supreme Court. At issue was whether the act of 1876 was constitutional. A majority of the Court found that it was. The First Amendment, however, was not mentioned in the opinion, but there seems to be an implied recognition that there is a right to engage in political activities. The law, the opinion states, "simply forbids [employees] receiving from or giving to each other,"

*Justice Douglas, dissenting in *Adler v. Board of Education,* 342 U.S. 485, 508 (1952).

funds for political purposes. "Beyond this no restrictions are placed on any of their political privileges." They are free to receive and solicit money for other purposes.

Justice Joseph P. Bradley objected.

> To deny to a man the privilege of associating and making joint contributions with such other citizens as he may choose, is an unjust restraint of his right to propagate and promote his views on public affairs. The freedom of speech and of the press, and that of assembling together to consult upon and discuss matters of public interest, and to join in petitioning for a redress of grievances, are expressly secured by the Constitution.

Despite Justice Bradley's view that restrictions upon public employees engaging in political activities burdens their freedom of speech, the justices have consistently upheld such restrictions. They did so in George Poole's case. Poole, a roller in the Philadelphia Mint, admitted having been a ward executive committeeman. He acknowledged that "both before and since . . . [his] employment in the United States Mint, [he had] taken an active part in political campaigns and political management."[64]

Poole and several others brought suit seeking a declaration that a federal law known as the Hatch Act was unconstitutional. The law in question prohibited federal government employees from taking "any active part in political management or political campaigns."

When the case came to the Supreme Court, a majority of the justices held the Hatch Act constitutional, even though they admitted that it was an infringement upon "what would otherwise be the freedom of the civil servant under the First, Ninth and Tenth Amendments." But such infringement is permissible in this case because "essential rights of the First Amendment in some instances are subject to the elemental need for order without which the guarantees of civil rights to others would be a mockery." In the case of governmental employees, the "need for order" rests in a determination by Congress "that the presence of government employees, whether industrial or administrative, in the ranks of political party workers is bad."

The decision did not go unchallenged. Justice Black expressed concern about the effect that the Hatch Act would have upon the political process of the country.

> Legislation which muzzles several million citizens threatens popular government, not only because it injures the individuals muzzled,

but also because of its harmful effect on the body politic in depriving it of the political participation and interest of such a large segment of our citizens.

The majority's acceptance of Congress' determination that political activities by all government employees, no matter what type of work they performed, was bad was challenged by Justice Douglas: "Poole, being an industrial worker, is as remote from contact with the public or from policy making or from the functioning of the administrative process as a chairwoman." Further, he argued, public employees "are not second-class citizens."

The Hatch Act was considered again twenty-six years later in a 1973 case, when only Justice Douglas remained of the Court in *Poole*. In a 6–3 decision, the act was upheld again. The majority declared:

> We unhesitatingly reaffirm the *Mitchell* holding that Congress had, and has, the power to prevent Mr. Poole and others like him from holding a party office, working at the polls, and acting as a paymaster for other party workers.[65]

In its opinion, delivered by Justice White, the majority notes that "early in our history, Thomas Jefferson was disturbed by the political activities of some of those in the Executive Branch. . . ." Congress may have had the same concern when it enacted the Hatch Act, for "it seems fundamental . . . that employees in the Executive Branch . . . or those working for any of its agencies, should administer the law in accordance with the will of Congress, rather than in accordance with their own or the will of a political party." Congress may also have been of "the conviction that the rapidly expanding Government work force should not be employed to build a powerful, invincible, and perhaps corrupt political machine."

As could be expected, Justice Douglas found the burden on the employees' First Amendment right to participate freely in political activities just as great in 1973 as in 1947:

> We deal here with a First Amendment right to speak, to propose, to publish, to petition Government, to assemble. Time and place are obvious limitations. Thus no one could object if employees were barred from using office time to engage in outside activities whether political or otherwise. But it is of no concern of Government what an employee does in his spare time, whether religion, recreation, social work, or politics is his hobby—unless what he does impairs efficiency or other facets of the merits of his job.

On the same day that the Court upheld the Hatch Act for the second time, it also approved a section of Oklahoma's Merit System Personnel Administration Act that "restricts the political activities of the State's classified civil service in much the same manner that the Hatch Act proscribes partisan political activities of federal employees."[66]

With the exception of the burden placed on First Amendment activities by laws such as the Hatch Act, the Court has generally held that public employment cannot be conditioned upon surrender of constitutionally protected freedom of expression. This does not mean, however, that a government employee may speak on any subject at any time he or she pleases.

Sheila Myers learned this lesson the hard way. Myers was an assistant district attorney in Orleans Parish, Louisiana. She had been employed there for five years and was considered competent and conscientious. When she was informed that she was to be transferred to a different position in the district attorney's office, she strongly protested and discussed her objections with the district attorney and one of his assistants. In hopes of changing the decision to transfer her, she prepared "a questionnaire soliciting the views of her fellow staff members concerning office transfer policy, office morale, the need for a grievance committee, the level of confidence in supervisors, and whether employees felt pressured to work in political campaigns."[67] When the district attorney heard that Myers was circulating the questionnaire, he called her into his office, and immediately discharged her for not accepting the transfer. "She was also told that her distribution of the questionnaire was considered an act of insubordination."

Myers brought suit in the federal district court, contending that her termination was in violation of her right of free speech. Judge Jack M. Gordon agreed and ordered her reinstated with back pay and damages. Judge Gordon's decision was affirmed by the court of appeals but reversed by the Supreme Court in a 5–4 decision, with Chief Justice Burger and justices White, Powell, Rehnquist, and O'Connor voting to sustain Myers's discharge. Justices Brennan, Marshall, Blackmun, and Stevens took the position that Myers' right of free expression should prevail and that she should not have been discharged.

The majority, acknowledging that public employees retain their right to free speech, held that its previous cases support the position "that if Myers' questionnaire cannot be fairly characterized as constituting speech on a matter of public concern, it is unnecessary for us to scrutinize the reasons for her discharge." In other words, "when employee expression cannot be fairly considered relating to any matter of political, social, or other concern to the community, government officials should enjoy wide latitude in managing their offices, without intrusive oversight by the judiciary in the name of the First Amendment."

The justices did not mean to imply, however, "that Myers' speech, even if not touching a matter of public concern, is totally beyond the protection of the First Amendment."

> We hold only that when a public employee speaks not as a citizen upon matters of public concern, but instead as an employee upon matters only of personal interest, absent the most unusual circumstances, a federal court is not the appropriate forum in which to review the wisdom of a personnel decision taken by a public agency allegedly in reaction to the employee's behavior.

The majority then concluded that only one question of the questionnaire seemed to relate to matters of public concern. "Question 11 inquires if assistant district attorneys 'ever feel pressured to work in political campaigns on behalf of office supported candidates.'" The majority concluded that overall the "questionnaire touched upon matters of public concern in only a most limited sense; her survey, in our view, is most accurately characterized as an employee grievance concerning internal office policy."

The minority's disagreement was with the finding that the survey was not a matter of public concern. "I would hold," Justice Brennan declared, "that Myers' questionnaire addressed matters of public concern because it discussed subjects that could reasonably be expected to be of interest to persons seeking to develop informed opinions about the manner in which the Orleans Parish District Attorney, an elected official charged with managing a vital governmental agency, discharges his responsibilities."

How tenuous the right of a public employee to speak freely is, is illustrated by the case of *Rankin v. McPherson*.[68] The headnote to this case sets forth the following facts:

> Ardith McPherson, "a data-entry employee in a county Constable's office, was discharged for remarking to a co-worker, after hearing of an attempt on the President's life, 'If they go for him again, I hope they get him.' . . . [McPherson] was not a commissioned peace officer, did not wear a uniform, was not authorized to make arrests or permitted to carry a gun, and was not brought by virtue of her job into contact with the public. Her duties were purely clerical. . . . Her statement was made during a private conversation

in a room not readily accessible to the public. The Constable fired
[McPherson] because of the statement."

McPherson's suit against Constable Rankin for reinstatement and
back pay followed a rather irregular path. District Judge Norman W.
Black, Jr., gave judgment for the constable, holding that McPherson's
speech was not protected and that therefore she had been properly
discharged. The court of appeals vacated the judgment and sent it back
for another hearing in the district court. Judge Black, after hearing the
matter again, came to the same conclusion. For a second time, the court
of appeals reversed. It held that the remark made by McPherson "addressed a matter of public concern" and therefore was entitled to be
weighed against "her employer's interest in maintaining efficiency and
discipline in the workplace."

Judge Patrick E. Higginbotham, writing for the court of appeals,
concluded that because McPherson was not a law enforcement officer
and her job did not bring her into contact with the public, the constable's "interest did not outweigh the First Amendment interest in protecting McPherson's speech."

The Supreme Court agreed. Believing that the remark addressed
a matter of public concern, the majority balanced McPherson's free
speech rights against the governmental interests in the workplace and
concluded that she had been wrongfully discharged. The justices could
find no evidence that other employees were disturbed or their work interrupted, or that any member of the public even heard the remark.

Justice Powell, concurring, did not think the case warranted all of
the attention it got from the judicial system.

> In my view, however, the case is hardly as complex as might be ex-
> pected in a dispute that now had been considered five separate times
> by three different federal courts. The undisputed evidence shows
> that McPherson made an ill-considered — but protected — comment
> during a private conversation, and the Constable made an instinc-
> tive, but intemperate, employment decision on the basis of this
> speech. I agree that on these facts, McPherson's private speech is pro-
> tected by the First Amendment.

But four justices, in an opinion written by Justice Scalia, viewed
the case from an entirely different perspective. "I agree," Justice Scalia
explained, "with the proposition, felicitously put by Constable
Rankin's counsel, that no law enforcement agency is required by the
First Amendment to permit one of its employees to 'ride with the cops

and cheer for the robbers.'" From the minority's point of view, McPherson's statement was not a matter of public concern but more like "statements that we have previously held entitled to no First Amendment protection even in the nonemployment context—including assassination threats against the President (which are illegal...)." Furthermore, "Constable Rankin's interest in maintaining both an esprit de corps and a public image consistent with his office's law enforcement duties outweighs any interest his employees may have in expressing on the job a desire that the President be killed, even assuming that such an expression addresses a matter of public concern it is not protected by the First Amendment from suppression."

Students, Teachers, and the Schoolhouse Gate

*"It can hardly be argued that either students or teachers shed their constitutional rights to freedom of speech ... at the schoolhouse gate."**
Having received word that some students intended to wear black armbands in support of a truce in the Vietnam War, the principals of some Des Moines, Iowa, schools "adopted a policy that any student wearing an armband to school would be asked to remove it, and if he refused he would be suspended until he returned without the armband."[69] What transpired thereafter is set forth in the Supreme Court's opinion.

> On December 16, [1965,] Mary Beth and Christopher [Tinker] wore black armbands to their schools. John Tinker wore his armband the next day. They were all sent home and suspended from school until they would come back without their armbands. They did not return to school until after the planned period for wearing armbands had expired—that is, until after New Year's Day.

Through their father, the Tinker children filed an action in the local federal district court asking for an injunction prohibiting school officials from disciplining them and nominal damages. Among the first questions Judge Roy L. Stephenson was required to answer was whether wearing the armband was a method of expression protected under the First Amendment. He answered that indeed it was. "The wearing of an arm band for the purpose of expressing certain views is a symbolic act and falls within the protection of the First Amendment's free speech clause."[70]

Tinker v. Des Moines School Dist., 393 U.S. 503, 506 (1969).

Judge Stephenson concluded, however, that the school rule was a reasonable one and not an infringement upon students' freedom of speech. "It was not unreasonable," he declared, "in this instance for school officials to anticipate that the wearing of arm bands would create some type of classroom disturbance. The school officials involved had a reasonable basis for adopting the arm band regulation."

The Eighth Circuit Court of Appeals sustained Judge Stephenson by an equally divided court (4–4), but the Supreme Court reversed. A majority viewed the issue as one involving First Amendment rights "closely akin to 'pure speech.'"[71]

> The school officials banned and sought to punish [the students] for a silent, passive expression of opinion, unaccompanied by any disorder or disturbance on [their] part. . . .

The justices were concerned that the action taken by the principals was based upon "undifferentiated fear or apprehension of disturbance" and pointed out that that "is not enough to overcome the right to freedom of expression."

The majority acknowledged that "any departure from absolute regimentation may cause trouble. Any variation from the majority's opinion may inspire fear. Any words spoken, in class, in the lunchroom, or on the campus, that deviate from the views of another person may start an argument or cause a disturbance. But our Constitution says we must take this risk."

The episode was seen much differently by Justice Black. As noted above, Justice Black has always been regarded as one of the great champions of the First Amendment, but in this case he fell back upon what has been a truism with regard to freedom of speech, "that the rights of free speech and assembly 'do not mean that everyone with opinions or beliefs to express may address a group at any public place and at any time.'" The school, at least at this particular time, was not, he believed, the proper place for a Vietnam protest. He pointed out that the record showed evidence that the "armbands caused comments, warnings by other students, the poking of fun at them, and a warning by an older football player that other, nonprotesting students had better let them alone." Justice Black also expressed concern that the armbands would distract the students from the learning process. "Nor are public school students," he noted, "sent to the schools at public expense to broadcast political or any other views to educate and inform the public."

The *Tinker* case sets forth the general principle that both students and teachers retain their constitutional rights on the school campus. As with all rights, however, rights of students and teachers are not absolute and at times must give way to greater interests of the rest of society. The case of Matthew N. Fraser, a student at Bethel High School, Pierce County, Washington, illustrates one of those instances where a Court majority decided that a student could be punished for freely expressing views that school officials thought objectionable.

Fraser gave a speech before approximately six hundred students, nominating another student for a school office. His speech, in full, was as follows:

> I know a man who is firm — he is firm in his pants, he's firm in his shirt, his character is firm — but most . . . of all, his belief in you, the students of Bethel, is firm.
> Jeff Kuhlman is a man who takes his point and pounds it in. If necessary, he'll take an issue and nail it to the wall. He doesn't attack things in spurts — he drives hard, pushing and pushing until finally — he succeeds.
> Jeff is a man who will go to the very end — even the climax, for each and every one of you.
> So vote for Jeff for A.S.B. vice-president — he'll never come between you and the best our high school can be.[72]

The next day, Fraser was notified that his speech violated a school rule that prohibited the use of "obscene, profane language or gestures" and that he would be suspended for three days and not allowed to speak at commencement. After seeking review of his suspension within the school's grievance procedures, he commenced an action in the federal district court requesting an order reinstating him and allowing him to speak at graduation, and monetary damages. Judge Jack E. Tanner held that "the school's sanctions violated [Fraser's] right to freedom of speech under the First Amendment." He awarded $278 in damages and $12,750 in litigation costs. He also ordered the school to allow Fraser to speak at graduation.

The court of appeals sustained Judge Tanner, but the Supreme Court reversed. Chief Justice Burger, who delivered the opinion of the Court, found a "marked distinction between the political 'message' of the armbands in *Tinker* and the sexual content of [Fraser's] speech in this case. . . ." He discussed the school's responsibilities in the educational process.

The process of educating our youth for citizenship in public schools is not confined to books, the curriculum, and the civics class; schools must teach by example the shared values of a civilized social order. Consciously or otherwise, teachers—and indeed the older students—demonstrate the appropriate form of civil discourse and political expression by their conduct and deportment in and out of class. Inescapably, like parents, they are role models. The schools, as instruments of the state, may determine that the essential lessons of civil, mature conduct cannot be conveyed in a school that tolerates lewd, indecent, or offensive speech and conduct such as that indulged in by this confused boy.

Justice Stevens started his dissenting opinion with Clark Gable's famous "Frankly, my dear, I don't give a damn" spoken in the movie *Gone with the Wind*. Justice Stevens continued that when he "was a high school student, the use of those words in a public forum shocked a Nation." Although agreeing that times have changed, he also agreed "that high school administrators may prohibit the use of [Gable's four-letter expletive] in classroom discussion and even in extracurricular activities that are sponsored by the school and held on school premises." His disagreement with the majority, therefore, was not that Fraser could be punished for his speech but that the procedure used by the school officials to discipline him did not meet procedural due process standards as required by the Fourteenth Amendment.

The justices, many years ago, held that teachers "have the right under our law to assemble, speak, think and believe as they will."[73] That freedom protects a teacher, even when he writes a lengthy letter to a local newspaper very critical of the local school board's tax and spending policies.

Marvin L. Pickering wrote such a letter and was subsequently dismissed as a teacher at Township High School District 205, Will County, Illinois. Pickering's claim that his dismissal violated his First Amendment rights was rejected by the Illinois Supreme Court, Justice Walter V. Schaefer dissenting. Concerning Pickering's letter, Justice Schaefer said: "To be entitled to the protection of the first amendment it is not necessary that [Pickering's] letter be a model of literary style, good taste and sound judgment. In my view it is not, but my view is irrelevant. The letter is substantially accurate, and more important it has not been shown to be knowingly false."[74]

A unanimous Supreme Court agreed with Justice Schaefer and reversed, holding that because the letter was protected by the First Amendment, the dismissal was in error.

To the extent that the Illinois Supreme Court's opinion may be read to suggest that teachers may constitutionally be compelled to relinquish the First Amendment rights they would otherwise enjoy as citizens to comment on matters of public interest in connection with the operation of the public schools in which they work, it proceeds on a premise that has been unequivocally rejected in numerous prior decisions of this Court.[75]

The right of public-school teachers to express their views without fear of retribution is subject to "a balance between the interests of the teacher, as a citizen, in commenting upon matters of public concern, and the interest of the State as an employer, in promoting the efficiency of the public services it performs through the employees."

Freedom of Speech in the Armed Forces

"This is the first case that presents to us a question of what protection, if any, the First Amendment gives people in the Armed Services."*

In 1890 Justice David Josiah Brewer described the changes that occur in a man's life when he becomes a soldier.

By enlistment the citizen becomes a soldier. His relations to the State and the public are changed. He acquires a new status, with correlative rights and duties; and although he may violate his contract obligations, his status as a soldier is unchanged. He cannot of his own volition throw off the garments he has once put on, nor can he, the State not objecting, renounce his relations and destroy his status on the plea that, if he had disclosed truthfully the facts, the other party, the State, would not have entered into the new relations with him, or permitted him to change his status.[76]

That description of what it means to be a member of the armed forces permeates court decisions relating to the constitutional rights of service personnel. The view "that the military is, by necessity, a specialized society separate from civilian society" was made clear to Captain Howard Levy. Captain Levy, a doctor, was stationed at the U.S. Army Hospital, Fort Jackson, South Carolina, when he found himself in difficulty with his superiors on two fronts.

As a dermatologist, he was supposed to conduct a clinic for Special Forces aides, and it appears that he was not doing that very well. Also,

---

*Justice Douglas, dissenting in *Parker v. Levy*, 417 U.S. 733, 768 (1974).

Captain Levy was very much opposed to the war in Vietnam and did not hesitate to express his views. Among the statements he is reported to have made is the following:

> The United States is wrong in being involved in the Viet Nam War. I would refuse to go to Viet Nam if ordered to do so. I don't see why any colored soldier would go to Viet Nam: they should refuse to go to Viet Nam and if sent should refuse to fight because they are discriminated against and denied their freedom in the United States, and they are sacrificed and discriminated against in Viet Nam by being given all the hazardous duty and they are suffering the majority of casualties. If I were a colored soldier and were sent I would refuse to fight. Special Forces personnel are liars and thieves and killers of peasants and murderers of women and children.[77]

Captain Levy was brought to court-martial and charged with (1) having "willfully disobeyed a lawful command of his superior commissioned officer"; (2) engaging in "conduct unbecoming an officer and a gentleman"; and (3) engaging in "disorders and neglects to the prejudice of good order and discipline in the armed forces." With regard to the accusation that he had engaged in "conduct unbecoming an officer and a gentleman," it was alleged that Levy "while in the performance of his duties at the United States Army Hospital . . . wrongfully and dishonorably [made] statements variously described as intemperate, defamatory, provoking, disloyal, contemptuous, and disrespectful to Special Forces personnel and to enlisted personnel who were patients or under his supervision."

The court-martial convicted Levy, and when he had exhausted all avenues of appeal within the military, he sought help from the federal district court. Judge Michael H. Sheridan denied relief. Levy appealed to the court of appeals, which reversed, principally because it "found little difficulty in concluding that 'as measured by contemporary standards of vagueness applicable to statutes and ordinances governing civilians,' the general articles [of the Military Code under which Levy was charged] 'do not pass constitutional muster.'" Laws that are so vague that a reasonable person cannot determine what is prohibited violate due process because such laws do not give adequate warning of the conduct that is punishable.

A majority of the Supreme Court concluded that Judge Sheridan was right in letting the court-martial conviction stand and that the court of appeals was wrong, and they therefore reversed.

The starting point for the majority was that "while the members of the military are not excluded from the protection granted by the First Amendment, the different character of the military community and of the military mission requires a different application of those protections. The fundamental necessity for obedience, and the consequent necessity for imposition of discipline, may render permissible within the military that which would be constitutionally impermissible outside it." As for Levy, "his conduct, that of a commissioned officer publicly urging enlisted personnel to refuse to obey orders which might send them into combat, was unprotected under the most expansive notions of the First Amendment."

Permitting the Army to discipline Levy for his speech gave Justice Douglas concern over the potential reach of this decision:

> The power to draft an army includes, of course, the power to curtail considerably the "liberty" of the people who make it up. But Congress in these articles [the ones under which Levy was convicted] has not undertaken to cross the forbidden First Amendment line. Making a speech or comment on one of the most important and controversial public issues of the past two decades cannot by any stretch of dictionary meaning be included in "disorders and neglects to the prejudice of good order and discipline in the armed forces." Nor can what Captain Levy said possibly be "conduct of a nature to bring discredit upon the armed forces."

The desire of Captain Albert Edward Glines, USAF Reserves, to shave his head brought him into conflict with an air force regulation prohibiting the "solicitation or collection of signatures on a petition by any person within an Air Force facility or by a member when in uniform . . . unless first authorized by the commander."[78] Captain Glines, while on active duty, objected to the air force's strict grooming code. He therefore drafted a petition to members of Congress and the secretary of defense requesting a change in policy. In support of the request, the petition stated: "We feel that the present regulations on grooming have caused more racial tension, decrease in morale and retention, and loss of respect for authorities than any other official Air Force policy."

Glines was aware of the rule prohibiting solicitation without approval of the commander, so at first he solicited off the base. Later, however, he gave the petition to a friend while on a training flight, who in turn obtained eight signatures. At that point, the military authorities stopped distribution of the petition and assigned Glines to standby duty.

Thinking that he was being unjustly punished for the exercise of his free speech rights, Glines brought an action against the secretary of defense seeking return to active duty and back pay. Federal Judge William H. Orrick agreed and declared the air force rule against solicitation a violation of the right to petition. Judge Orrick was sustained by the court of appeals but reversed by the Supreme Court.

In addressing the question of whether the air force regulation violated the First Amendment, the majority reiterated the previously established rule to the effect that "the rights of military men must yield somewhat 'to meet certain overriding demands of discipline and duty....'" And further, "speech likely to interfere with these vital prerequisites for military effectiveness therefore can be excluded from a military base."

Believing that it was necessary for the commander to know what materials were being distributed on the base, the Court also found:

> Since a commander is charged with maintaining morale, discipline, and readiness, he must have authority over distribution of materials that could affect adversely these essential attributes of an effective military force.

The decision did not meet with the approval of all of the justices. Justice Brennan was particularly disturbed, noting that "the maintenance of military discipline, morale, and efficiency are undeniably important, but they are not always, and in every situation, to be regarded as more compelling than a host of other governmental interests which we have found insufficient to warrant censorship."

Freedom to Speak Inside the Prison Gate

*"Prison walls do not form a barrier separating prison inmates from the protections of the Constitution."**

Robert Martinez and Wayne Earley, prison inmates, started an action in a federal district court challenging certain rules of the California Department of Correction relating to prisoners' mail. Prison policy permitted sending and receiving mail, subject to a prohibition that excluded "any writings ... expressing inflammatory political, racial, religious, or other views or beliefs ... which if circulated among other

*Turner v. Safley, 482 U.S. 78, 84 (1987).

inmates, would . . . tend to subvert prison order or discipline." Further, inmates "may not send or receive letters that pertain to criminal activity; are lewd, obscene, or defamatory; contain foreign matter, or are otherwise inappropriate."[79]

The district court struck down the rules as too broad, thus impeding prisoners' First Amendment rights.

> If censorship of out going personal mail is to continue, the regulations must be more narrowly and specifically drawn to prohibit only such communications as are obscene, . . . or as constitute a clear and present danger to the institution or its rehabilitation programs.

The Supreme Court affirmed in an opinion that gave greater weight to those corresponding with the prisoners than to the prisoners themselves. The justices did agree, however, that "when a prison regulation or practice offends a fundamental constitutional guarantee, federal courts will discharge their duty to protect constitutional rights."[80] But it is the interests of the outsider that must receive constitutional protection in mail censorship cases. "Whatever the status of a prisoner's claim to uncensored correspondence with an outsider, it is plain that the latter's interest is grounded in the First Amendment's guarantee of freedom of speech."

The majority used as an example the effect upon the wife of an inmate:

> The wife of a prison inmate who is not permitted to read all that her husband wanted to say to her has suffered an abridgement of her interest in communicating with him as plain as that which results from censorship of her letter to him.

Turning then for guidance to cases not dealing with prisoner's rights, the majority set forth several guidelines for prison authorities to follow in dealing with prison mail censorship. "First, the regulation . . . must further an important or substantial governmental interest unrelated to the suppression of expression." "Second, the limitation on First Amendment freedoms must be no greater than is necessary or essential to the protection of the particular governmental interest involved." Applying these criteria to the regulations at issue led the majority to conclude that "the regulations authorized censorship of prisoner mail far broader than any legitimate interest of penal administration demands and were properly found invalid by the District Court."

The justices specifically held that the power to censor with a standard as broad as "'inflammatory political, racial, religious, or other views,' and matter deemed 'defamatory' or 'otherwise inappropriate'" gave prison authorities the power "to apply their own personal prejudices and opinions as standards for prisoner mail censorship."

The justices who concurred would have gone further in defining rights of the prisoners. Justice Marshall wrote for himself and Justice Brennan that "prison authorities do not have a general right to open and read all incoming and outgoing prisoner mail." "A prisoner does not shed such basic First Amendment rights at the prison gate."

A somewhat different kind of freedom of speech issue was considered by the Court in a case that had "its humble origins in a complaint drafted by a lay prisoner serving time at San Quentin."[81] Booker T. Hillery, Jr., John Larry Spain, Bobby Bly, and Michael Shane Guile, all California prison inmates, sued Raymond K. Procunier, director of corrections. They were joined in the action by Eve Pell, Betty Segal, and Paul Jacobs, professional journalists. Their complaint concerned the constitutionality of Section 415.071 of the California Department of Corrections Manual:

> Press and other media interviews with specific individual inmates will not be permitted.

Pell, Segal, and Jacobs had requested permission to interview Spain, Bly, and Guile, and editors of another publication desired to talk to Hillery about publishing some of his writings. Relying on the above section, prison officials denied all requests. The inmates and journalists sought a declaration of their rights under the First Amendment and an order prohibiting enforcement of the regulation.

For many years, the Department of Corrections operated without a fixed policy regarding prisoner interviews. However, as prisoners began to voice complaints concerning prison conditions and the public became aware of such complaints, the media began to request more interviews. This created in the minds of prison authorities "the phenomenon of the 'prison celebrity' or 'big wheel' — the prisoner who, through his writings and media coverage, gained a certain notoriety both outside and inside the institution."

Judge Spencer Williams describes the department's response to what was taking place:

> It was against this background that the tragic events of August 21, 1971 took place. During an escape attempt at San Quentin three staff

members and two inmates were killed. This was viewed by the officials as the climax of mounting disciplinary problems caused, in part, by its liberal posture with regard to press interviews, and on August 23 Section 415.071 was adopted to mitigate the problem.

Judge Williams held that although the regulation did not infringe any constitutional right of the journalists, the section did unconstitutionally burden freedom of speech of the inmates. A majority of the Supreme Court agreed that no rights of the media were burdened but reversed regarding the rights of the inmates.

The majority opinion was delivered by Justice Stewart. He accepted "the hypothesis that under some circumstances the right of free speech includes a right to communicate a person's views to any willing listener, including a willing representative of the press for the purpose of publication by a willing publisher."[82] But he also pointed out that "a prison inmate retains [only] those First Amendment rights that are not inconsistent with his status as a prisoner or with the legitimate penological objectives of the corrections system."

Recognizing that "since most offenders will eventually return to society [and that therefore] . . . [a] paramount objective of the corrections system is the rehabilitation of those committed to its custody," some reasonable alternatives for communication are necessary. Here, the Court found, such alternatives were available by the ability of inmates to communicate with many other persons. "In this case the restriction takes the form of limiting visitations to individuals who have either a personal or professional relationship to the inmate—family, friends of prior acquaintance, legal counsel, and clergy." On that basis, the majority found that the restriction on communicating with media representatives was not unconstitutional.

Section 415.071 was far too broad and therefore unconstitutional, according to justices Douglas, Brennan, and Marshall. They agreed "with the court below that the State's interest in order and prison discipline cannot justify its total ban on all media interviews with any individual designated on any matter whatsoever. Such coarse attempt at regulation is patently unconstitutional in an area where 'precision of regulation must be the touchstone.'"

Prisoners' cases have presented the Court with the dilemma of trying to formulate a method of testing penal regulations that burden constitutional rights. In judging governmental burdens on fundamental rights of noninmates, the justices have required the government to prove that its regulation furthers "an important or substantial governmental interest" and "be no greater than is necessary or essential to the protection" of that interest.

The justices found themselves involved in that dilemma in the recent case of *Turner v. Safley*.[83] At issue was a ban on correspondence between nonfamily inmates at other correctional institutions unless "the classification/treatment team of each inmate deems it's in the best interest of the parties involved." A majority agreed upon a test that focuses on "whether a prison regulation that burdens fundamental rights is 'reasonably related' to legitimate penological objectives, or whether it represents an 'exaggerated response' to those concerns." This standard caused Justice Stevens to declare in dissent, "Application of the standard would seem to permit disregard for inmates' constitutional rights whenever the imagination of the warden produces a plausible security concern and a deferential trial court is able to discern a logical connection between the concern and the challenged regulation."

Corporations Have the Right to Speak

*"It is clear that . . . corporations possess certain rights of speech and expression under the First Amendment."**

Many years ago, the Court held that corporations were "persons" within the meaning of the Fourteenth Amendment, thereby assuring them of protection under the Due Process and Equal Protection clauses. Further, in considering cases involving First Amendment rights, the justices, heretofore, were not called upon to make a distinction between corporations and individuals in the exercise of such rights.

In 1978, however, that question was presented in a case involving the right of corporations in Massachusetts to participate in the political process. When a proposed constitutional amendment to permit the legislature to enact a graduated income tax was before the voters, Massachusetts had a law prohibiting corporations from spending money to influence the vote on such proposals. Several corporations, desiring to express their opposition to the proposed law, sued to have the law declared unconstitutional as an infringement upon their First Amendment right of freedom of expression.

The Massachusetts Supreme Judicial Court held that "the First Amendment rights of a corporation are limited to issues that materially

*First Nat. Bank of Boston v. Atty. General, 359 N.E.2d 1262, 1270 (1977).

affect its business, property, or assets. . . ."[84] Therefore, they could not publicize their views on the tax proposal, there being no evidence to show that if enacted, the tax would affect their businesses.

The U.S. Supreme Court, finding that the Massachusetts court had erroneously framed the question, concluded that it had therefore reached the wrong conclusion, and it reversed: "The court below framed the principal question in this case as whether and to what extent corporations have First Amendment rights." But that is not the issue, the Court said: "The question in this case, simply put, is whether the corporate identity of the speaker deprives this proposed speech of what otherwise would be its clear entitlement to protection."

After reviewing a number of its previous cases dealing with the First Amendment, a majority answered the question by declaring that "we find no support in the First or Fourteenth Amendment, or in the decisions of this Court, for the proposition that speech that otherwise would be within the protection of the First Amendment loses that protection simply because its source is a corporation that cannot prove, to the satisfaction of a court, a material effect on its business or property."

Because none of the First Amendment rights are absolute, the justices turned to an examination of the question of "whether [the law] can survive the exacting scrutiny necessitated by a state-imposed restriction on freedom of speech." In other words, were the interests asserted by the state compelling enough to outweigh the speech rights of corporations?

Noting that the state advanced two goals that the law was supposed to accomplish, the majority found both insufficient. Massachusetts interests were (1) to sustain "the active role of the individual citizen in the electoral process and thereby [prevent] diminution of the citizen's confidence in government" and (2) to give protection to "the rights of shareholders whose views differ from those expressed by management on behalf of the corporation."

> However weighty these interests may be in the context of partisan candidate elections, they either are not implicated in this case or are not served at all, or in any other than a random manner, by the prohibition in the law.

The majority pointed out in a footnote that although the law also prohibited corporate contributions and expenditures for promoting candidates, that was not at issue here.

The majority's analysis did not escape condemnation. In dissent, justices White, Brennan, and Marshall agreed with the majority that "there is now little doubt that corporate communications come within the scope of the First Amendment." Their difference with the majority was the fact that they had substituted their "judgment as to the proper balance for that of Massachusetts where the State has passed legislation reasonably designed to further First Amendment interests in the context of the political arena where the expertise of legislators is at its peak and that of judges is at its very lowest." The minority believed the corporate money in this factual situation posed a threat to the political process and further that the Massachusetts laws protected shareholders from supporting issues with which they did not agree.

Although this case deals with free speech rights of corporations concerning matters in the political arena (see discussion of political speech above), it is the landmark case upholding corporate speech generally. It was the precedent relied upon in *Consolidated Edison Co. v. Public Service Commission*.[85] During the Arab oil embargo in 1973, the New York Public Service Commission issued an order that prohibited electric corporations "from promoting the use of electricity through the use of advertising, subsidy payments . . . or employee incentives."[86] This order remained in effect after the embargo was lifted.

In 1976 Consolidated Edison sent written material with its electric bills, promoting nuclear power. Opponents of nuclear power immediately requested Con. Edison to enclose their contrary views in its next billing. The request was refused. The opponents then requested the PSC to order Edison to accept contrary "views on controversial issues of public importance." Rather than adopt that procedure, the commisison issued a ruling that "barred utility companies from including bill inserts that express 'their opinions or viewpoints on controversial issues of public policy.'"[87]

Con. Edison requested review of the commission's ruling in the New York courts. It won in the lower court, which held the order to be unconstitutional. However, it lost in both the state supreme court, appellate division, and in the New York Court of Appeals. It was again successful, however, in the Supreme Court, where a majority found that the lower New York court was right.

The justices characterized the PSC order prohibiting "discusion of controversial issues [as striking] at the heart of the freedom to speak." The questions to be answered, therefore, were "whether the prohibition is (i) a reasonable time, place, or manner restriction, (ii) a permissible subject-matter regulation, or (iii) a narrowly tailored means of serving a compelling state interest."

A "time, place, or manner [regulation] of speech," the majority stated, "may be imposed as long as it is reasonable." "But when regulation is based on the content of speech, governmental action must be scrutinized more carefully to insure that communication has not been prohibited 'merely because public officials disapprove the speaker's views.'" This is not a time, place, or manner restriction, however, because it is not content-neutral. Information may be sent to consumers "on certain subjects, such as energy conservation measures, but [the order] forbids the use of inserts that discuss public controversies."

The PSC next argued that its rule was permissible because it applied to "all discussion of nuclear power, whether pro or con, in bill inserts." The majority responded that "to allow a government the choice of permissible subjects for public debate would be to allow that government control over search for political truth."

Finally the state asserted that the rule was necessary "to avoid forcing Consolidated Edison's views on a captive audience," its customers. The Court answered by noting that its prior cases held that the First Amendment does not permit the government to prohibit speech as intrusive unless the "'captive audience' cannot avoid [the] objectionable speech." In this case, the "captive audience" can avoid the message "by simply transferring the bill insert from envelope to wastebasket."

"My dissent in this case," Justice Blackmun explained, "in no way indicates any disapprobation on my part of the precious rights of free speech (so carefully cataloged by the Court in its opinion) that are protected by the First and Fourteenth Amendments against repression by the States." He pointed out, however, that he could not agree that the ban on the inserts violated the First Amendment — "because of Consolidated Edison's monopoly status and its rate structure, the use of the insert amounts to an exaction from the utility's customers by way of forced aid for the utility's speech."

Both of the above cases relate to laws that prohibit certain kinds of corporate speech. Do the same rules apply when the government attempts to force a corporation to disseminate views contrary to its own? That was the question facing the courts when the California Public Utilities Commission ordered Pacific Gas and Electric Co. (PG&E) to give space in its customer newsletter to one of its critics. The critic was an organization named Toward Utility Rate Normalization (TURN). TURN was allowed to use space in the newsletter four times a year. The PUC was of the opinion that customers would benefit by being exposed to views other than those of PG&E.

When the California Supreme Court refused to hear PG&E's appeal from the commission's order, it turned to the U.S. Supreme Court for help. In a decision in which five justices concurred in the result but could not agree on the reasons therefor, the Court overturned the PUC's order.[88] The plurality, Chief Justice Burger and justices Brennan, O'Connor, and Powell, discussed some of the general principles that apply in cases like this one.

> The identity of the speaker is not decisive in determining whether speech is protected. Corporations and other associations, like individuals, contribute to the 'discussion, debate, and the dissemination of information and ideas' that the First Amendment seeks to foster.

Finding that PG&E's newsletter was therefore entitled to First Amendment protection, the plurality examined the commission's reasons for requiring it to give space to TURN. "The Commission's conclusion necessarily rests on one of two premises: (i) compelling [PG&E] to grant TURN access to a hitherto private forum does not infringe [PG&E's] right to speak; or (ii) [PG&E] has no property interest in the relevant forum, therefore has no constitutionally protected right in restricting access to it."

On the question of forcing PG&E to allow TURN to use its private forum, the plurality discusses prior cases dealing with laws that require a private property owner to open its property as "a forum for views other than its own. . . ." In most instances, such laws have been struck down.

> Just as the State is not free 'to tell a newspaper in advance what it can print and what it cannot,' . . . the State is not free either to restrict [PG&E's] speech to certain topics or views or to force [it] to respond to views that others may hold.

The justices also invoked the principle that the right of free expression includes "the right to refrain from speaking at all" (discussed in Chapter V). PG&E may be forced to respond to TURN's messages, and "that kind of forced response is antithetical to the free discussion that the First Amendment seeks to foster." The PUC's requirement, notes the plurality, presents PG&E with a dilemma. If it speaks out on a controversial issue, it is required to allow TURN to do the same in its newsletter. That may well influence PG&E to follow a "safe course" and "'avoid controversy', thereby reducing the free flow of information and ideas that the First Amendment seeks to promote."

We conclude that the Commission's order impermissibly burdens [PG&E's] First Amendment rights because it forces [it] to associate with the views of other speakers, and because it selects the other speakers on the basis of their viewpoints.

A minority of the justices did not believe that the order would in any way influence PG&E to reply, nor were they able to accept the premise that corporations should be given the same consideration as individuals in the application of First Amendment principles. Justice Rehnquist set forth their views: "I do not believe that the right of access here will have any noticeable deterrent effect. Nor do I believe that negative free speech rights [i.e., forced speech] applicable to individuals and perhaps to print media, should be extended to corporations."

Commercial Speech Is Less Valuable

*"Our decisions have recognized the 'commonsense' distinction between speech proposing a commercial transaction . . . and other varieties of speech."**

When first faced with the question whether a commercial advertisement was entitled to the protection of the First Amendment, the justices responded with a firm no. The case involved the circulation of a handbill advertising the opportunity to visit a former U.S. Navy submarine. Lewis J. Valentine owned the submarine and had attempted to have it docked at one of New York City's docks. When his request was denied, he obtained dockage at a state-owned pier in the East River. Valentine printed a handbill describing the sub as a "$2,000,000 fighting monster." The handbill also "contained a cut of the submarine, a statement that competent guides would take a person from one end of it to another, [and] insistent directions to see several featured points—the torpedo compartment, the sleeping quarters, [and] the kitchen."[89]

Officials of the city informed Valentine that distribution of the handbill would be unlawful because it contained "commercial and business advertising matter." He was also told "that bills containing only information or a public protest could be distributed." The submarine owner then reprinted the bill and included therein "a spirited

*Cen. Hudson G. & E. Corp. v. Pub. Ser. Comm'n., 447 U.S. 557, 562 (1980).

protest against the 'almost unbelievable' action of the 'dictatorial' subor-
dinates of 'a mayor who is one of the outstanding liberals of the United
States' in refusing ... permission to tie up to city-owned piers...."

Because this did not satisfy the city's agents, Valentine sought
relief from the federal district court. District Judge George M. Hulbert
granted an injunction against enforcement of the regulation. The court
of appeals, with one judge dissenting, sustained Judge Hulbert, but a
unanimous Supreme Court took a different view, and in a short four-
page opinion declared that "the Constitution imposes no ... restraint
on government as respects purely commercial advertising."[90] Nor did
the justices give much weight to Valentine's argument that "he was
engaged in the dissemination of matter proper for public information...." The justices said that "affixing of the protest against official
conduct to the advertising circular was with the intent, and for the purpose, of evading the prohibition of the ordinance."

For more than thirty years, because of the *Valentine* decision,
commercial messages enjoyed no First Amendment protection, even
though Justice Douglas, who participated in that case, would later say
that "the ruling was casual, almost offhand. And it has not survived
reflection."[91]

The Court directly faced the issue again when a newspaper editor
in Virginia, Jeffrey C. Bigelow, ran an ad offering assistance for abortions in New York. At that time, under Virginia law, it was a crime for
"any person, by ... advertisement, ... [to] encourage or prompt the
procuring of abortion or miscarriage...."[92] Bigelow was convicted of
violating the law, even though he claimed that it was unconstitutional
as an infringement upon his First Amendment rights. The Virginia
Supreme Court rejected Bigelow's constitutional argument and upheld
the conviction.

Justice Blackmun, for himself and six other justices, reversed, concluding that Bigelow's advertisement was protected speech. He referred
to the *Valentine* decison but said it applied only to "the manner in
which commercial advertising could be distributed" and was not relevant in this case.

Although the majority squarely held that hereafter commercial
speech was protected speech, it did not come to grips with the extent
of that protection.

> We need not decide in this case the precise extent to which the
> First Amendment permits regulation of advertising that is related to
> activities the State may legitimately regulate or even prohibit.

No matter what power a state may have to regulate advertisements, this regulation is unconstitutional because "Virginia is really asserting an interest in regulating what Virginians may *hear* or *read* about the New York services. It is, in effect, advancing an interest of shielding its citizens from information about activities outside Virginia's borders, activities that Virginia's police powers do not reach."

Justice Rehnquist took the majority to task for not giving greater weight to Virginia's interests in this matter. "Virginia's interest in this statute," he pointed out, "lies in preventing commercial exploitation of the health needs of its citizens."

The Court struck down laws regulating commercial speech in several cases following *Bigelow.* It found unconstitutional another Virginia law that provided that a pharmacist would be "guilty of unprofessional conduct if he '(3) publishes, advertises or promotes, directly or indirectly . . . any amount, price, fee, premium, discount, rebate or credit terms . . . for any drugs which may be dispensed only by prescription.'"[93] In this case the justices asked and answered their own question about commercial speech.

> Our question is whether speech which does "no more than propose a commercial transaction," . . . lacks all protection. Our answer is that it is not.

A year later, an ordinance of Willingboro, New Jersey, that banned *For Sale* and *Sold* signs on residential properties came to the Court. This law was passed in an attempt to prevent "panic selling" and "the flight of whites from the town." In finding the law a violation of the First Amendment, the majority did no more than determine that the town had "failed to establish that this ordinance is needed to assure that Willingboro remains an integrated community."[94]

In neither the *Virginia Pharmacy* case nor the *Willingboro* case do the justices give much guidance to lawyers and judges regarding when commercial speech may be burdened and when it may not. It is interesting to note, however, that by this point in the evolution of protection for commercial speech, all justices except Justice Rehnquist were agreeing that commercial speech was protected under the First Amendment.

The issue of how much freedom advertisers are entitled to was finally settled in *Central Hudson Gas & Elec. v. Public Service Commission.*[95] This case grew out of the same set of facts set forth in *Consolidated Edison,* discussed above. Here, Central Hudson attacked a

PSC ban on promotional advertising, claiming that it was a violation of its right of freedom of expression. The PSC policy "divided advertising expenses 'into two broad categories: promotional — advertising intended to stimulate the purchase of utility services — and institutional and informational, a broad category inclusive of all advertising not clearly intended to promote sales.'" The former was prohibited, the latter not.

Central Hudson challenged the above policy in the New York Supreme Court (a trial court) wherein Judge Roger J. Miner upheld the PSC Judge Miner's decision was affirmed by appellate courts, including New York's highest court, the court of appeals. A majority of the Supreme Court reversed in an opinion from which only Justice Rehnquist dissented.

The majority first acknowledged that the "Commission's order restricts only commercial speech, that is, expression related solely to the economic interests of the speaker and its audience." But the justices noted that "commercial expression not only serves the economic interest of the speaker, but also assists consumers and furthers the societal interest in the fullest possible dissemination of information." Even so, "the Constitution . . . accords a lesser protection to commercial speech than to other constitutionally guaranteed expression." The majority proceeded to outline a "four-part analysis" to be used hereafter by courts in commercial speech cases.

> At the outset, we must determine whether the expression is protected by the First Amendment. For commercial speech to come within that provision, it at least must concern lawful activity and not be misleading. Next, we ask whether the asserted governmental interest is substantial. If both inquiries yield positive answers, we must determine whether the regulation directly advances the governmental interst asserted, and whether it is not more extensive than is necessary to serve that interst.

In examining the PSC's policy and Central Hudson's advertising under this four-part test, the majority determined that (1) the advertising was neither inaccurate nor related to unlawful activity, (2) the state's interest in energy conservation was "substantial," (3) there was a "direct link between the state interest in conservation and the Commission's order," but (4) "the total ban on promotional advertising" was more restrictive than necessary to accomplish the state's goals.

> The Commission's order prevents [Central Hudson] from promoting electric services that would reduce energy use by diverting

demand from less efficient sources, or that would consume roughly the same amount of energy as do alternative sources. In neither situation would the utility's advertising endanger conservation or mislead the public. To the extent that the Commission's order suppresses speech that in no way impairs the State's interest in energy conservation, the Commission's order violates the First and Fourteenth Amendments and must be invalidated.

Justice Rehnquist continues to adhere to the position that commercial speech is not entitled to First Amendment protection but acknowledges that that issue has been foreclosed by prior decisions. However, even assuming commercial speech enjoys constitutional protection, he thinks "the Court nonetheless [is] incorrect in invalidating the carefully considered ban on promotional advertising in the light of pressing national and state energy needs." And he continues to find "that the Court unlocked a Pandora's Box when it 'elevated' commercial speech to the level of traditional political speech by according it First Amendment protection...."

One of the problems created by the decision not to give commercial speech the same protection as political speech is the determination of which speech is commercial and which is not. Justic Brennan illustrates the problem by giving the following examples of speech for which the answer to the question is not all that clear.

> "Because Joe thinks dairy products are good for you, please shop at Joe's Shoppe."
> "Be a patriot—do not buy Japanese-manufactured cars."
> "Support the San Diego Padres, a great baseball team."[96]

The justices have not been faced with the question whether any, all, or none of the above would be classified as commercial speech. But they were confronted with the question in a case involving material promoting the sale of prophylactics. Youngs Drug Products Corp., in an effort to increase sales of its prophylactic products, decided to engage in a direct-mail solicitation program. It prepared and intended to send out three types of materials:

> —multi-page, multi-item flyers promoting a large variety of products available at a drugstore, including prophylactics;
> —flyers exclusively or substantially devoted to promoting prophylactics;
> —informational pamphlets discussing the desirability and availability of prophylactics in general or Youngs' products in particular.[97]

When the Postal Service learned of these mailings, it warned Youngs that further mailings would be in violation of a federal law (39 U.S. Code, Section 3001(e)(2), which prohibits the mailing of "unsolicited advertisement . . . matter which is designed, adopted or intended to prevent conception"). Youngs furnished the Postal Service with copies of its materials and stated that they were constitutionally protected, an argument the service did not accept. Youngs therefore brought an action in federal district court for a declaration of its rights and an order preventing the service from enforcing the law against it. Judge John Garrett Penn found that all three of the mailers were commercial solicitations but nevertheless concluded that the law was "more extensive than necessary to the interests asserted by the Government, and . . . therefore . . . the statute's absolute ban on the three types of mailings violated the First Amendment."

The justices unanimously affirmed Judge Penn's decision. In an opinion written by Justice Marshall, the starting point of the analysis was a reiteration of the previously adopted rule "that the Constitution accords less protection to commercial speech than to other constitutionally safeguarded forms of expression." Among the arguments put forward by Youngs was that its "proposed mailings constitute 'fully protected speech,' so that [the law] amounts to an impermissible content-based restriction on such expression." Justice Marshall, however, held that with the exception of the "informational pamphlets," the mailings were no more than commercial advertisements. The "informational pamphlets, however, cannot be characterized merely as proposals to engage in commercial transactions. Their proper classification as commercial or noncommercial speech thus presents a closer question. The mere fact that these pamphlets are conceded to be advertisements clearly does not compel the conclusion that they are commercial speech." Furthermore, neither "the reference to a specific product" nor "that Youngs has an economic motivation" is sufficient to require the material to be labeled commercial. However, when all of these factors are considered together, they support Judge Penn's "conclusion that the informational pamphlets are properly characterized as commercial speech."

Determining that the mailings were all commercial speech did not end the inquiry. The question remained whether the government's interest in preventing the mailings was sufficient to justify the ban. The interests claimed to be served by the law according to the government were two:

The statute (1) shields recipients of mail from materials that they are likely to find offensive and (2) aids parents' efforts to control the manner in which their children become informed about sensitive and important subjects such as birth control.

The justices' response to the first contention was that "we have never held that the Government itself can shut off the flow of mailings to protect recipients who might potentially be offended." As to the second interest, the Court said there were two objections. First, under another federal law, parents can control the material that is sent to them, and further, the law in question here would "reduce the adult population . . . to reading only what is fit for children." "The level of discourse reaching the mailbox," Justice Marshall declared, "simply cannot be limited to that which would be suitable for a sandbox." This discussion therefore leads to only one conclusion — that the law cannot constitutionally be applied to Youngs' mailings.

Lawyers May Advertise

*"The heart of the dispute . . . today is whether lawyers . . . may constitutionally advertise the prices at which certain routine services will be performed."**

John R. Bates and Van O'Steen were attorneys licensed to practice law in Arizona. In March 1974 they opened a "legal clinic" in Phoenix. They hoped to be able to provide legal services at low cost and thereby attract clients from middle- and lower-income levels. In order to accomplish this, they concentrated their practice on uncontested divorces, adoptions, small bankruptcies, etc.

After a couple of years, they came to the conclusion they needed to attract more business or the "legal clinic" would not survive. In order to generate more business, they placed an ad in the *Arizona Republican,* a Phoenix newspaper. "The advertisement stated that [they] were offering 'legal services at very reasonable fees,' and listed their fees for certain services."[98]

Shortly thereafter, the president of the state bar association filed a complaint with the association against Bates and O'Steen, charging them with having violated a bar disciplinary rule:

(B) A lawyer shall not publicize himself, or his partner, or associate, . . . through newspaper or magazine advertisements, radio or tele-

Bates v. State Bar of Arizona, 433 U.S. 350, 367–68 (1977).

vision announcements, display advertisements in the city or telephone directories or other means of commercial publicity. . . .

A bar association committee held a hearing, and having found Bates and O'Steen in violation of the disciplinary rule, recommended that they be suspended from the practice of law for at least six months. The board of governors of the association, after reviewing the matter, reduced the recommended punishment to suspension for one week.

The Arizona Supreme Court rejected the argument that the rule violated the lawyers' First Amendment rights and sustained the bar association. Bates and O'Steen appealed to the U.S. Supreme Court, which held that the rule prohibiting members of the bar from advertising was a violation of the First Amendment.

Justice Blackmun, for the majority, began his analysis of the issue by referring to prior cases in which the Court had extended First Amendment protection to commercial advertising and noted that "the listener's interest is substantial: the consumer's concern for the free flow of commercial speech may often be far keener than his concern for urgent political dialogue." The narrow issue presented here was whether lawyers could "constitutionally advertise the *prices* at which certain routine services will be performed."

The bar association offered six justifications for its ban on advertising by its members.

1. Adverse effect on professionalism.
2. Inherently misleading nature of attorney advertising.
3. The adverse effect on the administration of justice.
4. The undesirable economic effects of advertising.
5. The adverse effect of advertising on the quality of service.
6. The difficulties of enforcement.

The Court found that none of these reasons, nor all of them taken together, were sufficient to uphold the state bar's rules. It found "the postulated connection between advertising and the erosion of true professionalism to be severely strained" and was "not persuaded that restrained professional advertising by lawyers inevitably will be misleading." With respect to the effect on the administration of justice, the majority said, "Although advertising might increase the use of the judicial machinery, we cannot accept the notion that it is always better for a person to suffer a wrong silently than to redress it by legal action."

Two arguments were advanced by the association with regard to the "economic effects of advertising": (1) It will increase the cost of legal services. (2) It will "create a substantial entry barrier, deterring or preventing young attorneys from penetrating the market...." To Justice Blackmun and the majority, "These two arguments seem dubious at best." Nor did they agree that the quality of service would be diminished. "An attorney who is inclined to cut quality will do so regardless of the rule on advertising." Further, "Even if advertising leads to the creation of 'legal clinics' like that of [Bates and O'Steen]— clinics that emphasize standardized procedures for routine problems— it is possible that such clinics will improve service by reducing the likelihood of error." Finally, it is argued that "because the public lacks sophistication in legal matters, it may be particularly susceptible to misleading or deceptive advertising by lawyers," thus creating enforcement problems.

> We suspect that, with advertising, most lawyers will behave as they always have: They will abide by their solemn oaths to uphold the integrity and honor of their profession and of the legal system. For every attorney who overreaches through advertising, there will be thousands of others who will be candid and honest and straightforward.

The decision that the First Amendment protects the right of attorneys to advertise did not come without great misgivings on the part of some justices and resulted in three dissenting opinions. Justice Powell was concerned about the effect advertising would have on the profession: "It is clear that within undefined limits today's decision will effect profound changes in the practice of law, viewed for centuries as a learned profession." Chief Justice Burger agreed and noted that "the exact effect of these changes cannot now be known, ... [and he found] that they will be injurious to those whom the ban on legal advertising was designed to protect—the members of the general public in need of legal services." Once again, Justice Rehnquist expressed his disagreement with the conclusion that commercial speech is protected by the First Amendment: "I continue to believe that the First Amendment speech provision, long regarded by this Court as a sanctuary for expressions of public importance or intellectual interest, is demeaned by invocation to protect advertisements of goods and services."

One of the issues left unanswered by the *Bates* decision was whether the right of attorneys to advertise included the right to make "in-person" solicitation of clients. That question was considered by the justices less than two years after *Bates*.

Albert Ohralik, a member of the Ohio Bar, upon hearing about an auto accident in the vicinity and learning that one of the passengers, Carol McClintock, was in the hospital, placed a call to her parents. He suggested that he visit their daughter, and the parents agreed but suggested that he come by their home first. Ohralik learned from the parents "that their daughter had been driving the family automobile on a local road when she was hit by an uninsured motorist."[99] At the time of the accident, Wanda Lou Holbert was a passenger in the McClintock car. The McClintocks mentioned to Ohralik a fear that Holbert might sue them because she too was hospitalized. Ohralik explained that under Ohio's "guest statute," passengers were prohibited from suing the driver of a car. "When [Ohralik] suggested to the McClintocks that they hire a lawyer, Mrs. McClintock retorted that such a decision would be up to Carol, who was 18 years old and would be the beneficiary of a successful claim."

Ohralik went to the hospital, where he found Carol McClintock in traction. After a short conversation, he suggested that he represent her and offered an agreement for her to sign. She refused to do so at the time, indicating that she wished to visit with her parents first. Ohralik tried to see Wanda Holbert before he left the hospital but was told that she had been discharged.

Ohralik's activities thereafter included visiting the scene of the accident and going to see the McClintocks again. On the way, he "picked up a tape recorder, which he concealed under his raincoat before arriving at the McClintocks' residence.... [Ohralik] discovered that the McClintocks' insurance policy would provide benefits of up to $12,500 each for Carol and Wanda Lou under an uninsured-motorist clause." After discussing the possibility that the passenger might sue them, Mrs. McClintock said that "Wanda swore up and down she would not do it."

Ohralik then went uninvited to see Wanda. He carried with him the concealed tape recorder and told her that McClintocks' insurance might provide compensation to her up to $12,500. He offered to represent her for one-third of any recovery, an offer Wanda accepted but later tried to repudiate. Ohralik insisted, however, that he had a binding agreement and eventually obtained one-third of her settlement by suing her for breach of contract.

Carol McClintock and Wanda Lou Holbert filed complaints against Ohralik with the county bar association, which referred them to the grievance committee of the state bar. That committee charged him with violating two sections of the Ohio Code of Professional Responsibility. Section 2-103(A): "A lawyer shall not recommend

employment, as a private practitioner, of himself, his partner, or associate to a non-lawyer who has not sought his advice regarding employment of a lawyer." Section 2-104(A): "A lawyer who has given unsolicited
advice to a layman that he should obtain counsel or take legal action shall
not accept employment resulting from that advice...."

Ohralik was found guilty of violating the disciplinary rules quoted
above, though he contended that his actions were protected by the First
Amendment. The Ohio Supreme Court affirmed the association's decision, "reiterated that [Ohralik's] conduct was not constitutionally protected, and increased the sanction of a public reprimand recommended
by the Board to indefinite suspension." After considering Ohralik's
contention that his actions were protected, a majority of the U.S.
Supreme Court sustained the Ohio court's decision.

Ohralik contended "that his solicitation of the two young women
as clients is indistinguishable, for purposes of constitutional analysis,
from the advertisement in *Bates*." He argued that his "conduct is
'presumptively an exercise of his free speech rights' which cannot be
curtailed in the absence of proof that it actually caused a specific harm
that the State has a compelling interest in preventing." The majority
refused to accept his arguments. Justice Powell, on behalf of the Court,
found personal solicitation not the same as advertising.

> But in-person solicitation of professional employment by a lawyer
> does not stand on a par with truthful advertising about the availability
> and terms of routine legal services, let alone with forms of speech
> more traditionally within the concern of the First Amendment.

The justices also took notice of the state's interest in regulating
solicitation activities of lawyers. "The state interests implicated in this
case are particularly strong. In addition to its general interest in protecting consumers and regulating commercial transactions, the State bears
a special responsibility for maintaining standards among members of
the licensed professions."

Finally, Justice Powell recited the evils flowing from solicitation by
lawyers.

> The substantive evils of solicitation have been stated over the years
> in sweeping terms: stirring up litigation, assertion of fraudulent
> claims, debasing the legal profession, and potential harm to the
> solicited client in the form of overreaching, overcharging, under-
> representation, and misrepresentation.

Justice Rehnquist agreed with the majority's decision.

Freedom of Speech — 1991 and Beyond

The evolution of the meaning of the Free Speech Clause started with the *Schenck* case, decided in 1919, when Justice Holmes wrote for the Court that words can be punished when they "create a clear and present danger that they will bring about the substantive evils [that the government] has a right to prevent."

Since that time, the justices have used this principle to sustain convictions of Communist leaders in the *Dennis* case, and for inflammatory speech to a hostile audience in *Feiner.* It could have played a part in the black armband case, except that the majority did not find any threat of disorder from the students' expression.

The clear and present danger test has also been used in cases where the justices seek to find a point at which advocacy can be punished, except that the wording of the test used there is somewhat different. Advocacy is protected until the "advocacy is directed to inviting or producing imminent lawless action and is likely to invite or produce such action."

Again using different language, the Court held in *Chaplinsky* that words spoken face-to-face "which by their very utterance inflict injury or tend to incite an immediate breach of the peace," can be punished.

Even in the case of flag desecration, the majority has been concerned that the message from the act not create a danger of a breach of peace.

This all leads to the conclusion that the justices are willing to allow speech to be punished when that speech creates a situation in which disorder is likely to occur. As the majority said in *Dennis,* the government need not "wait until the *putsch* is about to be executed."

With regard to the place where speech may take place, it is clear that one cannot exercise the right to speak at any time or place and that although streets and parks have "historically [been] associated with the free exercise of expressive activities," time, place, and manner regulations are permissible. Such regulations, however, must not give the permit issuer too much discretion so that he, she, or it can act as a censor. Furthermore, the regulation must be content-neutral. Regulations that are not can be sustained only by a showing of a "compelling governmental interest." That was the situation in *Boos v. Barry,* where a regulation prohibited any demonstration "designed . . . to intimidate, coerce or bring into public odium any foreign government." The justices held that unconstitutional because it banned only critical demonstrations and not demonstrations in support of the foreign government.

While the streets and parks are available for speech, some government property is not. Such was the case of the jailhouse grounds in *Adderley* and the Fort Dix military reservation in *Spock*. However, when government opens its property for speech activities, it must be open to all speakers. That was the message in *Widmar*, where the University of Missouri at Kansas City refused to allow Cornerstone, a religious group, use of its buildings.

One problem that has plagued the justices and does not appear to be going away is that of offensive speech as contrasted to obscenity. A majority has adopted a legal definition of the latter, but determining what is offensive has been more elusive. In the "seven dirty words" case, the Court disapproved not so much of the language but the time of day that the monologue was broadcast. In upholding punishment for Matthew Fraser for his campaign speech at Bethel School, the fact that this was a school-sponsored program played an important part in the decision. Also, even though the majority upheld Cohen's right to use the four-letter word on the back of his jacket in the courthouse, the decision might have been different if there had been a regulation prohibiting such use at that location. On the other hand, the justices seem not to want to interfere with offensive speech when the listener has some opportunity to avoid hearing it. Such was the dial-a-porn situation in *Sable Communications*.

This leads to a conclusion in offensive speech cases: (1) the time and place of the speech and (2) the opportunity of the recipient to avoid it will greatly influence the justices in reaching a decision.

Expenditures by a candidate to gain elective office are protected speech as are expenditures made by organizations (PACs) independent of candidates. The justices have also upheld the right of individuals to make unlimited contributions to groups supporting or opposing a ballot measure, but a ban on expenditures by a corporation from its own funds was held not to be a limit on First Amendment rights.

Speech by public employees, while guaranteed, is not as well protected as speech by civilians. The First Amendment does not protect public employees' participation in partisan political activites, and they can speak freely only when their speech relates to matters of public concern. Even then, the right to speak is weighed against the governmental interests in the workplace.

While students and teachers do not "shed their constitutional rights . . . at the schoolhouse gate," the balancing approach used by the justices does not guarantee that much security. The balance can swing in favor of school restrictions on speech.

The right of armed services personnel to speak freely is conditioned by the need for discipline and esprit de corps. This is a well-
established principle adhered to by most justices and is unlikely to be
abandoned.

Less secure than persons in the armed forces are free speech rights
of prisoners. Inmates' rights are dependent upon regulations that
prison authorities believe are reasonably related to legitimate
penological objectives. This principle is unlikely to change in the
future, especially if the prison population continues to grow and prison
conditions become more crowded.

The right of corporations to speak freely is safe, except that their
right to express their opinions through spending corporate funds for
campaign purposes can be limited.

A different approach to commercial speech has been taken by the
majority, although there is some dissent on this issue. The majority's
view is that such speech does not receive the same consideration as
political or individual speech, while some of the justices believe that
there should be no such distinction. The majority uses the same approach in judging advertising by lawyers and other professional persons.

What course the justices take in freedom of speech cases in the
future depends upon the attitude of the individual justices toward the
First Amendment. An adherence to a philosophy like Justice Black's
would guarantee that free expression will be well protected.

VII.
FREEDOM TO ASSEMBLE
AND PETITION

"The very idea of a government, republican in form, implies a right on the part of its citizens to meet peaceably for consultation in respect to public affairs and to petition for a redress of grievances."
United States v. Cruikshank, et al., 92 U.S. 542, 552 (1875).

We owe a debt of gratitude to the many angry English barons who forced King John to agree in the Magna Carta that

> if we or our justiciar or our bailiffs or any of our ministers are in any respect delinquent toward any one or transgress any article of the peace or security, and if the delinquency is shown to four barons of the aforesaid twenty-five barons, those four barons shall come to us, or to our justiciar if we are out of the kingdom, to explain to us the wrong, asking that without delay we cause this wrong to be redressed.

This pledge of a right to redress is part of Article 61 of the Magna Carta, which the king agreed to at Runnymede, England, in 1215.

It was not long after John Lackland became King John in 1199 that the English people knew that they had a tyrant for a monarch. By 1215, not only had he alienated the people, and especially the barons, but also Pope Innocent III. England at this time was a Catholic country, and having good relations with the pope was important.

King John was a ruthless and cruel ruler. "He seduced the wives and daughters of his subjects and was not averse to having enemies who thwarted him tortured and murdered."[1] He also exacted high taxes from the people, which he used for his own purposes and to support a war in France. It was against this background that King John met with representatives of the barons to seek a resolution of the many complaints against him. Little is known of what took place at Runnymede, except that during the few days that they met, the king and barons hammered out the Magna Carta, a document which is, as its title indicates, one of the "great charters" of freedom.

History tells us that the right of redress guaranteed in Article 61 was passed down through the reigns of subsequent English monarchs and eventually became that part of the First Amendment that protects the right "to petition the Government for a redress of grievances." As the right of redress evolved over the years, a right to assemble for that purpose was appended to it. The Declaration and Resolves of the First Continental Congress, 1774, for example, asserts that the people "have a right peaceably to assemble, consider their grievances, and petition the King. . . ."

Included in the amendments to the Constitution proposed by the Virginia ratifying convention in 1788 is one that suggests that a right to assemble exists separate from the right to petition. The proposed Fifteenth Amendment reads:

> 15th. That the people have a right peaceably to assemble together to consult for the common good, or to instruct their representatives; and that every freeman has a right to petition or apply to the legislature for redress of grievances.[2]

In the amendments that Madison proposed to be approved by the first Congress and sent to the states for adoption, he too separated the two rights. He suggested an amendment that read: "The people shall not be restrained from peaceably assembling and consulting for their common good; nor from applying to the Legislature by petitions, or remonstrances, for redress of their grievances."

After Madison's proposed amendments had been redrafted by a select committee of the House of Representatives, the rights of assembly and redress were included in an amendment that also protected freedom of speech and the press. That amendment then read: "The freedom of speech and of the press, and the right of the people peaceably to assemble and consult for their common good, and to apply to the Government for redress of grievances, shall not be infringed."

During the debate on this amendment, Congressman Sedgwick objected to the inclusion of a right of assembly. "He feared it would tend to make them appear trifling in the eyes of their constituents; what, said he, shall we secure the freedom of speech, and think it necessary, at the same time, to allow the right of assembling?" He then moved to strike the words *assemble and*. Congressman Benson responded that the committee had "proceeded on the principle that these rights belonged to the people; they conceived them to be inherent; and all that they meant to provide against was their being infringed by the Government."

This did not satisfy Sedgwick, who "replied, that if the committee were governed by that general principle, they might have gone into a very lengthy enumeration of rights; they might have declared that a man should have a right to wear his hat if he pleased; that he might get up when he pleased, and go to bed when he thought proper; but he would ask the gentleman whether he thought it necessary to enter this trifles in a declaration of rights, in a Government where none of them were intended to be infringed."

Congressman Page then entered the debate and pointed out that this was not a trivial matter, that "a man has been obliged to pull off his hat when he appeared before the face of authority; people have also been prevented from assembling together on their lawful occasions...." "If the people," he declared, "could be deprived of the power of assembling under any pretext whatsoever, they might be deprived of every other privilege contained in the clause."

When put to a vote, Sedgwick's motion was defeated. Congressman Tucker then moved to include the words *to instruct their Representatives*. This would have made the amendment similar to that proposed by Virginia during its ratifying convention. Although Tucker's motion was finally defeated, it brought forth extended debate, some members being concerned that if the amendment contained the words suggested, it might be interpreted to mean that the legislative was bound by instructions given by its constituents.

Another attempt was made, this time in the Senate, to include the words *to instruct their representative*, but that also failed. When the proposed amendments were finally approved by both the House and Senate and submitted to the states for adoption, the provision relating to assembly and redress was part of "Article III":

> Congress shall make no law respecting an establishment of religion, or prohibiting the free exercise thereof, or abridging the freedom of speech, or of the press, or the right of the people peaceably to assemble, and to petition the government for a redress of grievances.

Because the first two proposed amendments were never adopted by the required number of states, "Article III" became what we know as the First Amendment. The final wording of the First Amendment indicates that the first Congress intended to protect the right of the people to assemble for whatever purposes and at the same time to be assured of a separate right to petition the government if they chose to do so. The Supreme Court's first reference to the right of assembly, however, treats it as being for the sole purpose of petitioning the government. In the *Cruikshank* case referred to above, the Court stated that "the right of the people peaceably to assemble for the purpose of petitioning Congress for a redress of grievances, or for any thing else connected with the powers or the duties of the national government, is an attribute of national citizenship, and, as such, under the protection of, and guaranteed by, the United States."

Subsequent decisions of the Court, however, now treat the right to assemble peaceably as a right in and of itself, and the discussion that follows is consistent with that position.

To Petition the Government for Redress

In the Supreme Court

Federal District Judge Walter K. Stapleton has written that "the objective of the 'right to petition' clause is not merely to guarantee the opportunity for seeking redress. . . . It is also designed to provide some assurance that public decision-makers will be sufficiently informed to carry out their function."[3]

As the right was first implemented after the Magna Carta, it worked the way Judge Stapleton indicates. It became a method of informing the king and the House of Commons of the views of the petitioners and requests for relief.

Today, the rules of the House of Representatives set forth a similar procedure. Petitions received by members of the House can be delivered to the clerk, who, after screening them for obscenity and derogatory remarks, has them entered in the House Journal and published in the *Record*.

The right to petition as we know it today, however, encompasses more than just petitioning Congress. For example, some of the cases discussed in Chapter VI have within them an element of the right to petition, even though the Court chose to base its decision on freedom of speech.

In the *Adderley* case, when Harriett Adderley and her friends were demonstrating at the jail in Tallahassee, Justice Douglas saw that as a classic case of people petitioning the government (represented by the sheriff), for an end to segregation. He therefore would have upheld the right of the demonstrators to gather on the jailhouse grounds and in dissent wrote:

> The right to petition for the redress of grievances has an ancient history and is not limited to writing a letter or telegram to a congressman; it is not confined to appearing before the local city council, or writing letters to the President or Governor or Mayor.[4]

When Richard Grayned marched on the street near West Senior High School, Rockford, Illinois, as described in Chapter VI, he too was petitioning school authorities for redress of grievances concerning the treatment of black children at the school.

The Evils of Lobbying

*"To reach the real evils of lobbying without cutting into the constitutional right of petition is a difficult and delicate task...."**

The federal Regulation of Lobbying Act requires all persons who for pay attempt to influence the passage or defeat of legislation, to register with the clerk of the House of Representatives and the secretary of the Senate. The registration requires such persons to furnish their name and address, and give detailed information about who is paying them and how much they are being paid. Further, all persons receiving contributions or spending money for lobbying are required to file a report detailing such contributions and expenditures.

Mr. Harriss was charged with violating both of these requirements by failing to register and report certain expenditures allegedly paid "to others to communicate face-to-face with members of Congress, at public functions and committee hearings, concerning legislation affecting agricultural prices...."[5] Among the arguments asserted as a defense, Harriss challenged the validity of the laws, contending that they violated "the First Amendment guarantees of freedom of speech, freedom of the press, and the right to petition the Government...."

Although a majority of the justices acknowledged that First Amendment rights were involved, they construed the statutes to apply

*Justice Jackson, dissenting in *United States v. Harriss,* 347 U.S. 612, 636 (1954).

only to those persons whose lobbying efforts bring them into direct contact with members of Congress, and as so construed, the laws' requirements were justified. All that Congress had done, Chief Justice Warren wrote, was to require "a modicum of information from those who for hire attempt to influence legislation or who collect or spend funds for that purpose." Congress is therefore "not constitutionally forbidden to require the disclosure of lobbying activities."

Focusing upon the First Amendment's right of the people "to petition the Government for redress of grievances," Justice Jackson expressed concern over the decision.

> If this right is to have an interpretation consistent with that given to other First Amendment rights, it confers a large immunity upon activities of persons, organizations, groups and classes to obtain what they think is due them from government. Of course, their conflicting claims and propaganda are confusing, annoying and at times, no doubt, deceiving and corrupting. But we may not forget that our constitutional system is to allow the greatest freedom of access to Congress, so that the people may press for their selfish interests, with Congress acting as arbiter of their demands and conflicts.

The Lobbying Act, as construed in the *Harriss* case, is still the law of the land today.

There Is No Right to Commit Libel

"The right to petition is guaranteed; the right to commit libel with impunity is not."

David I. Smith was being considered by President Ronald Reagan for the position of U.S. Attorney in North Carolina. Robert McDonald, who operated several child-care centers, did not think that Smith was qualified for the position and therefore wrote two very derogatory letters to Reagan about Smith. Copies of the letters were mailed to a presidential adviser, Edwin Meese, North Carolina Senator Jesse Helms, several members of the House of Representatives, and William Webster, director of the Federal Bureau of Investigation.

When Smith learned of the letters and examined their contents, he sued McDonald in a North Carolina state court for libel, seeking compensatory and punitive damages in the amount of $1 million.

McDonald v. Smith, 472 U.S. 479, 485 (1985).

Because McDonald was not a resident of North Carolina, he had the case removed to federal court, where he made a motion for dismissal of the action on the grounds that "the Petition Clause of the First Amendment provides absolute immunity"[6] to him.

Smith's complaint against McDonald alleged "that these letters 'contained false, slanderous, libelous, inflammatory and derogatory statements'" about him.

> In particular, the complaint states that the letters falsely accused [Smith] of "violating the civil rights of various individuals while a Superior Court Judge," "fraud and conspiracy to commit fraud," "extortion or blackmail," and "violations of professional ethics."

District Judge Frank W. Bullock, Jr., while agreeing that the letters to the president were "petitions" within the meaning of the Petition Clause, held that that did not give McDonald an absolute privilege to defame Smith in this manner. The court of appeals affirmed, and all Supreme Court justices agreed except Justice Powell, who did not participate.

Chief Justice Burger, who delivered the opinion for the Court, started his analysis of the issue by stating that "the First Amendment guarantees 'the right of the people . . . to petition the Government for a redress of grievances.' The right to petition is cut from the same cloth as the other guarantees of that Amendment, and is an assurance of a particular freedom of expression." He then related part of the historical evolution of the right and concluded:

> To accept [McDonald's] claim of absolute immunity would elevate the Petition Clause to special First Amendment status. The Petition Clause, however, was inspired by the same ideals of liberty and democracy that gave us the freedoms to speak, publish, and assemble. . . . These First Amendment rights are inseparable, . . . and there is no sound basis for granting greater constitutional protection to statements made in a petition to the President than other First Amendment expressions.

Justice Brennan, for himself and justices Marshall and Blackmun, added a concurring opinion to emphasize their agreement that a petition, even if addressed to the president of the United States, should not be given greater protection than other communications.

> There is no persuasive reason for according greater or lessor protection to expression on matters of public importance depending on

whether the expression consists of speaking to neighbors across the backyard fence, publishing an editorial in the local newspaper, or sending a letter to the President of the United States.

Petitioning in the Library

*"The statute was deliberately and purposefully applied solely to terminate the reasonable, orderly, and limited exercise of the right to protest the unconstitutional segregation of a public facility."**

The parishes of East Feliciana, West Feliciana, and St. Helena, Louisiana, operated the Audubon Regional Library with three branches and two bookmobiles. "One of the bookmobiles was red, the other blue. The red bookmobile served only white persons. The blue bookmobile served only Negroes. It is a permissible inference that no Negroes used the branch libraries."[7]

Five young Negro males, all residents of East or West Feliciana Parishes, went into the adult reading or service room of the Audubon Regional Library at Clinton. The branch assistant, Mrs. Katie Reeves, was alone in the room. She met the men "between the tables" and asked if she "could help." Petitioner Brown requested a book, "The Story of the Negro" by Arna Bontemps. Mrs. Reeves checked the card catalogue, ascertained that the Branch did not have the book, so advised Mr. Brown, and told him that she would request the book from the State Library, that he would be notified upon its receipt and that "he could either pick it up or it would be mailed to him." She told him that "his point of service was a bookmobile or it could be mailed to him." Mrs. Reeves testified that she expected that the men would then leave; they did not, and she asked them to leave. They did not. Petitioner Brown sat down and the others stood near him. They said nothing; there was no noise or boisterous talking. Mrs. Reeves called Mrs. Perkins, the regional librarian, who was in another room. Mrs. Perkins asked the men to leave. They remained.

Neither Mrs. Reeves nor Mrs. Perkins had called the sheriff, but in "10 to 15 minutes" from the time of the arrival of the men at the library, the sheriff and deputies arrived. The sheriff asked the Negroes to leave. They said they would not. The sheriff then arrested them.

. . .

The Library obtained the requested book and mailed it to Mr. Brown. . . . An accompanying card said, "You may return the book either by mail or to the Blue Bookmobile." The reference to the color

Brown v. Louisiana, 383 U.S. 131, 142 (1966).

of the vehicle was obviously not designated to facilitate the identification of the library vehicle. The blue bookmobile is for Negroes and for Negroes only.

The men were charged under a breach of the peace law, which punishes anyone who "(1) crowds or congregates with others . . . in . . . a public place or building . . . and who fails or refuses to disperse and move on, . . . when ordered so to do by any law enforcement officer. . . ." Mr. Brown was found guilty and sentenced to pay a fine of $150 or to serve ninety days in jail.

When the case reached the Supreme Court, five justices agreed that the convictions must be reversed but issued three opinions setting forth their differing views, and four justices dissented.

Justice Fortas, in an opinion in which Chief Justice Warren and Justice Douglas joined, found two reasons why the convictions could not stand. First, "there was no violation of the statute which petitioners are accused of breaching; no disorder, no intent to provoke a breach of the peace and no circumstances indicating that a breach might be occasioned by petitioners' actions."

> But there is another and sharper answer which is called for. We are here dealing with an aspect of a basic constitutional right — the right under the First and Fourteenth Amendments guaranteeing freedom of speech and of assembly, and freedom to petition the Government for a redress of grievances.

The sit-in at the library was a protest against the segregation policies of the parish library system and was also in effect a petition to the government of the parish to end that segregated system.

Justice Brennan's reason for overturning the convictions was that the breach of the peace statute under which the men were charged was unconstitutional as written because of the possibility it could be used to punish free speech activities. Justice White, on the other hand, simply examined the facts and concluded that there was no breach of the peace.

The dissenting justices, led by Justice Black, thought that "the evidence in this case established every element in the offense charged against petitioners." It seems evident that what most concerned the dissenters was that this was a library and that the silent, peaceful protest upset the quiet functioning thereof.

Petitioning and Antitrust Laws

"The right of petition is one of the freedoms protected by the Bill of Rights, and we cannot . . . lightly impute to Congress an intent to invade those freedoms."*

A federal law, generally referred to as the Sherman Act, makes illegal "every contract, combination in the form of trust or otherwise, or conspiracy, in restraint of trade or commerce among the several States. . . ."[8] The purpose of the Sherman Act is to prevent businesses from banding together to create monopolies or to restrain trade. Persons found to engage in such conduct are not only subject to criminal penalties but may also be required to pay treble damages to those injured.

When a group of businesses, however, attempt to influence passage of legislation that would make it more difficult for competitors to carry on their business, a question arises whether those efforts are punishable under the Sherman Act. Such was the situation in the case of *Eastern R. Conf. v. Noerr Motors.*[9] In that case, Pennsylvania Motor Truck sued twenty-four eastern railroads, charging them with conducting "a publicity campaign against the truckers designed to foster the adoption and retention of laws and law enforcement practices destructive of the trucking business, to create an atmosphere of distaste for the truckers among the general public, and to impair the relationships existing between the truckers and their customers."

The railroads admitted that "they had conducted a publicity campaign designed to influence the passage of state laws relating to truck weight limits and tax rates on heavy trucks, and to encourage a more rigid enforcement of state laws penalizing trucks for overweight loads and other traffic violations. . . ." The railroads insisted that they had the right "to inform the public and the legislatures of the several states of the truth with regard to the enormous damage done to the roads by the operators of heavy and especially of overweight trucks, . . . [and] with regard to their repeated and deliberate violations . . ." of the laws regulating the weight and speed of trucks.

District Judge Thomas J. Clary held in favor of the truck association, granted damages to it, and enjoined the railroads from engaging in further activities against the trucking industry. He was not persuaded that the railroads were entitled to First Amendment protection.

*_Eastern R. Conf. v. Noerr Motors,_ 365 U.S. 127, 138 (1961).

What the defendants have combined to do is something more than free speech; something more than freedom to assemble; something more than a petition to the legislature. They have engaged in a course of conduct designed to destroy the good will of a competitor in order to secure a monopoly—all of this in violation of a valid public policy set down many years ago by the Congress of the United States.[10]

The court of appeals affirmed, but a unanimous Supreme Court held that "no violation of the Act can be predicated upon mere attempts to influence the passage or enforcement of laws." The justices were of the opinion that Congress did not intend to regulate political activity of businesses because "such a construction of the Sherman Act would raise important constitutional questions" relating to the right to petition the government.

We think it clear that the Sherman Act does not apply to the activities of the railroads at least insofar as those activities comprised mere solicitation of governmental action with respect to the passage and enforcement of laws.[11]

Even though the truck association had argued that the "sole purpose [of the railroads] in seeking to influence the passage and enforcement of laws was to destroy the truckers as competitors for the long-distance freight business," the justices concluded that that was irrelevant. "The right of the people," Justice Black said, "to inform their representatives in government of their desires with respect to the passage or enforcement of laws cannot properly be made to depend upon their intent in doing so."

Although the *Noerr* opinion clearly protects the right to petition, it also sends a warning that if a publicity campaign that is "ostensibly directed toward influencing governmental action, is a mere sham to cover what is actually nothing more than an attempt to interfere directly with the business relationships of a competitor . . . the application of the Sherman Act would be justified."

The question of whether truckers were really petitioning the government came to the Court when one group of carriers sued another in a federal district court in California. Truckers Unlimited and others had brought suit against California Motor Transport Co., alleging that California Motor, together with other trucking companies, had conspired to put "their competitors, including plaintiff, out of business, of weakening such competitors, of destroying, eliminating and weakening existing and potential competition, and of monopolizing the highway common carriage business in California and elsewhere."[12]

Among the actions allegedly done by the defendants were "instituting state and federal proceedings to resist and defeat applications by [plaintiff] to acquire, transfer, or register operating rights." Federal District Judge William T. Sweigert, believing that under the holding of *Noerr,* the actions of California Motor were protected by the Right to Petition Clause, dismissed the case. The court of appeals reversed and reinstated the case.

The Supreme Court affirmed, holding that the plaintiff was entitled to the opportunity to prove that the defendant's actions were a sham and therefore not protected by the Petition Clause. Justice Douglas, writing for the majority, pointed out that the right to petition "governs the approach of citizens or groups of them to administrative agencies [which are both creatures of the legislature and arms of the executive] and to courts, the third branch of Government. Certainly the right to petition extends to all departments of the Government. The right of access to the courts is indeed but one aspect of the right of petition."

He went on to point out that "in the present case, however, the allegations are not that the conspirators sought 'to influence public officials,' but that they sought to bar their competitors from meaningful access to adjudicatory tribunals and so to usurp that decision-making process." Because "First Amendment rights may not be used as the means or the pretext of achieving 'substantive evils,'" Truckers Unlimited was entitled to present evidence showing the real pupose of the defendant's actions.

Justices Stewart and Brennan concurred only in the result. They believed that the majority's reasoning "retreats from *Noerr,* and in the process tramples upon important First Amendment values."

In the Lower Courts

Hustler *and Members of Congress*

"Larry Flynt sent Hustler *to Members of Congress 'to express my political and social views to public officials.'"**

When the U.S. government sought to enjoin Larry Flynt from sending copies of his *Hustler* magazine to members of Congress,

---

*United States Postal Service v. Hustler *Magazine,* 630 F.Supp. 867, 871, 872 (986).

federal District Judge John H. Pratt expressed the view that "this case presents the novel question of whether the statutory prohibition against mailing certain pandering advertisements . . . is constitutional where the 'addressee' is a Member of Congress."[13]

In early September 1983 Larry Flynt mailed a copy of *Hustler* to all members of Congress with a letter describing the magazine as containing "the latest news, sex reviews, political satire, pornography, and in-depth investigative articles."

A substantial number "did not . . . appreciate Larry Flynt's munificence on their behalf," and 264 of them complained to the Postal Service. The service, in compliance with a federal law that permits an addressee to request that the sender be notified to discontinue sending mail that the addressee does not want, sent 264 orders to Flynt ordering him to stop the mailings. Because Flynt ignored the requests and continued to send the magazines, the service brought this action seeking to enjoin further mailings.

The Supreme Court some years earlier had upheld the federal law, even though it acknowledged the existence of a conflict between the right of one person to communicate with another and the right of the other person to be let alone. It had resolved that conflict by balancing the respective rights and concluding that the right to be let alone outweighed the right to communicate. In commenting upon the Supreme Court's decision, Judge Pratt noted that "this emphasis on the householder's right to be let alone reflects the privileged constitutional status of the home. It is beyond dispute that the walls of one's house enclose a unique zone of privacy."

But that "zone of privacy" did not exist in this case, where the recipients of the communication were members of Congress.

> Members of Congress are in a different category from "addressees" who are householders. As elected representatives of the people, they cannot simply shield themselves from undesirable mail in the same manner as an ordinary addressee. Private citizens bear no obligation even to acknowledge the views of others. Members of Congress, on the other hand, are chosen to speak for those who elected them. As the framers of the Constitution expressly contemplated, a Senator or Congressman should naturally "take care to inform himself of [his fellow citizens'] dispositions and inclinations..."

Turning then to the argument made by Flynt that his mailings were protected by the First Amendment, Judge Pratt declared that "the right to petition the Government is part of our heritage from earliest times and represents a cornerstone of our national liberty." He concluded that "a prohibitory order under [the law] would effectively deny defendants' right to petition Congress at all." He pointed out that "Members are not forced to read the magazine or other of the mail they receive in volume. We cannot imagine that Congressional offices all lack wastebaskets."

NOW's Economic Boycott

"The goal and sole purpose of NOW's economic boycott campaign is the ratification of the ERA...."

Beginning in 1977, the National Organization for Women (NOW) commenced a boycott of conventions, directed at states that had not ratified the Equal Rights Amendment.

Activities undertaken by NOW included (1) sending letters to many organizations urging them to adopt a convention boycott resolution; (2) printing and distributing literature that asked individuals to join and support the boycott; (3) creating a campaign-style button for supporters of the boycott to wear; (4) and preparing a boycott kit for distribution to persons interested in the movement.

NOW's actions had substantial economic effect upon hotels, motels and restaurants, which depend upon the patronage of conventioneers. Because of this economic impact, the state of Missouri brought an action against NOW in federal district court seeking an injunction to prohibit NOW from continuing the boycott. Missouri argued that the boycott was a violation of federal antitrust laws and should therefore be prohibited. Federal District Judge Elmo B. Hunter disagreed and dismissed the action. Judge Hunter reasoned that "NOW's activities were political and thus not within the scope of the Sherman Act...."[14]

The state appealed to the court of appeals, which recognized that the case posed "serious questions concerning the First Amendment's right of petition and the scope of the antitrust laws." After extensive analysis of the legislative history of the Sherman Act and cases from the Supreme Court and other courts, Judge Roy L. Stephenson, writing for himself and Judge J. Smith Henley, concluded that the act did not cover NOW's activities.

State of Missouri v. Nat. Organ. for Women, 620 F.2d 1301, 1302 (1980).

We hold that NOW's boycott activities are privileged on the basis of the First Amendment right to petition and the Supreme Court's recognition of that important right when it collides with commercial effects of trade restraints.

Senior Circuit Judge Floyd R. Gibson, in reaching a different conclusion, would have given greater weight to the harmful effects of the boycott, than to NOW's right to petition. "When the interference with first amendment rights is minimal," Judge Gibson asserted, "and the governmental interest in regulation is great, the mere presence of some first amendment interest cannot prevent the federal government from exercising its constitutionally granted power to regulate commerce."

Harassment by Petition

*"As exasperating as Silvey's conduct must have been to Smith, Silvey was constitutionally protected in exercising his right to petition. . . ."**

Most everyone would agree that Harold R. Silvey, Jr., was a "pain in the neck" to Kenneth D. Smith. Smith owned the Paradise Ranch Mobile Home Park where Silvey had been a tenant. After having lived in the park for about three years, Silvey became dissatisfied with its operation and began to make complaints. One complaint was made to the alcoholic beverage control board and may have resulted in a raid on the park's Halloween party. "In 1975, Silvey's agitation concerning water quality in the Park also apparently led to the filing of a criminal action to enforce certain regulations concerning water quality and to cause modification of a well Smith dug on the property."[15]

Silvey left the park, but this did not end his harassment of Smith. "He conducted a complaint campaign with various governmental agencies he thought to be responsible for the regulation of the Park, writing numerous letters, making phone calls and meeting personally with officials." When he was not getting the reponse that he thought he should from local officials, he sought a court order to require the board of supervisors to act. This action was dismissed when the officials agreed to hold hearings concerning permits and variances at the park.

When Smith had had about all that he could take, he sued Silvey for harassment and requested a restraining order prohibiting him from continuing his activities. Temporary Superior Court Judge Donald W.

*Smith v. Silvey, 149 Cal. App. 3d 400, 406 (1983).

Pike, after examining the declarations of each party, issued an order barring Silvey "from directly or indirectly initiating complaints by phone, in writing, or personally appearing at any agency with authority to grant or revoke, or approve or disapproves [sic] of permits of construction. . . ."

Silvey filed an appeal with the California Court of Appeals, arguing that the terms of the order violated his constitutional right of speech and right to petition for redress of grievances. In an opinion written by Presiding Judge Joan Dempsey Klein, the court of appeals agreed and ordered the injunction dissolved.

Not only did the appeals court find that Silvey's contacts with the officials were protected, but it also held that "his filing of the mandamus action against the board of supervisors was likewise an exercise of this same right to petition the judicial branch of government."

Charles Aknin found himself in a similar exasperating situation and fared no better than did Kenneth Smith. Aknin was the owner of a discotheque in the village of Mamaroneck, New York, called Zazou, which was doing well financially. But Zazou's financial success meant nothing but trouble for the neighbors, who took offense to activities of some of its patrons.

The neighbors' feelings about the "discotheque" were described by Judge Charles L. Brieant, Jr., as follows:

> Since we assume that in the early hours of the morning in Mamaroneck, New York the good burghers are sleeping, and readying themselves for their contest with the Penn Central commuter trains on the following day, we assume that this resentment was a natural and reasonable outgrowth of the noise and related activities of the revelers attending the discotheque, and that their ethnicity is of no particular relevance.[16]

When the residents complained about the patrons' parking and blocking their driveways, Aknin secured permission from a nearby A&P supermarket to use their parking lot after hours. The residents responded by asking the market not to allow Zazou's customers to park there, and as could be expected, the market agreed. The noise and activities of the revelers caused some of the neighbors to seek help from local officials. They wanted to know what the officials were going to do about the discotheque.

The residents also complained about fire exits, and as a result the state Labor Department cited Aknin for not having the required number and gave him thirty days to take corrective action. But this did not satisfy the neighbors. They "persuaded the Village Building Department to issue an order revoking the certificate of occupancy, and directing a closing down of this place of public assembly until the exits were installed. . . . This was done on the eve of the July 4th weekend, at which time it was admitted that there would probably be a substantial crowd in attendance at the discotheque."

Realizing that having to close on the fourth would mean serious financial loss, Aknin did not do so and was therefore arrested for violating the order. He was later acquitted of the charge.

This, however, did not end Aknin's woes. When it was determined that the village had ordinances prohibiting noise and the playing of music or dancing "after 1:00 A.M. on weekday morning and after 2:00 A.M. on Sunday and holiday mornings," local officials arrested Aknin for violating these laws, and he was convicted on these charges.

Aknin finally retaliated by suing the officials of the village, the chairman of the liquor authority, Edith Sideman, a housewife and resident of the village, and other unnamed persons. He asked for injunctive relief and money damages.

In his complaint, Aknin alleged that "Mrs. Sideman, together with her [unnamed] conspirators, persuaded the defendant Village officials to invoke the cabaret ordinance against [him], and likewise the unnecessary noise ordinance." Sideman moved the court for an order dismissing her from the action. When this motion came before Judge Brieant, he agreed that whatever part Sideman played in this episode, her actions were protected by the First Amendment.

> To permit maintenance of this type of civil rights lawsuit against a private individual would under the circumstances and uncontested facts shown in this case, have an unfortunate and unjust chilling effect upon the exercise by members of the public of their First Amendment right to complain about a public nuisance.

The Right of the People Peaceably to Assemble

In *De Jonge v. Oregon*,[17] Chief Justice Hughes wrote that "the right of peaceable assembly is a right cognate to those of free speech and free press and is equally fundamental." By this statement, the justice acknowledged the existence of two qualities concerning the right of assembly—first, that it is a right separate and distinct from freedom of speech and of the press; second that it is just as fundamental as those rights.

In spite of this characterization, the right of assembly is frequently connected with the right to speak freely, leaving the impression that only one First Amendment right is involved. The discussion that follows will focus on those cases in which the Court addressed the right of people peaceably to assemble, separately and distinct from other First Amendment rights.

Peaceably Assembling Is No Crime

*"It follows from these considerations that, consistently with the Federal Constitution, peaceable assembly for lawful discussion cannot be made a crime."**

In September 1934, Dirk De Jonge, Don Cluster, Edward R. Denny, and Earl Stewart were indicted by the Multnomah County, Oregon, Grand Jury for "unlawfully and feloniously presid[ing] at, conduct[ing] and assist[ing] in conducting an assemblage of persons, organizations, society, and group, to wit: The Communist Party. . . ."[18] The indictment grew out of a meeting held in Portland under the auspices of the Communist party, which was attended by approximately 150 people, although it was estimated that only about 10 or 15 percent were members of the party. "De Jonge, who admitted that he was and for several years had been a member of the Communist Party, was the second speaker on the program, and in his talk protested against conditions at the county jail, the action of city police in relation to the maritime strike then in progress in Portland, and numerous other matters."

The Oregon statute under which he was charged provides that a person "commits a crime of criminal syndicalism if he presides at, conducts, or assists in conducting a meeting of an organization or group which teaches or advocates criminal syndicalism or sabotage."[19] He was found guilty and sentenced to prison for seven years.

The Oregon Supreme Court, "having limited the charge to the defendant's participation in a meeting called by the Communist Party, . . . sustained the conviction upon that basis regardless of what was said or done at the meeting." A unanimous Supreme Court reversed. In reaching its conclusion, the Court first explained what De Jonge had not been charged with:

> It appears that, while the defendant was a member of the Communist Party, he was not indicted for participating in its organization,

De Jonge v. Oregon, 299 U.S. 353, 365 (1937).

or for joining it, or for soliciting members or for distributing literature. He was not charged with teaching or advocating criminal syndicalism or sabotage or any unlawful acts, either at the meeting or elsewhere. . . . His sole offense as charged, and for which he was convicted and sentenced to imprisonment for seven years, was that he had assisted in the conduct of a public meeting, albeit otherwise lawful, which was held under the auspices of the Communist Party.

The justices recognized that states have the right to protect themselves when force and violence are used as a substitute for advocacy of peaceful change. But Chief Justice Hughes pointed out that "we are not called upon to review the findings of the state court as to the objectives of the Communist Party. Notwithstanding those objectives, the defendant still enjoyed his personal right of free speech and to take part in a peaceable assembly having a lawful purpose, although called by that Party."

By its decision in the *De Jonge* case, the Court made the Petition and Assembly Clauses applicable to actions of state governments under the doctrine of incorporation discussed in Chapter III.

Assembling for Business Purposes

"The grievances for redress of which the right of petition was insured, and with it the right of assembly, are not solely religious or political ones."*

The state of Texas required labor union organizers to apply for, receive, and carry an organizer's card before soliciting persons to join a union. During the latter part of 1943, the Congress of Industrial Organizations and the Oil Workers Industrial Union were attempting to organize the employees of the Humble Oil & Refining Company in Bay Town, Texas. R.J. Thomas, a vice president of the CIO, came to Bay Town to speak at an organizational meeting. Shortly before he was to speak, Thomas was served with a court order restraining him, "while in Texas, from soliciting members for or memberships in specified labor unions and others affiliated with the Congress of Industrial Organizations, without first obtaining an organizer's card as required" by law.[20]

Upon receiving the order, Thomas, after consulting with his attorneys, decided to speak at the meeting as planned. Near the end of his speech, he invited those not already members of the union to join, and extended a personal invitation to "Pat O'Sullivan, a nonunion man

---

**Thomas v. Collins,* 323 U.S. 516, 531 (1945).

in the audience whom he previously had never seen." Shortly thereafter, he was arrested for violating the court order and taken before a justice of the peace, formally charged, and released. He was later tried, convicted, and sentenced for contempt of court. Thomas sought release by filing a writ of habeas corpus with the Texas Supreme Court, but that was denied.

In presenting its case before the U.S. Supreme Court, Texas argued that no right of free assembly was presented and that the statute was "directed at business practices, like selling insurance, dealing in securities, acting as commission merchant, pawnbrokering, etc. . . . ." Thomas maintained that "the right to make the speech includes the right to ask members of the audience, both generally and by name, to join the union."

Justice Rutledge, who delivered the opinion for the majority, identified the case before the Court as one that "confronts us again with the duty our system places on this Court to say where the individual's freedom ends and the State's power begins." He continued: "Choice on that border, now as always delicate, is perhaps more so where the usual presumption supporting legislation is balanced by the preferred place given in our scheme to the great, the indispensable democratic freedoms secured by the First Amendment." In this balancing process, "it is . . . in our tradition to allow the widest room for discussion, the narrowest range for its restriction, particularly when this right is exercised in conjunction with peaceable assembly."

Justice Rutledge then addressed Texas's assertion that because this was a business matter, a different rule ought to prevail. "The idea is not sound," he wrote, ". . . that the First Amendment's safeguards are wholly inapplicable to business or economic activity." Referring to cases in which the Court had approved requirements for permits to engage in certain business, the majority noted that such requirements were upheld when necessary for identification purposes — but more is involved in this case.

> As a matter of principle a requirement of registration in order to make a public speech would seem generally incompatible with an exercise of the rights of free speech and free assembly. Lawful public assemblies, involving no element of grave and immediate danger to an interest the State is entitled to protect, are not instruments of harm which require previous identification of the speakers. And the right either of workmen or of unions under these conditions to assemble and discuss their own affairs is as fully protected by the Constitution as the right of businessmen, farmers, educators, political

party members or others to assemble and discuss their affairs and to enlist the support of others.

The majority then held that "a requirement that one must register before he undertakes to make a public speech to enlist support for a lawful movement is quite incompatible with the requirements of the First Amendment."

In a concurring opinion, Justice Jackson explained that there is a difference between protecting the public from unethical business practices and protection against being propagandized by speech or the press. "Very many are the interests which the state may protect against the practice of an occupation, very few are those it may assume to protect against the practice of propagandizing by speech or press. These are thereby left great range of freedom."

Four justices dissented in an opinion written by Justice Owen J. Roberts. Their view of the Texas registration law was very different from the marjority's. They saw the law as doing nothing more than requiring union solicitors to register in the same way that "doctors and nurses, lawyers and notaries, bankers and accountants, insurance agents and solicitors of every kind in every State of this Union have traditionally been under duty to make some identification of themselves as practitioners of their calling."

Assembling May Be Annoying to Others

*"The First [Amendment does] not permit a State to make criminal the exercise of the right of assembly simply because its exercise may be 'annoying' to some people."**

No facts are given as to the specific conduct of defendant Coates except that he was a student involved in a demonstration when he was arrested and charged as "being one of a group of more than two persons assembled on the sidewalk on or about April 11, 1968, at and in the city of Cincinnati, [who] did unlawfully conduct himself in a manner annoying to persons passing by contrary to and in violation of Section 901-L6 of the Code of Ordinances of the City of Cincinnati."[21] Coates was convicted, and his conviction was upheld by two Ohio appellate courts, including the Ohio Supreme Court, although three justices of that court dissented.

The issue was the validity of the Cincinnati law, which "makes it

---

*Coates v. City of Cincinnati, 402 U.S. 611, 615 (1971).

a criminal offense for 'three or more persons to assemble . . . on any of the sidewalks . . . and there conduct themselves in a manner annoying to persons passing by. . . .'"[22]

In his appeal to the Supreme Court, Coates raised two constitutional issues: (1) that the law was unconstitutionally vague and therefore a violation of the Due Process Clause of the Fourteenth Amendment; (2) that the law violated the Right to Assemble Clause of the First Amendment.

Six justices agreed with both positions, and reversed. "In our opinion," Justice Stewart declared for the majority, "this ordinance is unconstitutionally vague because it subjects the exercise of the right of assembly to an unascertainable standard, and unconstitutionally broad because it authorizes the punishment of constitutionally protected conduct."

The majority conceded that "the city is free to prevent people from blocking sidewalks, obstructing traffic, littering streets, committing assaults, or engaging in countless other forms of antisocial conduct." But this ordinance does much more. It "violates the constitutional right of free assembly and association. Our decisions establish that mere public intolerance or animosity cannot be the basis for abridgment of these constitutional freedoms."

Justice White, for himself, Chief Justice Burger, and Justice Blackmun, dissented on the ground that the law was neither vague nor violated freedom of assembly rights.

A Courtroom Is a Place to Assemble

*"A trial courtroom is a public place where the people generally . . . have a right to be present, and where their presence historically has been thought to enhance the integrity and quality of what takes place."**

Chief Justice Burger commenced his opinion in *Richmond Newspapers*[23] by noting that "the narrow question presented in this case is whether the right of the public and press to attend criminal trials is guaranteed under the United States Constitution."

The *Richmond Newspapers* case involved the trial of John Paul Stevenson for murder of a hotel manager. Stevenson was convicted of second-degree murder, but that decision was reversed by the Virginia Supreme Court because "a bloodstained shirt purportedly belonging to Stevenson had been improperly admitted into evidence." His "second

---

*Richmond Newspapers, Inc. v. Virginia, 448 U.S. 555, 556 (1980).

trial ended in a mistrial . . . when a juror asked to be excused after trial had begun and no alternate was available." A third trial also ended in a mistrial because "a prospective juror had read about Stevenson's previous trials in a newspaper and had told other prospective jurors about the case before the retrial began." At the beginning of the fourth trial, Stevenson's attorney asked that "everybody be excluded from the Courtroom because I don't want any information being shuffled back and forth. . . ." When the prosecution offered no objection, the judge granted the request. Richmond Newspapers, Inc., which had two reporters in the courtroom at the time, sought to have the order reversed, but the judge refused to do so. After the prosecution had presented its evidence against Stevenson, his counsel asked the judge to find Stevenson not guilty, which the judge did.

In the meantime, Richmond Newspapers petitioned the Virginia Supreme Court to reverse the closure order, which it refused to do. An appeal was then taken to the U.S. Supreme Court, which did reverse, but in so doing, the justices were unable to agree upon a majority opinion. While seven justices agreed that "the right to attend criminal trials is implicit in the guarantees of the First Amendment, . . ." six opinions were written to explain how the justices individually came to that conclusion.

Chief Justice Burger, in an opinion concurred in by justices White and Stevens, acknowledged the correctness of the state's position "that neither the Constitution nor the Bill of Rights contains any provision which by its terms guarantees to the public the right to attend criminal trials." But he did not see that as a stumbling block because "there remains the question whether, absent an explicit provision, the Constitution [still] affords protection against exclusion of the public from criminal trials."

In searching for an answer to that question, the Chief Justice noted that "the right of access to places traditionally open to the public, as criminal trials have long been, may be seen as assured by the amalgam of the First Amendment guarantees of speech and press; and their affinity to the right of assembly is not without relevance. From the outset, the right of assembly was regarded not only as an independent right but also as a catalyst to augment the free exercise of the other First Amendment rights with which it was deliberately linked by the draftsmen." And further: "People assemble in public places not only to speak or to take action, but also to listen, observe, and learn; indeed, they may 'assemble for any lawful purpose.' . . ."

Justice Brennan, in an opinion joined by Justice Marshall, took a straightforward position on the application of the First Amendment but did not specifically identify which part required open trials.

> Because I believe that the First Amendment—of itself and as applied to the States through the Fourteenth Amendment—secures such a public right of access, I agree with those of my Brethren who hold that, without more, agreement of the trial judge and the parties cannot constitutionally close a trial to the public.

Because the Sixth Amendment guarantees the right to a "public trial," Justice Blackmun based his decision that trials must be open on that amendment. However, he went on to say that "I am driven to conclude, as a secondary position, that the First Amendment must provide some measure of protection for public access to the trial."

Justice Rehnquist dissented because he could find no provision in the Constitution that could "fairly be read to prohibit what the trial judge in the Virginia state-court system did in this case." Justice Powell did not participate in the case.

The Right Peaceably to Assemble and to Petition the Government—1991 and Beyond

It is now clear that the right of assembly and the right to petition are separate constitutional rights and have equal status with other First Amendment rights. However, because the Court often combines its discussion of these rights with the right of free speech, few cases are decided by reference only to the right to petition or the right to assemble. Even if the justices were more specific in identifying which right they were relying upon, it should make little difference in the ultimate outcome because, as Chief Justice Burger points out in the *McDonald* case, "The First Amendment rights are inseparable...."

Giving these rights equal status with the other First Amendment rights means that the government must accord them a "great range of freedom." How great that freedom will be, however, will depend upon the depth of commitment of the present and future justices to all First Amendment rights, including the right peaceably to assemble and the right to petition.

VIII.
FREEDOM OF ASSOCIATION

"It is beyond debate that freedom to engage in association for the advancement of beliefs and ideas is an inseparable aspect of the 'liberty' assured by the Due Process Clause of the Fourteenth Amendment, which embraces freedom of speech."
NAACP v. Alabama, 357 U.S. 449, 460 (1958)

No specific provision of the First Amendment protects the right of people to associate with other people. But it seems to follow logically that the right to speak, to petition, and to assemble impliedly includes the right to associate together for those purposes. This is the approach the Court has taken in recognizing the existence of a specific constitutional right of freedom of association. That recognition, however, did not come until 1958 in the *NAACP* case.

As early as 1927, however, references to a right of association began to appear in Court opinions. The 1927 case involved Charlotte A. Whitney, who was found guilty of the crime of "criminal syndicalism" because she participated in organizing the Communist Labor party in California. Whitney had been a member of the local Oakland (California) Socialist party, but when that party decided to form a branch of the Communist Labor party, she not only attended the organizational meeting but actively participated as a member of the credentials and resolutions committees.

Criminal syndicalism acts were aimed at punishing persons who advocated, taught, aided, or abetted, among other things, "unlawful methods of terrorism as a means of accomplishing a change in industrial ownership or control, or affecting any political change."[1] A person who "organizes or assists in organizing, or is or knowingly becomes a member of, any organization . . . organized . . . to advocate, teach, aid and abet criminal syndicalism," could be found guilty of violating the California Criminal Syndicalism Act.

Because of her organizational activities, Whitney was found guilty. She appealed to the California appellate courts, which upheld the conviction. A unanimous Supreme court affirmed in a decision that the Court overruled forty-two years later in the *Brandenburg* case (discussed in Chapter VI).

In upholding the decision of the California courts, the justices, without a great deal of discussion, concluded that "the Syndicalism Act as applied in this case, [was not] repugnant to the due process clause as a restraint of the rights of free speech, assembly, and association." While this seems to acknowledge a right of association, the Court goes on to hold that it was "the combining with others in an association for the accomplishment of the desired ends through the advocacy and use of criminal and unlawful methods" that made Whitney guilty.

Justices Brandeis and Holmes concurred but were concerned that the opinion did not give sufficient recognition to the First Amendment rights involved. "I am unable," Justice Brandeis declared, "to assent to the suggestion in the opinion of the Court that assembling with a political party, formed to advocate the desirability of a proletarian revolution by mass action at some date necessary far in the future, is not a right within the protection of the Fourteenth Amendment." He was referring to the Fourteenth Amendment Due Process Clause, which, as pointed out in Chapter III, encompasses most of the provisions of the first ten amendments.

In spite of their concern that First Amendment rights were involved in this case, justices Brandeis and Holmes voted to uphold the conviction because "there was evidence on which the court or jury might have found that . . . danger" to the government did exist from the association of Whitney and the others in the formation of the Communist Labor party.

The power of the state to punish persons for their association with others came before the Court again in *Bryant v. Zimmerman*.[2] Although the Court also made reference to associational interests in this case, it upheld a conviction based solely upon associational membership. George W. Bryant was charged with having "attended meetings and remained a member of the Buffalo [New York] Provisional Klan of the Knights of the Ku Klux Klan, . . . he then having knowledge that such association had wholly failed to comply with the requirement" of registering with the secretary of state.

Under the law, an organization having twenty or more members and requiring "an oath as a prerequisite or condition of membership" was required to file "a sworn copy of its constitution, by-laws, regulations and oath of membership, together with a roster of its membership and a list of its officers for the current year. . . ." A member who knew that the association had not filed the proper documents could be found guilty of a misdemeanor.

After Bryant was arrested and while he was in custody of the sheriff, he attempted to secure his release by a writ of habeas corpus, arguing that the law under which he was being held was unconstitutional. The writ was denied by a New York trial court, and that decision was affirmed by two New York appellate courts and the Supreme Court.

Bryant argued that "under the due process clause . . . the statute deprive[d] him of liberty in that it prevent[ed] him from exercising his right of membership in the association." Without directly holding that there was a right of association implicit within the concept of liberty, Justice Willis Van Devanter wrote for the Court that Bryant's "liberty in this regard, like most other personal rights, must yield to the rightful exertion of the police power." The police power was rightfully used in this case against associations "to confine their purposes and activities within limits which are consistent with the rights of others and the public welfare."

The Court had an opportunity in 1950 to establish a right of association and define its parameters, but again failed to do so. At issue was the constitutionality of Secton 9(h) of the National Labor Relations Act, which denied unions use of certain procedures under the act "unless there is on file with the [National Labor Relations] Board an affidavit . . . by each officer of such labor organization . . . that he is not a member of the Communist Party . . . and that he does not believe in, and is not a member of or supports any organization that believes in or teaches, the overthrow of the United States Government by force or by any illegal or unconstitutional methods."[3]

In discussing the constitutionality of Section 9(h), the Court noted that "by exerting pressures on unions to deny office to Communists and others identified therein, Section 9(h) undoubtedly lessens the threat to interstate commerce, but it has the further necessary effect of discouraging the exercise of political rights protected by the First Amendment." Throughout the rest of its opinion, in which a majority sustained Section 9(h), the Court focused on First Amendment rights generally, and never came to grips with the burden of this law upon associational rights. The justices saw "the problem . . . [as] one weighing the probable effects of the statute upon the free exercise of the right of speech and assembly against the congressional determination that political strikes are evils of conduct which cause substantial harm to interstate commerce and that Communists and others identified by Section 9(h) pose continuing threats to that public interest when in positions of union leadership."

Justice Jackson, in a concurring and dissenting opinion, discussed why he thought the law applicable to the Communist party but not to other parties.

> If the statute before us required labor union officers to forswear membership in the Republican Party, the Democratic Party or the Socialist Party, I suppose all agree that it would be unconstitutional. But why, if it is valid as to the Communist Party?

Justice Jackson did not explain why the statute would be unconstitutional if imposed on members of our dominant political parties, but implicit in what he said is that the First Amendment may protect some kinds of association but not others. The answer for him, therefore, was not difficult. There are, he wrote, "decisive differences between the Communist Party and every other party of any importance in the long experience of the United States with party government."

Justice Jackson then discussed the Communist party at great length describing it as "a satrap party, which to the threat of civil disorder, adds the threat of betrayal into alien hands." He noted that it was a party under the command of the Kremlin, not native to this country, and believed in violent and undemocratic means to achieve their ends. That being true, it was easy to downplay any alleged First Amendment rights and opt in favor of the law and industrial peace, which the law is supposed to achieve.

Justice Black took exception to the majority's characterization of the question as not a substantial one.

> The Court assures us that today's encroachment on liberty is just a small one, that this particular statutory provision "touches only a relative handful of persons, leaving the great majority of persons of the identified affiliations and beliefs completely free from restraint."

"But not the least of the virtues of the First Amendment," Justice Black declared, "is its protection of each member of the smallest and most unorthodox minority." He expressed concern for the possible reach of the majority's decision. He was confident that it would not be applied to the major political parties but might be to lesser organizations that advocated unpopular ideas. He quoted Thomas Jefferson's First Inaugural Address:

If there be any among us who would wish to dissolve this Union or to change its republican form, let them stand undisturbed as monuments of the safety with which error of opinion may be tolerated where reason is left free to combat it.

Association May Be for Many Purposes

"It is immaterial whether the beliefs sought to be advanced by association pertain to political, economic, religious or cultural matters. . . ."*

An order by Alabama Circuit Court Judge Walter B. Jones set in motion the circumstances that brought the question of the existence of a constitutional right of freedom of association squarely before the Supreme Court.

The NAACP, a nonprofit corporation organized under the laws of New York, received its first charter in Alabama in 1918 and opened its first regional office there in 1951. It never qualified to do business as a foreign corporation in Alabama, assuming that it was exempt from such requirements. In 1956, however, the Alabama attorney general commenced an action against the association seeking to stop its activities and to oust it from the state. The attorney general alleged that "the Association had opened a regional office and had organized various affiliates in Alabama; had recruited members and solicited contributions within the State; had given financial support and furnished legal assistance to Negro students seeking admission to the state university; and had supported a Negro boycott of the bus lines in Montgomery to compel the seating of passengers without regard to race."[4]

The same day that the complaint was filed, Judge Jones ordered the association to cease its activities in the state and not to attempt to qualify to do business there. He also ordered it to produce many of its records, including "records containing the names and addresses of all Alabama 'members' and 'agents' of the Association." When the NAACP refused to comply with the order, Judge Jones held them in contempt and levied a fine of $10,000, which might be reduced or suspended if the records were forthcoming within five days. If the records were not produced, the fine would be increased to $100,000.

The Association then agreed to furnish most of the information requested but refused to submit its membership lists. When the Alabama Supreme Court later upheld Judge Jones' order of contempt, it characterized this refusal as a "brazen defiance of the order of the

**NAACP v. Alabama*, 357 U.S. 449, 460 (1958).

court." In response to an appeal by the association, a unanimous Supreme Court reversed Judge Jones' contempt order and the decision of the Alabama Supreme Court upholding that order.

The opinion of Justice Harlan for the Court states that "the question presented is whether Alabama, consistently with the Due Process Clause of the Fourteenth Amendment, can compel petitioner [NAACP] to reveal to the State's Attorney General the names and addresses of all its Alabama members and agents, without regard to their positions or functions in the Association."

By referring to the Fourteenth Amendment's Due Process Clause, Justice Harlan is in reality questioning the validity of Judge Jones' order because of its effect upon First Amendment rights. "It is beyond debate," Justice Harlan notes, "that freedom to engage in association for the advancement of beliefs and ideas is an inseparable aspect of the 'liberty' assured by the Due Process Clause of the Fourteenth Amendment, which embraces freedom of speech." He then concludes that "the production order . . . must be regarded as entailing the likelihood of a substantial restraint upon the exercise by petitioner's members of their right to freedom of association."

> Petitioner has made an uncontroverted showing that on past occasions revelation of the identity of its rank-and-file members has exposed these members to economic reprisal, loss of employment, threat of physical coercion, and other manifestations of public hostility.

Because First Amendment rights are not absolute, finding an infringement upon associational rights does not end the inquiry. Still to be determined is whether Alabama had sufficient interest in having the membership lists to justify forced disclosure. Alabama argued that Judge Jones' order was necessary to assist it in determining whether the association was lawfully doing business in the state. The Court's reply to this argument was that it was "unable to perceive that the disclosure of the names of the petitioner's rank-and-file members has a substantial bearing" on the queston at hand, and therefore "whatever interest the State may have in obtaining names of ordinary members had not been shown to be sufficient to overcome petitioner's constitutional objections to the production order."

In support of the court's order, Alabama cited the decision in the *Bryant* case, where the Court had upheld a New York law under which the Ku Klux Klan was required to disclose its membership. The Court's response was that the Klan was an entirely different kind of organization.

The decision [in *Bryant*] was based on the particular character of the Klan's activities, involving acts of unlawful intimidation and violence, which the Court assumed was before the state legislature when it enacted the statute, and of which the Court itself took judicial notice.

Since 1909, the NAACP has been striving to eliminate "all racial barriers which deprive Negro citizens of the privileges and burdens of equal citizenship rights in the United States."[5] In furtherance of these goals, the association has provided legal assistance to persons involved in litigation the outcome of which could enhance civil rights for blacks.

The Virginia Conference of the NAACP provided such assistance through a staff of attorneys and by paying the costs of litigation.

Typically, a local NAACP branch will invite a member of the legal staff to explain to a meeting of parents and children the legal steps necessary to achieve desegregation. The staff member will bring printed forms to the meeting authorizing him . . . to represent the signers in legal proceedings to achieve desegregation. . . . It is usual, after obtaining authorizations, for the staff lawyer to bring into the case the other staff members in the area where suit is to be brought and sometimes to bring in lawyers from the national organization. . . . In effect, then the prospective litigant retains not so much a particular attorney as the "firm" of NAACP lawyers.

In 1956, the Virginia Assembly amended the state laws dealing with attorney malpractice "to broaden the definition of solicitation of legal business to include acceptance of employment . . . from any person . . . not a party to a judicial proceeding and having no pecuniary right or liability in it. It also made it an offense for any such person or organization to solicit business for any attorney." Shortly after these changes were made, the NAACP sued the state attorney general to enjoin enforcement of the laws, contending that they were unconstitutional under the First Amendment.

The trial court upheld the prohibitions and concluded that they were applicable to NAACP activities. The Virginia Supreme Court of Appeals agreed, but a majority of the U.S. Supreme Court reversed the Virginia courts' decisions.

The NAACP's argument for reversal was that "the [change in the law] infringes the right of the NAACP and its members and lawyers to associate for the purpose of assisting persons who seek legal redress for infringement of their constitutionally guaranteed and other rights."

Justice Brennan, for the majority, agreed: "We hold that the activities of the NAACP, its affiliates and legal staff shown on this record are modes of expression and association protected by the First and Fourteenth Amendments which Virginia may not prohibit, under its power to regulate the legal profession. . . ."

The justices who dissented in this case did not deny the existence of a constitutional right freely to associate with others for lawful purposes. Justice Harlan, writing for himself and justices Clark and Stewart, declared:

> Freedom of expression embraces more than the right of an individual to speak his mind. It includes also his right to advocate and his right to join with his fellows in an effort to make that advocacy effective. . . . And just as it includes the right jointly to petition the legislature for redress of grievances, . . . so it must include the right to join together for the purposes of obtaining judicial redress.

But because First Amendment rights are not absolute, the dissenters found it necessary "to weigh the legitimate interest of the State against the effect of the regulation on individual rights," and because litigation is conduct that is associated with the right to speak and associate together, "the area of legitimate governmental interest expands."

> Although the State surely may not broadly prohibit individuals with a common interest from joining together to petition a court for redress of their grievances, it is equally certain that the State may impose reasonable regulations limiting the permissible form of litigation and the manner of legal representation within its borders. Thus the State, may without violating protected rights, restrict those undertaking to represent others in legal proceedings to properly qualified practitioners.

The dissenters then concluded that because of the state's interest in "maintaining high professional standards among those who practice law within its borders," the laws were justifiable and could be applied against the NAACP.

Relying upon the *Button* case, a majority of the justices upheld a plan whereby the Brotherhood of Railroad Trainmen recommended to its "members and their families the names of lawyers whom the Brotherhood believe to be honest and competent."[6]

> When a worker was injured or killed, the secretary of his local lodge would go to him or to his widow or children and recommend that the

claim not to be settled without first seeing a lawyer, and that in the Brotherhood's judgment the best lawyer to consult was the counsel selected by it for that area.

The Court also upheld a practice of the United Mine Workers of America whereby the union "employed a licensed attorney on a salary basis to represent any of its members who wished his services to prosecute workmen's compensation claims before the Illinois Industrial Commission."[7]

The majority summed up their position in these cases by stating that "the First Amendment would, however, be a hollow promise if it left government free to destroy or erode its guarantees by indirect restraints so long as no law is passed that prohibits free speech, press, petition or assembly as such."

Association with Unpopular Causes Is Protected

*"The Court has consistently disapproved governmental action imposing criminal sanctions or denying rights . . . solely because of a citizen's association with an unpopular organization."**

While the above statement represents the present position of the Court, it was not always that way. Following World War II, many federal and state laws were enacted that either criminalized or placed severe penalties upon membership in the Communist party and other so-called subversive organizations.

Lists of organizations considered subversive were made, and public employees were subject to discharge for membership in listed organizations. Loyalty oaths were required of civil servants, and aliens who were members of the Communist party could be deported. Further, a member of such an organization could not apply for or use a U.S. passport, and it was a federal crime to be a member of any organization that advocated the overthrow of the government by force or violence.

The judicial response to the question of the constitutionality of these laws during the 1950s and 60s was to uphold them. With regard to public employment and associational membership, Justice Sherman Minton summed up the Court's position by pointing out that there is no right to work for the government on one's own terms. "If they do not choose to work [on the government's] terms," he declared, "they

Healy v. James, 408 U.S. 169, 185–186 (1972).

are at liberty to retain their beliefs and associations and go elsewhere. Has the State thus deprived them of any right to free speech or assembly? We think not."[8]

Regarding whether membership in a "subversive" organization could be made a federal crime, a majority of the justices held that it could in the case of *Scales v. United States.*[9] Scales, a member of the Communist party, was convicted of being a member "with knowledge of the Party's illegal purpose and [having] a specific intent to accomplish overthrow of the Government 'as speedily as circumstances would permit.'"

In answer to Scale's argument that his membership in the party was protected by the First Amendment, the majority pointed out that in the *Dennis* case (discussed in Chapter VI) the Court had upheld the conviction of members of the Communist party for knowingly and intentionally advocating the overthrow of the government. "We can discern no reason why membership, when it constitutes a purposeful form of complicity in a group engaging in this same forbidden advocacy, should receive any greater degree of protection from the guarantees of that Amendment." The majority did emphasize, however, that "the member for whom the organization is a vehicle for the advancement of legitimate aims and policies does not fall within the ban of the statute; he lacks the requisite specific intent 'to bring about the overthrow of the government as speedily as circumstances would permit.' Such a person may be foolish, deluded, or perhaps merely optimistic, but he is not by this statute made a criminal."

Four justices dissented from the *Scales* decision and wrote three strongly worded dissenting opinions. What disturbed Justice Douglas was that the Court was legalizing "guilt by association, sending a man to prison when he committed no unlawful act." He recognized that a fear that the government could be overthrown by alleged subversive activities prevailed throughout the land but expressed the hope that "what we lose by majority vote today may be reclaimed at a future time when the fear of advocacy, dissent, and non-conformity no longer cast a shadow over us."

That a person could not be punished "solely [for] association with an unpopular organization" was finally approved by a majority of the justices in *United States v. Robel.*[10] Eugene Frank Robel, a Communist party member, worked in a shipyard, which was a defense facility. A federal law made it a crime for a communist to work in a such a facility as long as the party had not registered with the government.

When Robel was indicted for violating this law, Chief Judge William J. Lindberg of the federal district court dismissed the indictment, concluding that it was faulty because it did not allege that defendant Robel was an active member of the party and had a "specific intent" to carry out its illegal aims. The government appealed to the Supreme Court, arguing that such an allegation was not necessary because the law specifically made it a criminal offense for *any* member of the party, active or not, to work in a defense facility.

A majority of the justices disagreed. Chief Justice Warren, for the majority, first noted that "the operative fact" of the crime was "the exercise of an individual's right of association, which is protected by the provisions of the First Amendment." In other words, Robel, by exercising his right of association and joining the Communist party, had committed a crime by working at the shipyard. The government attempted to justify this result by asserting that (1) Congress, acting under its "war power," had a right to enact the law, and (2) the law was necessary in the interest of national defense. In response, the majority said that "the war power does not remove constitutional limitations safeguarding essential liberties," and that the "concept of 'national defense' cannot be deemed an end in itself, justifying any exercise of legislative power designed to promote such a goal."

> For almost two centuries, our country has taken singular pride in the democratic ideals enshrined in its Constitution, and the most cherished of those ideals have found expression in the First Amendment. It would indeed be ironic if, in the name of national defense, we would sanction the subversion of one of those liberties—the freedom of association—which makes the defense of the Nation worthwhile.

But, the government argued, the purpose of the law is "to reduce the threat of sabotage and espionage in the Nation's defense plants." While acknowledging that this was indeed a very substantial interest, Chief Justice Warren was concerned that the "statute quite literally established guilt by association alone, without any need to establish that an individual's association poses the threat feared by the Government in proscribing it."

> Our decision today simply recognizes that, when legitimate legislative concerns are expressed in a statute which imposes a substantial burden on protected First Amendment activities, Congress must achieve its goal by means which have a 'less drastic' impact on the continued vitality of First Amendment freedoms.

Justices White and Harlan were disturbed that the majority was giving too much weight to the right of association (which they agreed existed) and not enough to the potential danger to the country. They pointed out that the "right of association is not mentioned in the Constitution, [and] it has only recently blossomed as the controlling factor in constitutional litigation; its contours as yet lack delineation." Because of this, the dissenters argued, the majority should not substitute its judgment regarding "threats to the security of the country" for that of Congress and the executive branch.

The constitutional prohibition against guilt by association was applied by the Court in a case involving a boycott of white merchants in Claiborne County, Mississippi, during a seven-year period from 1966 through 1972. The Court describes the case as begining in 1966 when "black citizens of ... Claiborne County presented white elected officials with a list of particularized demands for racial equality and integration."[11]

> The petition included 19 specific demands. It called for the desegregation of all public schools and public facilities, the hiring of black policemen, public improvements in black residential areas, selection of blacks for jury duty, integration of bus stations so that blacks could use all facilities, and an end to verbal abuse by law enforcement officers. It stated that "Negroes are not to be addressed by terms as 'boy,' 'girl,' 'shine,' 'uncle,' or any other offensive term, but as 'Mr.,' 'Mrs.,' or 'Miss,' as in the case with other citizens."

An additional demand that "all stores must employ Negro clerks and cashiers," was added later.

When the black citizens received no response to their demands, a boycott of white merchants was organized. While most of the boycott was conducted peacefully, some violence did occur when some of the blacks ignored the boycott and continued to trade with the merchants. Shots were fired into the homes of some who refused to participate, a brick was thrown through a windshield, and a flower garden was damaged.

In an action brought by white merchants seeking damages from the organizers of the boycott, the court gave judgment against the NAACP and the other defendants in an amount in excess of $1.25 million and ordered that the boycott be discontinued. The Mississippi Supreme Court affirmed the judgment but remanded the case for a recomputation of damages. The defendants appealed to the U.S.

Supreme Court, which reversed in an opinion in which seven justices joined. Justice Rehnquist concurred only in the result, and Justice Marshall did not participate.

At the outset the justices were confronted with the question of "whether petitioners' [the NAACP and other defendants] activities are protected in any respect by the Federal Constitution and, if they are, what effect such protection has on a lawsuit of this nature." In finding that the defendants' activities were protected by the First Amendment, Justice Stevens, writing for the majority, explained that "the right to associate does not lose all constitutional protection merely because some members of the group may have participated in conduct or advocated doctrine that itself is not protected." Further, in this case the participants did more than just associate together; they peacefully picketed, marched, and demonstrated, and made speeches exhorting others to join the boycott. All of these nonviolent activities, the Court said, were "entitled to the protection of the First Amendment."

The question then to be decided was how to reconcile the fact that there had been violence with the right of the defendants to exercise their constitutionally protected right to join together to protest being treated as second-class citizens. Justice Stevens stated that while "the First Amendment does not protect violence" and "the State legitimately may impose damages for the consequences of violent conduct, it may not award compensation for the consequences of nonviolent, protected activity." Further, the state may not "impose liability on an individual solely because of his association with another."

> Civil liability may not be imposed merely because an individual belonged to a group, some members of which committed acts of violence. For liability to be imposed by reason of association alone, it is necessary to establish that the group itself possessed unlawful goals and that the individual held a specific intent to further those illegal aims. "In this sensitive field, the State may not employ 'means that broadly stifle fundamental personal liberties when the end can be more narrowly achieved.'"

Therefore, to impose liability on all of the participants simply because some members thereof engaged in acts of violence would be assigning guilt by association, contrary to the commands of the First Amendment.

Compelling Disclosure of Membership

"It is hardly a novel perception that compelled disclosure of affiliation with groups engaged in advocacy may constitute ... a restraint on freedom of association...."

In *NAACP v. Alabama*, the justices unanimously found that compelled disclosure of the names and addresses of NAACP members would have caused irreparable injury to both the association and the individuals involved, thus violating freedom of association rights. When the government has sought to determine whether certain individuals are members of the Communist party, however, the Court has required disclosure, or in lieu thereof, criminal punishment.

During testimony before the House Subcommittee on Un-American Activities in 1954, Lloyd Barenblatt was identified as a member of the Communist party. At the time Barenblatt was a 31-year-old teacher of psychology whose teaching contract at Vassar College had expired and had not been renewed. When called for questioning before the subcommittee, he refused to answer the following questions:

> Are you now a member of the Communist Party?
> Have you ever been a member of the Communist Party?
> Were you ever a member of the Haldane Club of the Communist Party while at the University of Michigan?[12]

He "objected generally to the right of the Subcommittee to inquire into his 'political' and 'religious' beliefs or any 'other personal and private affairs' or 'associational activites.'" Because refusal to answer questions "pertinent" to the inquiry before the subcommittee was a criminal offense, Barenblatt was convicted for contempt of Congress fined, and sentenced to imprisonment for six months. His conviction was affirmed by the court of appeals and by a majority of the Supreme Court.

In support of the conviction, Justice Harlan, for the majority, explained that Congress "has wide power to legislate in the field of Communist activity in this country, and to conduct appropriate investigations in aid thereof...."

> Justification for [the] exercise [of its power] rests on the long and widely accepted view that the tenets of the Communist Party include the ultimate overthrow of the Government of the United

NAACP v. Alabama, 357 U.S. 449, 462 (1958).

States by force and violence, a view which has been given formal expression by the Congress.

This danger to the survival of the country was therefore sufficient to override Barenblatt's associational rights. "We conclude," wrote Justice Harlan, "that the balance between the individual and the governmental interests here at stake must be struck in favor of the latter, and therefore the provisions of the First Amendment have not been offended."

But this balancing of fundamental rights brought a strong protest from Justice Black in which Chief Justice Warren and Justice Douglas joined. "I do not agree," Justice Black declared, "that laws directly abriding First Amendment freedoms can be justified by a congressional or judicial balancing process." Additionally, the dissenters were concerned that if associational rights of the Communist party and its members could be so easily balanced away, no organization or membership was really safe.

> History should teach us then, that in times of high emotional excitement minority parties and groups which advocate extremely unpopular social or governmental innovations will always be typed as criminal gangs and attempts will always be made to drive them out.

"Today's holding," he concluded, "marks another major step in the progressively increasing retreat from the safeguards of the First Amendment."

The extent to which a majority of justices approved government inquiry into membership in the Communist party during those turbulent times, even though such inquiry admittedly infringed First Amendment rights, is illustrated in the case of *In re Anastaplo*.[13]

> [George Anastaplo's] early life had been spent in a small town in southern Illinois where his parents, who had immigrated to this country from Greece before his birth, still resided. After having received his precollege education in the public schools of his home town, he had discontinued his education, at the age of eighteen, and joined the Air Force during the middle of World War II—flying as a navigator in every major theater of the military operations of that war. Upon receiving an honorable discharge in 1947, he had come to Chicago and resumed his education, obtaining his undergraduate degree at the University of Chicago and entering immediately into the study of law at the University of Chicago Law School. His record throughout his life, both as a student and as a citizen, was unblemished.

In 1954, while an instructor and research assistant at the University of Chicago and after having successfully passed the Illinois bar examination, Anastaplo was denied admission to the bar because he refused to answer certain questions put to him by the committee on character and fitness. When asked "whether he was a member of the Communist Party or of any other group named in the Attorney General's list of 'subversive' organizations including the Ku Klux Klan and the Silver Shirts of America," he refused to answer, asserting that that information was protected by his rights of free speech and association. Although the "Committee already had before it uncontroverted evidence as to Anastaplo's 'good moral character,' in the form of written statements and affidavits,"it refused to admit him to membership in the bar because it concluded "that there is a strong public interest in our being free to question applicants for admission to the bar on their adherence to our basic institutions and form of government and that such public interest in the character of its attorneys overrides an applicant's private interest in keeping such views to himself."

The Illinois Supreme Court upheld the committee's decision, three justices, including Justice Walter V. Schaefer, dissenting. A majority of the U.S. Supreme Court affirmed, four justices dissenting. Justice Harlan's opinion for the majority points out that a state may "adopt a rule that an applicant will not be admitted to the practice of law, if, . . . by refusing to answer material questions, he obstructs a bar examining committee in its proper functions of interrogating and cross-examining him upon his qualifications." And further, "the State's interest in enforcing such a rule as applied to refusals to answer questions about membership in the Communist Party outweighs any deterrent effect upon freedom of speech and association, and hence such state action does not offend the Fourteenth Amendment."

Because Anastaplo had "followed a high moral, ethical and patriotic course in all of the activities of his life [and because] he combines these more common virtues with the uncommon virtue of courage to stand by his principles at any cost," Justice Black, Chief Justice Warren, and justices Douglas and Brennan dissented. To the dissenters, the use of the balancing process in this case was an anathema.

> The effect of the Court's "balancing" here is that any State may now reject an applicant for admission to the Bar if he believes in the Declaration of Independence as strongly as Anastaplo and if he is willing to sacrifice his career and his means of livelihood in defense of the freedoms of the First Amendment. But the men who founded this country and wrote our Bill of Rights were strangers neither to a

belief in the "right of revolution" nor to the urgency of the need to be free from the control of government with regard to political beliefs and associations.

Subsequent Court decisions have continued to approve government inquiry into Commuist party membership in spite of assertions that such inquiry violates freedom of association rights. However, questions seeking information about membership or participation in any other organization that advocates overthrow of the government by force or violence must be directed at whether the person questioned is a knowing, active member of such an organization. If the person responds that he or she is such a member, the questioning may continue without violating the First Amendment.

The country's obsession with the perceived dangers of communism during the 1950s caused the Arkansas legislature to enact a statute that compelled "every teacher, as a condition of employment in a state-supported school or college, to file annually an affidavit listing without limitation every organization to which he has belonged or regularly contributed within the preceding five years."[14] Another statute made it unlawful for any member of the NAACP to work for the state or any part thereof, or for any school district. This section of the law was motivated by a belief that the NAACP had caused racial strife and turmoil in the state.

B.T. Shelton, who had been employed as a teacher in Little Rock, refused to file the required affidavit, and therefore his contract for the next school year was not renewed. He brought an action in the federal district court seeking a declaration that the Arkansas laws deprived "teachers in Arkansas of their rights to personal, associational, and academic liberty, protected by the [First Amendment] from invasion by state action." At that time, he was a member of the NAACP but not of the Communist party. The district court struck down the law relating to NAACP members working for the state but upheld the affidavit requirement.

The Supreme Court, in a 5–4 decision written by Justice Stewart, reversed. To put the case in proper perspective, Justice Stewart described what the affidavit required:

> The statute requires a teacher to reveal the church to which he belongs, or to which he has given financial support. It requires him to disclose his political party, and every political organization to which he may have contributed over a five-year period. It requires him to list, without number, every conceivable kind of associational

tie—social, professional, political, avocational, or religious. Many such relationships could have no possible bearing upon the teacher's occupational competence or fitness.

This led the majority to conclude that "the statute's comprehensive interference with associational freedom goes far beyond what might be justified in the exercise of the State's legitimate inquiry into the fitness and competency of its teachers."

However, it was the state's need for competent teachers that caused four justices to dissent. For Justice Frankfurter the disclosure requirement was permissible because "presumably, a teacher may have so many divers associations, so many divers commitments, that they consume his time and energy and interest at the expense of his work of even of his professional dedication." For the other dissenters, the question was simply one of balancing the state's need for the information against the associational rights of teachers. Starting from the position that free speech and association "are not absolute," it was an easy step to conclude that the state had an overriding interest in knowing which organizations its teachers belonged to. "Since I believe," Justice Harlan declared, "that such a requirement cannot be said to transgress the constitutional limits of a State's conceded authority to determine the qualifications of those serving it as teachers, I am bound to consider that Arkansas had the right to pass the statute in question, and therefore conceive it my duty to dissent."

The Federal Election Campaign Act, discussed in Chapter VI, imposing limitations upon campaign contributions and expenditures, also required political committees to keep records of the contributions received and expenditures made. These records were to include the name and address of the person making a contribution in excess of $10, and if the contribution amounted to more than $100, the occupation and principal place of business of the contributor was required.

In an action brought by Senator Buckley and others, the constitutionality of the act's disclosure requirements was questioned. In upholding these requirements, the Court acknowledged that it had "repeatedly found that compelled disclosure, in itself, can seriously infringe on privacy of association and belief guaranteed by the First Amendment" and "that significant encroachments on First Amendment rights of the sort that compelled disclosure imposes cannot be justified by a mere showing of some legitimate governmental interest."[15] "But," the Court held, "we have acknowledged that there are governmental interests sufficiently important to outweigh the possibilty of infringement, particularly when the 'free functioning of our national institutions' is involved."

The governmental interests to be served by disclosure here were (1) assisting in evaluating candidates by knowing where their contributions came from, (2) preventing corruption by exposing contributions and expenditures, and (3) providing data that may show a violation of contribution limitations. Senator Buckley's concern was the application of the disclosure requirements not to major political parties but to minor parties "because the governmental interest in this information is minimal and the danger of significant infringement on First Amendment rights is greatly increased." But the Court pointed out that "a minor party sometimes can play a significant role in an election. Even when a minor-party candidate has little or no chance of winning, he may be encouraged by major-party interests in order to divert votes from other major-party contenders."

Chief Justice Burger took issue with the decision of the majority to uphold the record keeping as it applied to minor parties. He could find no legitimate interest for such disclosure and found the situation here much different from those in the cases requiring disclosure of membership in subversive organizations. "To hold, as the Court has," he wrote, "that privacy must sometimes yield to congressional investigations of alleged subversion is quite different from making domestic political partisans give up privacy.... In any event, the dangers to First Amendment rights here are too great."

A majority of the justices found the "dangers to First Amendment rights ... too great" when Ohio attempted to apply the disclosure provisions of its Campaign Expense Reporting Law to the Socialist Workers Party (SWP). The majority did not retreat from the *Buckley* decision but simply recognized that a threat to First Amendment rights existed when minor parties were required to disclose the source of contributions and recipients of expenditures. This was particularly true with regard to the Socialist Workers Party, which had been subjected to harassment from both government and private sources.

> These incidents, many of which occurred in Ohio and neighboring States, included threatening phone calls and hate mail, the burning of SWP literature, the destruction of SWP members' property, police harassment of a party candidate, and the firing of shots at an SWP office.[16]

Under such circumstances, the majority declared, "the First Amendment prohibits a State from compelling disclosures by a minor party that will subject those persons identified to the reasonable probability of threats, harassment, or reprisals."

Patronage Is a Restraint on Association

"The cost of the practice of patronage is the restraint it places on freedoms of belief and association."*

> In December 1970, the Sheriff of Cook County [Illinois], a Republican, was replaced by Richard Elrod, a Democrat. At that time, [John Burns, Frank Vargas, Fred L. Buckley, and Joseph Dennard], all Republicans, were employees of the Cook County Sheriff's Office.
>
> . . .
>
> It has been the practice of the Sheriff of Cook County, when he assumes office from a Sheriff of a different political party, to replace non-civil-service employees . . . with members of his own party when the existing employees lack or fail to obtain requisite support from, or fail to affiliate with, that party. Consequently, subsequent to Sheriff Elrod's assumption of office, [Burns, Vargas, and Dennard] were discharged . . . solely because they did not support and were not members of the Democratic Party and had failed to obtain the sponsorship of one of its leaders.[17]

Following their discharge, Burns, Vargas, and Dennard brought suit in the federal district court against Sheriff Elrod and others. They were joined by Buckley, who believed that his discharge was imminent. District Judge William J. Bauer dismissed the action, holding that the complaint failed to state a lawful claim upon which relief could be granted. The court of appeals reversed, concluding that the plaintiffs' complaint did state a legally cognizable claim. In a decision that split the justices into three factions, the Supreme Court affirmed. Three justices (the plurality) met the First Amendment question head-on and held that because "the patronage dismissals severely restrict political belief and association, . . . government may not, without seriously inhibiting First Amendment rights, force a public employee to relinquish his right to political association as the price of holding a public job." While two justices concurred in the result, they did not reach the question of the constitutionality of the patronage system but simply held

**Elrod v. Burns*, 427 U.S. 347, 355 (1976).

"that a nonpolicymaking, nonconfidential government employee may not be discharged from a job he is satisfactorily performing, upon the sole ground of his political beliefs. . . ."

At the outset, the plurality conceded that the patronage system was deeply ingrained in our politial structure.

> Patronage practice is not new to American politics. It has existed at the federal level at least since the Presidency of Thomas Jefferson, although its popularization and legitimation primarily occurred later, in the Presidency of Andrew Jackson.

Simply because a practice or procedure has a long history, however, does not necessarily mean that it is constitutional. Segregated schools, for example, were a fact of life for blacks in many parts of the United States until the Supreme Court held that such schools violated the Equal Protection Clause of the Fourteenth Amendent and the Due Process Clause of the Fifth Amendment.

Noting that the Court had previously held that "the government 'may not deny a benefit to a person on a basis that infringes his constitutionally protected interests—especially, his interest in freedom of speech,'" the plurality declared that "patronage practice falls squarely within" that rule. "For if the government could deny a benefit to a person, because of his constitutionally protected speech or associations, his exercise of those freedoms would in effect be penalized and inhibited."

But of course the right of association is not absolute, and recognition that patronage is an infringement on that right simply raises the question of whether there is a governmental interest that outweighs the right. The state asserted three interests served by patronage and sufficient to override the infringement upon freedom of association. First, employees of different political persuasions do not work effectively together; second, effective representative government requires politically loyal employees; and third, the patronage system preserves the democratic process and makes it work.

Justice Brennan, for the plurality, responded that while these were all valid interests, they could be achieved by means less drastic than discharging an employee with different political beliefs. A merit system, for example, would be "less intrusive than patronage" and still achieve "effective and efficient government." Further "limiting patronage dismissals to policymaking positions is sufficient to achieve" political loyalty from employees. And finally, the plurality was not convinced that the elimination of patronage dismissals "will bring about the demise of party politics."

Patronage dismissals thus are not the least restrictive alternative to achieving the contribution they make to the democratic process. The process functions as well without the practice, perhaps even better, for patronage dismissals clearly also retard that process.

"In summary," the opinion states, "patronage dismissals severely restrict political belief and association. Though there is a vital need for government efficiency and effectiveness, such dismissals are on balance not the least restrictive means for fostering that end."

The decision to strike down the patronage system that had prevailed in the country for such a long time was troublesome for Chief Justice Burger and justices Powell and Rehnquist, who dissented. "The Court strains the rational bounds of First Amendment doctrine," the Chief Justice argued, "and runs counter to longstanding practices that are part of the fabric of our democratic system to hold that the Constitution *commands* something it has not been thought to require for 185 years."

Justice Powell agreed: "The Court holds unconstitutional a practice as old as the Republic, a practice which has contributed significantly to the democratization of American politics." Justice Powell did not dispute the holding of the plurality that First Amendment interests were involved in patronage dismissals but concluded that "patronage hiring practices sufficiently serve important state interests, including some interests sought to be advanced by the First Amendment, to justify a tolerable intrusion on the First Amendment interests of employees or potential employees."

Although their was no majority opinion in the *Elrod* case, the position of the plurality that "the practice of patronage is [a] restraint . . . on freedoms of belief and association," has been affirmed by a majority of the justices in two subsequent cases. In *Branti v. Finkel*,[18] decided in 1980, a majority held that "it is manifest that continued employment of an assistant public defender cannot properly be conditioned upon his allegiance to the political party in control of the county government."

In June 1990, even though the makeup of the Court had substantially changed since 1980, a majority again approved both *Elrod* and *Branti* in *Rutan v. Republican Party of Illinois*.[19] Justice Brennan, who delivered the *Rutan* opinion, wrote: "To the victor belong only those spoils that may be constitutionally obtained." And further: "The rule of *Elrod* and *Branti* extends to promotion, transfer, recall, and hiring decisions based on party affiliation and support. . . ."

Election Laws May Impinge on Association

"Unduly restrictive state election laws may so impinge upon freedom of association as to run afoul of the First and Fourteenth Amendments."*

State election laws may clash with associational rights in several different ways. A candidate may have difficulty getting on the ballot, a voter's attempt to associate with the party of his or her choice may be restricted, and a political party's rules may conflict with state regulations.

On April 24, 1980, John Anderson declared himself a candidate for president of the United States. Although his supporters were able to gather enough signatures to meet the general filing requirements in all fifty states, the Ohio March 20 filing deadline had passed. Ohio Secretary of State Anthony J. Celebrezze therefore rejected Anderson's nominating petition. Anderson and three of his supporters, claiming that the Ohio laws violated their constitutional rights, filed an action in federal district court seeking an order placing Anderson's name on the general election ballot.[20] District Judge Robert M. Duncan granted the request and ordered Celebrezze to place Anderson's name on the ballot. Judge Duncan held that "the statutory deadline was unconstitutional on two grounds. It imposed an impermissible burden on the First Amendment rights of Anderson and his Ohio supporters and . . . violated the Equal Protection Clause of the Fourteenth Amendment . . ." because independent candidates were treated differently than nominees of a political party. The court of appeals saw the issue differently and reversed, holding that "the early deadline served the State's interest in voter education by giving voters a longer opportunity to see how Presidential candidates withstand the close scrutiny of a political campaign." A majority of the Supreme Court agreed with Judge Duncan and reversed the court of appeals. So that there would be no doubt that election laws like Ohio's had an effect upon freedom of association, Justice Stevens, writing for the majority, specifically noted that their decision was based "directly on the First and Fourteenth Amendments and [that they would] not engage in a separate Equal Protection Clause analysis."

Not all laws regulating elections violate constitutional rights. Quoting from a prior case, Justice Stevens explained that the Court had "recognized that, 'as a practical matter, there must be a substantial

*Kusper v. Pontikes, 414 U.S. 51, 57 (1973).

regulation of elections if they are to be fair and honest and if some sort of order, rather than chaos, is to accompany the democratic processes.'" Turning then to the effect of Ohio's filing deadline, the majority pointed out that it prevented "indepdenent candidates from entering the . . . political arena . . . any time after mid to late March," while "campaigns for the major-party nominations have only begun, and the major parties will not adopt their nominees and platforms for another five months."

> Not only does the challenged Ohio statute totally exclude any can-
> didate who makes the decision to run for President as an indepen-
> dent after the March deadline, it also burdens the signature-
> gathering efforts of independents who decide to run in time to meet
> the deadline. When the primary campaigns are far in the future and
> the election itself is even more remote, the obstacles facing an in-
> dependent candidate's organizing efforts are compounded. Volun-
> teers are more difficult to recruit and retain, media publicity and
> campaign contributions are more difficult to secure, and voters are
> less interested in the campaign.

The state's interest, however, must be considered, and these were identified as three: "voter education, equal treatment for partisan and independent candidates, and political stability." Justice Stevens discussed each of these interests and found them all insufficient to outweigh associational rights. With regard to the need for more time for education of voters, he acknowledged that interest as "one of the concerns that motivated the Framers' decision not to provide for direct popular election of the President." But times have changed substantially since then, and "a State's claim that it is enhancing the ability of its citizenry to make wise decisions by restricting the flow of information to them must be viewed with some skepticism."

Neither was there merit in the state's claim, Justice Stevens declared, "that the early filing deadline serves the interest of treating all candidates alike." The nominees of the two national parties would ap-pear on the Ohio general election ballot "even if they did not decide to run until after Ohio's March deadline had passed, but the independent is simply denied a position on the ballot if he waits too long."

The majority also saw "Ohio's asserted interest in political stability [as] a desire to protect existing political parties from competition— competition for campaign workers, voter support, and other campaign resources—generated by independent candidates who have previously been affiliated with the party." This analysis led the majority to conclude that "the Ohio filing deadline not only burdens the associational rights of independent voters and candidates, it also places a significant state-imposed restriction on a nationwide electoral process."

Four justices dissented in an opinion written by Justice Rehnquist. Conceding that Anderson and his supporters were harmed by the Ohio law because "Anderson would have been excluded from Ohio's 1980 general election ballot," Justice Rehnquist pointed out that "the Constitution does not require that a State allow any particular Presidential candidate to be on its ballot, and so long as the Ohio ballot access laws are rational and allow nonparty candidates reasonable access to the general election ballot, this Court should not interfere with Ohio's exercise" of its power to appoint presidential electors under Article II, Section 1, Clause 2, of the Constitution.

How state election laws implicate associational rights of individuals is illustrated by the attempt of Harriet G. Pontikes to vote in the Illinois Democratic primary in 1972. Pontikes had voted in the Republican primary in February 1971 and therefore under Illinois law was prohibited from voting in a primary election of another political party for a period of twenty-three months from that date.[21]

> [Pontikes] filed a complaint for declaratory and injunctive relief in the United States District Court for the Northern District of Illinois, alleging that [the Illinois law] unconstitutionally abridged her freedom to associate with the political party of her choice by depriving her of the opportunity to vote in the Democratic primary. A statutory three-judge court was convened, and held, one judge dissenting, that the 23-month rule is unconstitutional.

The State, represented by the Chicago Board of Election Commissioners, appealed to the Supreme Court, which affirmed. As a starting point, a majority asserted that "the right to associate with the political party of one's choice is an integral part of [the] basic constitutional freedom" protected by the First Amendment. The Illinois law did not prevent Pontikes from associating with the Democratic party; however it did prevent her from participating in the selecting of Democratic candidates for a period of twenty-three months.

> Under our political system, a basic function of a political party is to select the candidates for public office to be offered to the voters at general elections. A prime objective of most voters in associating themselves with a particular party must surely be to gain a voice in that selection process.

In support of the law, the state argued that "the 23-month rule serves the purpose of preventing 'raiding'—the practice whereby voters in sympathy with one party vote in another's primary in order to distort the primary's results." Further, the state was able to cite another of the Court's decisions holding that curtailing raiding was a legitimate state interest and upholding a New York law that "required a voter to enroll in the party of his choice at least 30 days before a general election in order to be eligible to vote in the next party primary." As far as New York voters were concerned, this created almost an eleven-month waiting period from the time a voter chose a party until that party's primary.

The majority, however, did not think that the two laws (Illinois' and New York's) created the same problem. Under New York law, "a person who wanted to vote in a different party primary every year . . . had only to meet the requirement of declaring his party allegiance 30 days before the preceding general election." But "the Illinois law," Justice Stewart explained, "unlike that of New York, . . . 'locks' voters into a pre-existing party affiliation from one primary to the next, and the only way to break the 'lock' is to forgo voting in *any* primary for a period of almost two years."

Justice Blackmun did not think that Pontikes suffered a great infringement on her rights by the law's waiting period. "Apart from this meager restraint," he wrote, ". . . Pontikes is fully free to associate with the party of her varying choice. She is, and has been, completely free to vote as she chooses in any general election. And she was free to vote in the primary of the party with which she had affiliated and voted in the preceding primary."

Generally speaking, political parties have their own rules specifying who can participate as delegates in their national conventions and how those delegates are chosen.

> The [Democratic] National Party's Delegate Selection Rules provide that only those who are willing to affiliate publicly with the Democratic Party may participate in the process of selecting delegates to the Party's National Convention.[22]

The party's rules came in conflict with the laws of Wisconsin when delegates to the 1980 national convention were to be chosen. Wisconsin had an "open" primary, one in which a person may vote in either party's primary without regard to or disclosure of party preference.

The voters in Wisconsin's "open" primary express their choice among Presidential candidates for the Democratic Party's nomination; they do not vote for delegates to the National Convention. Delegates to the National Convention are chosen separately, after the primary, at caucuses of persons who have stated their affiliation with the Party. But these delegates, under Wisconsin law, are bound to vote at the National Convention in accord with the results of the open primary election.

When the Democratic party indicated that it would not recognize delegates chosen in accordance with Wisconsin law, the state brought suit against the party in the Wisconsin Supreme Court seeking a judgment that its laws were constitutional and that therefore the party must seat its delegates. The court upheld the state's requirements and concluded that the party could not bar Wisconsin delegates from participation in the convention. On appeal to the U.S. Supreme Court, that decision was reversed in a decision supported by six justices.

Justice Stewart, who wrote the majority opinion, framed the question as follows:

> The question on this appeal is whether Wisconsin may successfully insist that its delegates to the Convention be seated, even though those delegates are chosen through a process that includes a binding state preference primary election in which voters do not declare their party affiliation.

Recognizing that the party and its members had "a constitutionally protected right of political association," Stewart stated that that "necessarily presupposes the freedom to identify the people who constitute the association, and to limit the association to those people only."

In response to the state's argument that its laws infringe only minimally upon associational rights, the majority noted that "even if the State were correct, a State, or a court, may not constitutionally substitute its own judgment for that of the Party."

> A political party's choice among the various ways of determining the makeup of a State's delegation to the party's national convention is protected by the Constitution. And as is true of all expression of First Amendment freedoms, the courts may not interfere on the ground that they view a particular expression as unwise or irrational.

Justice Powell, joined by Blackmun and Rehnquist, would have upheld the Wisconsin procedure. "Because I believe," wrote Powell, "that this law does not impose a substantial burden on the associational freedom of the National Party, and actually promotes the free political activity of the citizens of Wisconsin, I dissent."

The goal of the Democratic Party's rules was to give assurance that only those persons willing to associate openly with the party were allowed a voice in selection of the party's candidates for president and vice president. The Republican Party of Connecticut took the opposite approach and amended its rules so that not only party members but independent voters could vote for its candidates in the party's primary election.[23] It appears that the party was "motivated in part by the demographic importance of independent voters in Connecticut politics...." Nevertheless, this rule change was in direct conflict with a Connecticut law that only registered members of a party could vote in the party's primary. When the Republican Party challenged the validity of the law, the federal district court, the court of appeals, and a majority of the Supreme Court all agreed that the law violated the First Amendment:

> The statute here places limits upon the group of registered voters whom the Party may invite to participate in the "basic function" of selecting the Party's candidates.... The State thus limits the Party's associational opportunities at the crucial juncture at which the appeal to common principles may be translated into concerted action, and hence to political power in the community.

But "the Court's opinion," wrote Justice Scalia in dissent, "exaggerates the importance of the associational interest at issue, if indeed it does not see one where none exists." "The Connecticut voter who, while steadfastly refusing to register as a Republican, casts a vote in the Republican primary, forms no more meaningful an 'association' with the Party than does the independent or the registered Democrat who responds to questions by a Republican Party pollster."

Private Associations Must Give Way

"The Court has held that the Constitution protects against unjustified government interference with an individual's choice to enter into and maintain certain intimate or private relationships."*

Among the "intimate relationships to which [the Court has] accorded constitutional protection [are] marriage, ... the begetting and

---

**Bd. of Dirs. of Rotary Int'l. v. Rotary Club*, 481 U.S. 537, 544 (1987).

bearing of children, . . . child rearing and education, . . . and cohabita-
tion with relatives. . . ." As discued above, the Court has also "upheld
the freedom of individuals to associate for the purpose of engaging in
protected speech or religious activities."[24]

When called upon to apply these two constitutional principles to
civic organizations that excluded women from membership, all the
justices concluded that the associational freedom of such organizations
must give way to the broader goal of eliminating discrimination against
women. Such was the decision of the Court in cases involving the
Jaycees[25] and Rotary International.

These cases contain some similarities. Local chapters of the Jaycees
in Minnesota and the Rotary in California had begun to admit women
as members, and that practice had been challenged by their respective
national organizations. Further, both states had civil rights statutes that,
in the words of the California law, "entitle all persons, regardless of sex,
to full and equal accommodations, advantages, facilities, privileges,
and services in all business establishments in the State."

When the national organizations of the Jaycees and Rotary International sought to enforce their "men only" rules, the local chapters,
and the states argued that such discrimination was prohibited by the
states' civil rights acts. And all the justices agreed, first determining that
membership in the Jaycees or the Rotary Club did not involve "the kind
of intimate or private relation that warrants constitutional protection,"
under the first principle noted above. They recognized that membership in these organizations did involve "the right of expressive association." Nevertheless, "Minnesota's [and California's] compelling interest in eradicating discrimination against its female citizens justifies
the impact that application of the Act to [the Jaycees and Rotary Club]
may have on [their] male members' freedom of expressive association."
Justice Blackmun did not participate in either of these cases.

Colleges Must Honor Associational Rights

*"At the outset we note that state colleges and universities are not
enclaves immune from the sweep of the First Amendment."**

In order to put the above statement in proper focus, it is necessary
to examine the social and political climate in the country in the late
1960s and early 70s.

Healy v. James, 408 U.S. 169, 180 (1972).

A climate of unrest prevailed on many college campuses in this country. There had been widespread civil disobedience on some campuses, accompanied by the seizure of buildings, vandalism, and arson. Some colleges had been shut down altogether, while at others files were looted and manuscripts destroyed. SDS [Students for a Democratic Society] chapters on some campuses had been a catalytic force during this period.[26]

In September 1969, Catherine J. Healy, together with some other students at Central Connecticut State College (CCSC), organized a chapter of SDS and petitioned the student affairs committee for official campus recognition, which brought with it special privileges such as use of campus facilities for meetings and use of bulletin boards and the student newspaper for announcements concerning meetings, rallies, etc.

After the students gave assurance that they would be independent from the national SDS organization, the committee, by a 6–2 vote, approved SDS's request "and recommended to the President of the College, Dr. James, that the organization be accorded official recognition."

> In approving the application, the majority indicated that its decision was premised on the belief that varying viewpoints should be represented on campus and that since the Young Americans for Freedom, the Young Democrats, the Young Republicans, and the Liberal Party all enjoyed recognized status, a group should be available with which "left wing" students might identify.

But President James rejected the committee's recommendation. He was concerned that the local chapter, in spite of its statement to the contrary, would be inclined to follow the national organization. The policies of that organizatin, he believed, were contrary to the policies of the college, which stated: "Students do not have the right to invade the privacy of others, to damage the property of others, to disrupt the regular and essential operation of the college, or to interfere with the rights of others."

Healy and the others then turned to the district court for help, seeking a declaration of their rights and an injunction against the college. District Judge T. Emmet Clarie refused to order the college to give recognition to the SDS because he "found [the group] 'likely to cause violent acts of disruption' [and that such refusal] did not violate the petitioners' [students'] associational rights."

The court of appeals affirmed, but a unanimous Supreme Court reversed. Justice Rehnquist concurred only in the result.

Justice Powell, who delivered the opinion for the Court, recognized on the one hand "the need for affirming the comprehensive authority . . . of school officials, consistent with fundamental safeguards to prescribe and control conduct in the schools," at the same time noting that "precedents of this Court leave no room for the view that, because of the acknowledged need for order, First Amendment protections should apply with less force on college campuses than in the community at large." Powell then found that nonrecognition burdened the associational rights of the SDS, and that "was demonstrated . . . when, several days after the President's decision was announced, petitioners were not allowed to hold a meeting in the campus coffee shop because they were not an approved group."

The Court sent the case back to the district court for further inquiry into the willingness of the students to abide by campus rules and regulations. The justices wanted it understood, however, that it was not retreating from its dedication to the principles of the Bill of Rights.

> Though we deplore the tendency of some to abuse the very constitutional privileges they invoke, and although the infringement of rights of others certainly should not be tolerated, we affirm this Court's dedication to the principles of the Bill of Rights upon which our vigorous and free society is founded.

Freedom of Association — 1991 and Beyond

After the Court held that it was "beyond debate that freedom to engage in association . . . was an inseparable aspect of . . . 'liberty' . . . which embraces freedom of speech," a majority of justices refused to apply that principle when dealing with membership in the Communist Party. The passage of time and changes in the political climate in the world, however, makes those cases anachronisms today. But even at the time, the cases involving Lloyd Barenblatt and George Anastaplo were contrary to the spirit of liberty from which the freedom to associate came.

Cases decided since the early 1970s indicate that a majority of justices have viewed the right of association in the same way they do "all expression of First Amendment freedoms." Recent cases like *Healy v. James, Tashjian v. Republican Party,* and *Rutan v. Republican Party* support this view. This gives hope that infringement on associational rights will be permitted by the justices *only* when asserted governmental interests are compelling and the government's actions are least restrictive of freedom of association.

IX.
FREEDOM OF THE PRESS

"The point of criticism has been 'that the mere exemption from previous restraints cannot be all that is secured by [freedom of the press]'; and that the 'liberty of the press might be rendered a mockery and a delusion, and the phrase itself a by-word, if, while every man was at liberty to publish what he pleased, the public authorities might nevertheless punish him for harmless publications.'"

Near v. Minnesota, 283 U.S. 697, 715 (1931)

Prior to 1931 when *Near* was decided, there were only a few references in the cases to freedom of the press, and those could be characterized as being made by "voices crying in the wilderness."

For example, in 1907, a majority of the justices upheld the conviction of Thomas M. Patterson for contempt of court because he published "certain articles and a cartoon, which, it was charged, reflected upon the motives and conduct of the Supreme Court of Colorado in cases still pending and were intended to embarrass the court in the impartial administration of justice."[1] In response to Patterson's argument that he was protected by freedom of the press, Justice Holmes, for the majority, declined to hold that the First Amendment applied to the states. But even assuming that it did apply, he followed the narrow view of freedom of the press by pointing out that "the main purpose of such constitutional provisions is 'to prevent all such *previous restraints* upon publications,' . . . and they do not prevent the subsequent punishment of such as may be deemed contrary to the public welfare."

This brought forth a strong dissent from the first Justice Harlan, who wrote that he could not agree with Holmes's view "if it meant that the legislature may impair or abridge the rights of a free press and of free speech whenever it thinks that the public welfare requires that to be done." In words that truly were from a voice crying in the wilderness in 1907, Harlan declared:

I go further and hold that the privileges of free speech and of a free press, belonging to every citizen of the United States, constitute essential parts of every man's liberty, and are protected against violation by that clause of the Fourteenth Amendment forbidding a State to deprive any person of his liberty without due process of law. It is, I think, impossible to conceive of liberty, as secured by the Constitution against hostile action, whether by the Nation or by the States, which does not embrace the right to enjoy free speech and the right to have a free press.

Prior Restraints Are Presumed Unconstitutional

"Any system of prior restraints of expression comes to this Court bearing a heavy presumption against its constitutional validity."*

The idea that freedom of the press prohibits "previous restraints upon publications" is attributed to Sir William Blackstone, an English jurist and writer who wrote *Blackstone's Commentaries* on the law between 1765 and 1769.

Although Blackstone's view of a free press is considerably narrower than that later adopted by the Supreme Court, the concept that prior restraints are presumed a violation of the First Amendment is firmly implanted in our constitutional law. The Court first made this clear when the state of Minnesota brought charges against J. Near, Howard A. Guilford, and others for violating a statute that made it a nuisance for persons to produce, publish, or circulate "a malicious, scandalous and defamatory newspaper, magazine or other periodical. . . .'"[2] The law further provided that "the State [may] enjoin perpetually the persons committing . . . any such nuisance from further committing . . . it."

Near and his colleagues published a newspaper in Minneapolis, the *Saturday Press.* The state alleged that during the latter part of 1927 the editions of the *Press* "were 'largely devoted to malicious, scandalous and defamatory articles' concerning Charles G. Davis [a law enforcement officer], Frank W. Brunskill [chief of police], . . . George E. Leach [mayor of Minneapolis], the Jewish Race, [and] the members of the Grand Jury of Hennepin County. . . ."

The Supreme Court's opinion in this case summarizes these articles thus:

> The articles charged in substance that a Jewish gangster was in control of gambling, bootlegging and racketeering in Minneapolis, and

**Bantam Books, Inc. v. Sullivan*, 372 U.S. 58, 70 (1963).

that law enforcing officers and agencies were not energetically performing their duties. Most of the charges were directed against the Chief of Police; he was charged with gross neglect of duty, illicit relations with gangsters, and with participation in graft. . . . The Mayor was accused of inefficiency and dereliction. One member of the grand jury was stated to be in sympathy with the gangsters.

In the district court, Near admitted that he was the owner of the *Press* and that the articles were indeed printed therein. He denied that they "were malicious, scandalous or defamatory," and "expressly invoked the protection of the due process clause of the Fourteenth," in effect arguing that the protection of liberty in that clause included the right of freedom of the press.

After a trial in the Minnesota District Court, the judge, finding that the articles were "malicious, scandalous, and defamatory," held that the *Press* constituted a public nuisance and entered judgment against the defendants. "The judgment perpetually enjoined the defendants 'from producing, editing, publishing, circulating, . . . any publication whatsoever which is a malicious, scandalous, or defamatory newspaper, . . .' and also 'from further conducting said nuisance under the name and the title of said *The Saturday Press* or any other name or title.'" The Minnesota Supreme Court affirmed.

Although the U.S. Supreme Court had not specifically held, as Justice Harlan would have in 1907, that the Due Process Clause protected freedom of the press from infringement by the states, it did so in this case. Chief Justice Hughes, delivering the opinion for a majority, declared that "it is no longer open to doubt that the liberty of the press, and of speech, is within the liberty safeguarded by the due process clause of the Fourteenth Amendment from invasion by state action."

Turning then to an analysis of what this case was all about, Hughes described the effect of the statute upon the press.

> If we cut through mere details of procedure, the operation and effect of the statute in substance is that public authorities may bring the owner or publisher of a newspaper or periodical before a judge upon a charge of conducting a business of publishing scandalous and defamatory matter — in particular that the matter consists of charges against public officers of official dereliction — and unless the owner or publisher is able and disposed to bring competent evidence to satisfy the judge that the charges are true and are published with good motives and for justifiable ends, his newspaper or periodical is suppressed and further publication is made punishable as a contempt. This is the essence of censorship.

On that basis the majority held that "the statute, so far as it authorized the proceedings in this action, [is] an infringement of the liberty of the press guaranteed by the Fourteenth Amendment."

Justice Pierce Butler dissented. The majority was giving "to freedom of the press a meaning and a scope not heretofore recognized and construes 'liberty' in the due process clause of the Fourteenth Amendment to put upon the States a federal restriction that is without precedent." He did not consider the law a prior restraint. "The restraint authorized," he asserted, "is only in respect of continuing to do what has been duly adjudged to constitute a nuisance."

In Chapter II, reference was made to the case of *New York Times Co. v. United States,*[3] where a majority of the Court held that enjoining the *New York Times* and the *Washington Post* from publishing the so-called Pentagon Papers would be a violation of freedom of the press. Although there was no majority opinion in that case, a majority of the justices agreed that "'any system of prior restraints of expression comes to this Court bearing a heavy presumption against its constitutional validity;' . . . [that the] Government 'thus carries a heavy burden of showing justification for the imposition of such a restraint,' [and that] the Government has not met that burden."

This case did not produce a majority opinion because the six justices who agreed with the decision had conflicting views on how freedom of the press should be applied to the facts here. Justices Black and Douglas took an absolutist position — that *all* prior restraints upon the press are a violation of the First Amendment. "I believe," Black stated, "that every moment's continuance of the injunctions against these newspapers amounts to a flagrant, indefensible, and continuing violation of the First Amendment." Further, he wrote, "it is unfortunate that some of my Brethren are apparently willing to hold that the publication of news may sometimes be enjoined. Such a holding would make a shambles of the First Amendment."

Justice Brennan was not quite so absolutist. He did agree, however, that there should be no restraint on the publication of the Pentagon Papers because he could not say that "disclosure of any of them will surely result in direct, immediate, and irreparable damage to our Nation or its people."

Even though they concurred in the decision, justices White and Stewart thought that "the First Amendment [under some circumstances would] permit an injunction against publishing information about government plans or operations."

But for Chief Justice Burger and justices Harlan and Blackmun this case was "conducted in unseemly haste." "We all crave speedier judicial process," the Chief Justice explained, "but when judges are pressured as in these cases the result is a parody of the judicial function."

The short period the Court had to consider this case is stressed by Justice Harlan in his dissenting opinion. The courts of appeals that heard these cases rendered their judgments on June 23, 1971, and the newspapers filed appeals in the Supreme Court the next day. The Court immediately set a hearing for June 26 at 11:00 A.M., and the briefs of the parties did not arrive until two hours before argument. Therefore, one can understand Harlan's statement that "I consider that the Court has been almost irresponsibly feverish in dealing with these cases."

Harlan summed up his concern by noting: "This frenzied train of events took place in the name of the presumption against prior restraints created by the First Amendment. Due regard for the extraordinarily important and difficult questions involved in these litigations should have led the Court to shun such a precipitate timetable."

"None of our decided cases on prior restraint," wrote Chief Justice Burger in *Nebraska Press Assn. v. Stuart*,[4] "involved restrictive orders entered to protect a defendant's right to a fair and impartial jury, but the opinions on prior restraint have a common thread relevant to this case." The facts of the case referred to by the Chief Justice are given in his opinion:

> On the evening of October 18, 1975, local police found the six members of the Henry Kellie family murdered in their home in Sutherland, Neb., a town of about 850 people. Police released the description of a suspect, Erwin Charles Simants, to the reporters who had hastened to the scene of the crime. Simants was arrested and arraigned in Lincoln County Court the following morning, ending a tense night for this small rural community.

Because this crime received widespread local and national press coverage, the county attorney together with Simants' attorney sought and obtained an order from the county court that "prohibited everyone in attendance from 'releas[ing] or authoriz[ing] the release for public dissemination in any form or manner whatsoever any testimony given or evidence adduced....'"

After a preliminary hearing, which the public was allowed to attend, Simants was ordered by the county court to stand trial in the district court. Before that trial commenced, the Nebraska Press Association was allowed to intervene. District Judge Hugh Stuart then entered his own restrictive order, which "applied only until the jury was impaneled." Being of the opinion that Judge Stuart's order violated their free press rights, the press association appealed to the Nebraska Supreme Court. That court, in balancing Simants' right to a trial by an impartial jury against freedom of the press, upheld Judge Stuart's order in a modified form. "The order as modified prohibited reporting of only three matters: (a) the existence and nature of any confessions or admissions made by the defendant to law enforcement officers, (b) any confessions or admission made to any third parties, except members of the press, and (c) other facts 'strongly implicative' of the accused."

With this order in effect, Simants was tried and convicted. In the meantime, the press association appealed to the U.S. Supreme Court, which unanimously concluded that Judge Stuart's order was unconstitutional. The majority opinion by Chief Justice Burger starts by noting that

> the problems presented by this case are almost as old as the Republic. Neither in the Constitution nor in contemporaneous writings do we find that the conflict between these two important rights [fair trial and freedom of the press] was anticipated, yet it is inconceivable that the authors of the Constitution were unaware of the potential conflicts between the right to an unbiased jury and the guarantee of freedom of the press.

Pointing out that the Sixth Amendment guarantees "trial by an impartial jury," the Chief Justice also noted that "in the overwhelming majority of criminal trials, pretrial publicity presents few unmanageable threats to this important right. But when the case is a 'sensational' one, tensions develop between the right of the accused to a trial by an impartial jury and the rights guaranteed others by the First Amendment."

The Court then had to find some balance between the two rights to accommodate both. The majority recognized that making "prior restraints" presumptively unconstitutional created a substantial barrier to the validity of "gag orders" like the one under consideration. Further, even though the accused's rights are substantial, there are alternatives a trial judge may adopt that will protect those rights. Burger listed these alternatives: "a change of trial venue to a place less exposed to intense publicity that seemed imminent in Lincoln county; (b) postponement of the trial to allow public attention to subside; (c) searching questioning of prospective jurors; . . . [and] (d) the use of emphatic and clear instructions on the sworn duty of each juror to decide the issues only on evidence presented in open court. Sequestration of jurors is, of course, always available."

After examining the record to see if these alternatives or some of them would have been effective, the Court concluded that "there was no finding [by the Nebraska Supreme Court] that alternative measures would not have protected Simants' rights. . . ."

This brought the Chief Justice to the majority's disposition of the case.

> Our analysis ends as it began, with a confrontation between prior restraint imposed to protect one vital constitutional guarantee and the explicit command of another that the freedom to speak and publish shall not be abridged. . . . We hold that, with respect to the order entered in this case prohibiting reporting or commentary on judicial proceedings held in public, the barriers have not been overcome; to the extent that this order restrained publication of such material, it is clearly invalid.

Concurring only in the judgment of the Court, Justice Brennan wrote for himself and Justices Stewart and Marshall: "I would hold . . . that resort to prior restraints on freedom of the press is a constitutionally impermissible method of enforcing [the right to a fair trial]; judges have at their disposal a broad spectrum of devices for ensuring that fundamental fairness is accorded the accused. . . ."

As the above cases indicate, the burden of justifying a prior restraint is almost insurmountable.

However, in the area of obscenity, the Court has approved laws requiring prior submission of films to a censor, provided there is a prompt hearing on the issue. The censor, however, has the burden of proving that the film is obscene, and if the film is not licensed, the censor must apply to a court for an order that the film is obscene and should not be shown.[5] As more fully discussed hereafter, obscenity is *not* entitled to First Amendment protection; however, the procedural requirements set forth above are necessary so that films that are not obscene can be shown.

The Press and Defamatory Material

"This Court has struggled for nearly a decade to define the proper accommodation between the law of defamation and the freedoms of speech and press protected by the First Amendment."

The struggle started when L.B. Sullivan's case against the *New York Times* came to the Court in 1974.[6] Sullivan, commissioner of public affairs for the city of Montgomery, Alabama, brought an action for civil libel against the *New York Times* and Ralph D. Abernathy, Fred L. Shuttlesworth, S.S. Seay, Sr., and J.E. Lowery. He claimed that he was libeled by an ad that the individuals named above had placed in the *Times* on March 29, 1960. The Court's opinion in the *Times* case describes the ad as follows:

> Entitled "Heed Their Rising Voices," the advertisement began by stating that "As the whole world knows by now, thousands of Southern Negro students are engaged in widespread non-violent demonstrations in positive affirmation of the right to live in human dignity as guaranteed by the U.S. Constitution and the Bill of Rights." It went on to charge that "in their efforts to uphold these guarantees, they are being met by an unprecedented wave of terror by those who would deny and negate that document which the whole world looks upon as setting the pattern for modern freedom...."

Although Sullivan was not personally named in the ad, he contended that references therein to the "police" and that Dr. Martin Luther King, Jr., had been "arrested ... seven times" indirectly referred to him because he was the police commissioner. The two paragraphs in question read as follows:

Third paragraph:
"In Montgomery, Alabama, after the students sang 'My Country, 'Tis of Thee' on the State Capitol steps, their leaders were expelled from school, and truckloads of police armed with shotguns and teargas ringed the Alabama State College Campus. When the entire student body protested to state authorities by refusing to re-register, their dining hall was padlocked in an attempt to starve them into submission."
Sixth paragraph:
"Again and again the Southern violators have answered Dr. King's peaceful protests with intimidation and violence. They have bombed

Gertz v. Robert Welch, Inc., 418 U.S. 323, 325 (1974).

his home almost killing his wife and child. They have assaulted his person. They have arrested him seven times — for 'speeding,' 'loitering' and similar 'offenses.' And now they have charged him with 'perjury' — a *felony* under which they could imprison him for *ten years....*"

Sullivan sued for libel, claiming that some of the statements made in the ad were not accurate. At the trial he did not prove that he had been injured in any way, but the jury awarded him damages in the amount of $500,000. The trial judge "rejected [the] contention that his rulings [during the trial] abridged the freedoms of speech and of the press that are guaranteed by the First and Fourteenth Amendments." The Alabama Supreme Court agreed and upheld the jury's decision. All justices of the U.S. Supreme Court, however, held that the decision violated the First Amendment.

The Court's opinion, written by Justice Brennan and joined by five other justices, held that "the rule of law applied by the Alabama courts is constitutionally deficient for failure to provide the safeguards for freedom of speech and of the press that are required by the First and Fourteenth Amendments in a libel action brought by a public official against critics of his official conduct."

What concerned these justices was that "a rule compelling the critic of official conduct to guarantee the truth of all his factual assertions — and to do so on pain of libel judgments virtually unlimited in amount — leads to ... 'self-censorship.'" "The constitutional guarantees," Justice Brennan wrote "require, we think, a federal rule that prohibits a public official from recovering damages for a defamatory falsehood relating to his official conduct unless he proves that the statement was made with 'actual malice' — that is, with knowledge that it was false or with reckless disregard of whether it was false or not."

Examining the evidence in the case, the Court could find none that supported a finding of "malice" or "reckless disregard" of the truth on the part of the *Times* or the individual defendants.

The three justices who concurred in the Court's decision were even more adamant that the First Amendment protected the publication of the ad. "Unlike the Court," Justice Black asserted for himself and Justice Douglas, "I vote to reverse exclusively on the ground that the *Times* and the individual defendants had an absolute, unconditional constitutional right to publish in the *Times* advertisement their criticisms of the Montgomery agencies and officials." Justice Goldberg agreed, and quoting Justice Brandeis, noted that "sunlight is the most powerful of all disinfectants."

The *Times* case established the rule that when *public officials* sue the press for defamation, they must prove that the publisher acted with "malice" or with "reckless disregard" of the truth before they can recover damages. Shortly thereafter, a majority of the justices agreed that the same rule should apply to public *figures* in a case involving the *Saturday Evening Post* and football coach Wally Butts, of the University of Georgia. The *Post* had published an article claiming that Coach Butts and Coach "Bear" Bryant, of the University of Alabama, had conspired to fix a football game between the two schools. In an action brought by Coach Butts against the *Post* for defamation, the jury awarded Butts $60,000 in actual damages and $3 million in punitive damages, which trial judge Lewis R. Morgan reduced to $400,000. In affirming the judgment, the majority agreed that because Butts was a well-known coach, he was a "public figure." The justices also held, however, that the *Post* had "acted in reckless disregard of the truth."[7]

If a person is neither a public official nor a public figure, the *Times* rule does not apply. Elmer Gertz was just such a person. Gertz, an attorney, represented the family of a youth who had been shot and killed by a Chicago policeman, Nuccio. He brought suit against Nuccio on behalf of the youth's family and attended the inquest into the shooting. Nuccio was later convicted of murder in the second degree.

In March 1969, the *American Opinion,* a publication of the John Birch Society, published an article entitled "FRAME-UP: Richard Nuccio and the War on Police."[8]

> Notwithstanding [Gertz's] remote connection with the prosecution of Nuccio, [the] magazine portrayed him as an architect of the "frame-up." According to the article, the police file on [Gertz] took a "big, Irish cop to lift." The article stated that [Gertz] had been an official of the "Marxist League for Industrial Democracy, . . . which has advocated the violent seizure of our government." It labeled Gertz a "Leninist" and a "Communist-fronter." It also stated that Gertz had been an officer of the National Lawyers Guild, described as a Communist organization that "probably did more than any other outfit to plan the Communist attack on the Chicago police during the 1968 Democratic Convention."
> These statements contained serious inaccuracies.

In an action against Robert Welch, Inc., the publisher of *American Opinion,* the jury awarded Gertz $50,000. Judge Bernard M.

Decker of the federal district court set the verdict aside. He agreed that Gertz was neither a public official nor public figure but held that *American Opinion* was protected by the *Times* rule because the article was a discussion of a "public issue." The court of appeals affirmed, also finding that the "article concerned a matter of public interest." With four justices dissenting, the Supreme Court reversed.

"The principal issue in this case," Justice Powell explained for the majority, "is whether a newspaper or broadcaster that publishes defamatory falsehoods about an individual who is neither a public official nor a public figure may claim a constitutional privilege against liability for the injury inflicted by those statements." In other words, must a *private individual* prove that the publisher acted with "malice" or with "reckless disregard" of the truth in order to recover damages? The majority answered no, and explained its answer: "So long as they do not impose liability without fault, the States may define for themselves the appropriate standard of liability for a publisher or broadcaster of defamatory falsehood injurious to a private individual."

The majority acknowledged that although "there is no constitutional value in false statements of fact," they are "nevertheless inevitable in free debate." One solution, therefore, is to protect a publisher for false statements innocently made but permit damages for such statements negligently made. But even then, damages may be allowed only for "actual injury," and "the States may not permit recovery of presumed or punitive damages, at least when liability is not based on a showing of knowledge of falsity or reckless disregard for the truth."

Chief Justice Burger and Justice White would not have "constitutionalized" the law of defamation but let it develop as it has for centuries. Justices Brennan and Douglas, however, would have extended protection under the *Times* rule to the press when the material published concerned matters of public affairs.

More than two decades have now passed since the *Times* case, and the justices are still divided upon the "proper accommodation between the law of defamation and the freedoms of speech and press protected by the First Amendment." A majority of the justices now agree, however, that "breathing space [for the First Amendment] is provided by a constitutional rule that allows public figures to recover for libel or defamation only when they can prove *both* that the statement was false and that the statement was made with the requisite level of culpability," i.e., with "malice" or "reckless disregard" of the truth.[9]

The Press and the Right to Privacy

"Such privacy as a person normally has ceases when his life has ceased to be private."*

In 1890, long before he became a justice of the Supreme Court, Louis D. Brandeis, together with Samuel D. Warren, published an article in the *Harvard Law Review* entitled "The Right to Privacy." This article discussed the need for legal protection against invasion of personal privacy by the press. This was needed, the authors declared, because "the press is overstepping in every direction the obvious bounds of propriety and of decency."[10]

This right to privacy is recognized by many states, either by statute or as a right existing under the common law. It has been described as "the right to be let alone; to live one's life as one chooses, free from assault, intrusion or invasion except as they can be justified by the clear needs of community living under a government of law."[11]

Sometimes this right to privacy collides with the right of the press to publish truthful information lawfully obtained. Such a situation occurred when television station WSB-TV in Georgia reported the name of a rape and murder victim. Under Georgia law, publication of the name of identity of a rape victim was a misdemeanor. Shortly after the rape and murder had occurred, six youths were arrested and charged with the crime. When these defendants appeared in court, Wassell, a reporter for the station was in attendance and obtained the victim's name from the indictments. Five of the youths pleaded guilty to rape, and the murder charge against them was dropped. One defendant pleaded not guilty.

The victim's name was broadcast that day during a newscast concerning the court proceedings. It was broadcast again during a similar newscast the next day. Martin Cohn, the father of the victim, brought an action for damages against the owner of the station, "claiming that his right to privacy had been invaded by the television broadcasts giving the name of his deceased daughter."[12]

Judge Durwood T. Pye, of the Georgia Superior Court, granted judgment for the father but did not make a determination of damages. The Georgia Supreme Court affirmed, a majority holding that the father's privacy had been violated and that the First Amendment did not protect the station from liability.

Eight justices of the U.S. Supreme Court voted to reverse. Justice

*Justice Douglas, concurring in *Time, Inc. v. Hill*, 385 U.S. 374, 401 (1967).

White, for himself and five other justices, focused on the essence of the case: "Because the gravamen of the claimed injury is the publication of information, whether true or not, the dissemination of which is embarrassing or otherwise painful to an individual, it is here that claims of privacy most directly confront the constitutional freedoms of speech and press."

The majority was concerned about the consequences of establishing a rule of law that would prohibit the publication of public records "if offensive to the sensibilities of the supposed reasonable man."

> Such a rule would make it very difficult for the media to inform citizens about the public business and yet stay within the law. The rule would invite timidity and self-censorship and very likely lead to the suppression of many items that would otherwise be published and that should be made available to the public.

In balancing the station's press rights against the privacy rights of Cohn in this case, the majority opted in favor of the First Amendment because the information that was broadcast was part of the public record. West Virginia, however, attempted by statute to prohibit the publication of the name of juvenile offenders unless written permission had been given by the juvenile court, making it a crime to publish such information whether is was part of the public record or not. This law was challenged by two West Virginia newspapers when they published the name of a 14-year-old boy who shot and killed a classmate at school.

> The *Charleston Daily Mail* and the *Charleston Gazette* . . . learned of the shooting by monitoring routinely the police band radio frequency; they immediately dispatched reporters and photographers to the junior high school. The reporters for both papers obtained the name of the alleged assailant simply by asking various witnesses, the police, and an assistant prosecuting attorney who were at the school.[13]

The *Gazette* published the juvenile's name and picture the next day. The *Daily Mail* published a story about the shooting but did not print the alleged attacker's name; however, it did so in a later edition of its paper. The juvenile's name was also broadcast over several radio stations.

Shortly thereafter, the newspapers were indicted for a violation of the law. Before they were brought to trial, they filed a petition with the West Virginia Supreme Court of Appeals for an order prohibiting the prosecuting attorney and the circuit court judges of the county from taking any action against them. The order was granted, and an appeal was taken to the U.S. Supreme Court, which unanimously affirmed, Justice Powell not participating.

To put the question in proper perspective, Chief Justice Burger noted that "our recent decisions demonstrate that state action to punish the publication of truthful information seldom can satisfy constitutional standards." And this is true in this case, even though "the sole interest advanced by the State to justify its criminal statute is to protect the anonymity of the juvenile offender."

The Court had some misgivings about the state's sincerity because the statute applied only to newspapers and not to electronic media. But even assuming that the state's interest in protecting the juvenile was substantial, the Court pointed out that there was "no evidence to demonstrate that the imposition of criminal penalties is necessary to protect the confidentiality of juvenile proceedings." Most states rely upon cooperation between the juvenile courts and the press to accomplish this goal. And the Court wanted it understood that it favored that approach. "At issue," Chief Justice Burger declared, "is simply the power of a state to punish the truthful publication of an alleged juvenile delinquent's name lawfully obtained by a newspaper. The asserted state interest cannot justify the statute's imposition of criminal sanctions on this type of publication."

Justice Rehnquist reached the same conclusion, but by a different route. He did not see the law as accomplishing its purpose, because it applied only to newspapers and not other parts of the media. However, he thought that preserving the anonymity of juvenile offenders was an interest of the "highest order" and "that a generally effective ban on publication that applied to all forms of mass communication, electronic and print media alike, would be constitutional."

Criminal Trials Are Open to the Public

*"The narrow question presented . . . is whether the right of the public and press to attend criminal trials is guaranteed under the United States Constitution."**

Of paramount concern to those involved in the criminal justice system is that an accused receives a fair trial as guaranteed by the Sixth

*Richmond Newspapers, Inc. v. Virginia, 448 U.S. 555, 558 (1980).

Amendment. The murder trials of John Paul Stevenson illustrate this concern. In March 1976, Stevenson was charged with the murder of a hotel manager. He was tried and found guilty of second-degree murder in a circuit court in Virginia, but the Virginia Supreme Court set aside the conviction because a bloodstained shirt had been improperly admitted into evidence. A second trial ended in a mistrial when one juror was excused and no alternate was available. A third trial had hardly gotten under way when it too was ended, apparently because a prospective juror had read about the previous trials and had discussed them with others on the jury panel. At the beginning of the fourth trial, Stevenson's attorney requested the trial judge to close the trial to the public. The prosecutor did not object, nor did news reporters Wheeler and McCarthy, who were in the courtroom at the time. The judge therefore "ordered 'that the Courtroom be kept clear of all parties except the witnesses when they testify.'"[14]

Richmond Newspapers, Inc., and its reporters Wheeler and McCarthy (appellants) filed a motion seeking to have the closure order vacated, which the trial judge denied. The next day, after the prosecutor for the commonwealth had presented evidence against Stevenson, his counsel moved the court to strike the evidence and find Stevenson not guilty, which the court did. Shortly thereafter, the appellants filed an appeal with the Virginia Supreme Court seeking a determination that the trial court's closure order was unconstitutional. The appeal was denied, and the appellants sought review in the U.S. Supreme Court. That Court reversed in a decision with which seven justices concurred but did not produce a majority opinion.

With Justice Rehnquist dissenting and Justice Powell not participating, the other justices agreed that the First Amendment protects the right of the public to attend trials. The justices, however, had differing views about the extent of the protection given by the First Amendment. For Chief Justice Burger and justices White and Stevens, closure in this case was not appropriate because "despite the fact that this was the fourth trial of the accused, the trial judge made no findings to support closure; no inquiry was made as to whether alternative solutions would have met the need to ensure fairness; there was no recognition of any right under the Constitution for the public or the press to attend the trial." These justices might have voted to uphold closure but concluded that without "an overriding interest articulated in findings, the trial of a criminal case must be open to the public."

By concurring only in the judgment, justices Brennan and Marshall made it clear that for them, the First Amendment guaranteed

open trials in almost every case. "Popular attendance at trials...,"
Justice Brennan asserted, "substantially furthers the particular public
purposes of that critical judicial proceeding. In that sense, public access
is an indispensable element of the trial itself. Trial access, therefore,
assumes structural importance in our 'government of laws.'"

But Justice Rehnquist would have none of that: "I do not believe
that either the First or Sixth Amendment, as made applicable to the
States by the Fourteenth, requires that a State's reasons for denying
public access to a trial, where both the prosecuting attorney and the
defendant have consented to an order of closure approved by the judge,
are subject to any additional constitutional review at our hands."

These differences surfaced again when the Court reviewed a
Massachusetts statute that required "trial judges, at trials for specified
sexual offenses involving a victim under the age of 18, to exclude the
press and general public from the courtroom during the testimony of
that victim."[15]

The case arose when the Globe Newspaper Co. (Globe) sought to
attend a trial of a defendant "charged with forcible rape and forced un-
natural rape of three girls who were minors at the time of trial—two
16 years of age and one 17." Although neither the defendant nor the
prosecution desired the trial to be closed during the testimony of the
victims, the trial judge, over Globe's objection, ordered closure, relying
upon the Massachusetts law. Globe immediately applied to one of the
justices of the supreme judicial court for an injunction against the
closure order. When this was denied, it took an appeal to the full
supreme judicial court. By that time, the rape trial had been held and
the defendant acquitted.

The Massachusetts court examined the statute and concluded that
there were two legislative purposes for it: (1) "to encourage young victims of sexual offenses to come forward"; (2) "once they have come forward ... [to] preserve their ability to testify by protecting them from
undue psychological harm at trial." Based upon these two legislative
purposes, the court held that the statute "*required* the closure of sex-
offense trials only during the testimony of minor victims; during other
portions of such trials, closure was 'a matter within the judge's sound
discretion.'"

Globe appealed to the U.S. Supreme Court, which reversed,
holding "that the mandatory closure rule ... violates the First Amendment." The Court noted that a majority of the justices in the *Richmond
Newspapers* case had agreed "that the press and general public have a
constitutional right of access to criminal trials" but also acknowledged

that that right was not absolute and that closure could be justified by a compelling need. In examining the reasons given for the *mandatory* closure rule here, the majority held that they were not compelling. On the claim that the rule would encourage victims of sex crimes to come forward, the majority replied that "the Commonwealth has offered no empirical support for the claim that the rule of automatic closure . . . will lead to an increase in the number of minor sex victims coming forward and cooperating with state authorities." Further, as for protecting the physical and psychological well-being of the minor, trial courts, should be able to make the decision to close or not to close the trial on a case-by-case basis. "Among the factors to be weighed are the minor victim's age, psychological maturity and understanding, the nature of the crime, the desires of the victim, and the interests of parents and relatives."

"Massachusetts," Justice O'Connor wrote, concurring in the judgment, "has demonstrated no interest weighty enough to justify application of its automatic bar to all cases, even those in which the victim, defendant, and prosecutor have no objection to an open trial."

The decision brought forth a strong dissent from Chief Justice Burger and Justice Rehnquist. "The Court's decision . . . is . . . a gross invasion of state authority and a state's duty to protect its citizens — in this case minor victims of crime." The Chief Justice stressed that the Commonwealth was not denying access to the information given at the trial and the trial transcript was available to the press and public.

Relying upon its decisions in *Richmond Newspapers, Inc.,* and *Globe Newspaper Co.,* the Court has held that the pretrial examination of potential jurors in a rape and murder cases must be open to the public and press[16] and that the First Amendment right to access applied to preliminary hearings conducted in California.[17]

Reporters May Be Required to Reveal Their Sources

"The issue in these cases is whether requiring newsmen to appear and testify before . . . grand juries abridges the freedom of speech and press guaranteed by the First Amendment."[*]

When the Court was called upon to answer the above question, it had before it several cases where newsmen claimed a First Amendment right not to testify before a grand jury.

Branzburg v. Hayes, 408 U.S. 665, 667 (1972).

Paul Branzburg, a reporter, after witnessing two individuals making hashish, wrote an article about his experience. "The article included a photograph of a pair of hands working above a laboratory table on which was a substance identified by the caption as hashish. The article stated that [Branzburg] had promised not to reveal the identity of the two hashish makers."[18] In another article, Branzburg "reported that in order to provide a comprehensive survey of the 'drug scene' in Frankfort, [Kentucky,] . . . [he] had 'spent two weeks interviewing several dozen drug users in the capital city' and had seen some of them smoking marijuana. A number of conversations with and observations of several unnamed drug users were recounted."

Paul Pappas, a newsman-photographer, had gained access to Black Panther headquarters in New Bedford, Massachusetts, upon condition that he not reveal what he saw or heard. "[Earl] Caldwell, a black, [was] a reporter for the *New York Times* and was assigned to San Francisco with the hope that he could report on the activities and attitudes of the Black Panther Party. Caldwell in time gained the complete confidence of its members and wrote in-depth articles about them."

All of these newsmen were summoned to appear before grand juries. Branzburg appeared before a grand jury in Jefferson County but refused to identify the individuals making the hashish. When Judge J. Miles Pound ordered him to answer, he petitioned the Kentucky Court of Appeals for relief, which that court denied. Branzburg was then summoned before another grand jury, this time in Franklin County, to testify about drug use in that county. He attempted to have the summons quashed, but that motion was denied, and that denial was upheld by the Kentucky Court of Appeals.

When Pappas appeared before a grand jury in Massachusetts, he answered some questions about his activities "but refused to answer any questions about what had taken place inside the headquarters while he was there.'" Superior Court Judge Smith held that he must respond to the grand jury's questions, and the Massachusetts Supreme Judicial Court agreed.

Caldwell's journey through the judicial system was somewhat different. He was subpoenaed to appear before a federal grand jury but moved to quash the subpoena. District Judge Alfonso J. Zirpoli ordered him to appear but held that he did not have to reveal "confidential information until there had been 'a showing by the Government of a compelling and overriding national interest in requiring Mr. Caldwell's testimony.'" The court of appeals dismissed Caldwell's appeal without opinion. A subsequent grand jury issued a subpoena for Caldwell, which Judge Zirpoli refused to quash. When Caldwell refused to appear, he was held in contempt. This time the court of appeals agreed with Caldwell and held that he did not have to appear, "absent some special showing of necessity by the Government."

Branzburg and Pappas appealed to the Supreme Court, as did the United States in Caldwell's case. The Court stated and answered the question as follows:

> The issue in these cases is whether requiring newsmen to appear and testify before state or federal grand juries abridges the freedom of speech and press guaranteed by the First Amendment. We [five justices] hold that it does not.

The majority therefore upheld the others requiring Branzburg and Pappas to appear and testify, and struck down the court of appeals protective order given Caldwell.

Justice White, for the majority, outlined the arguments advanced by the newsmen why they should not be required to reveal information that they had gained in confidence.

> Petitioners Branzburg and Pappas and respondent Caldwell press First Amendment claims that may be simply put: that to gather news it is often necessary to agree either not to identify the source of information published or to publish only part of the facts revealed, or both; that if the reporter is nevertheless forced to reveal these confidences to a grand jury, the source so identified and other confidential sources of other reporters will be measurably deterred from furnishing publishable information, all to the detriment of the free flow of information protected by the First Amendment.

The newsmen did not claim that the privilege not to testify was absolute but argued that they should not be required to testify unless "the information the reporter has is unavailable from other sources, and that the need for the information is sufficiently compelling to override the claimed invasion of First Amendment interests occasioned by the disclosure."

To put the matter in proper focus, Justice White explained that here there was

> no prior restraint or restriction on what the press may publish, and no express or implied command that the press publish what it prefers to withhold. No exaction or tax for the privilege of publishing, and no penalty, civil or criminal, related to the content of published

material is at issue here. The use of confidential sources by the press is not forbidden or restricted; reporters remain free to seek news from any source by means within the law."

Furthermore, freedom of the press is not absolute, and some infringement is justified when there are compelling reasons for doing so.

Even though a number of states have adopted statutes that give news personnel a privilege against compelled testimony in some cases, the majority refused to create a constitutional testimonial privilege for them because

fair and effective law enforcement aimed at providing security for the person and property of the individual is a fundamental function of government, and the grand jury plays an important, constitutionally mandated role in this process.

Summing up the majority's position, Justice White held that "we cannot seriously entertain the notion that the First Amendment protects a newsman's agreement to conceal the criminal conduct of his source, or evidence thereof, on the theory that it is better to write about crime than to do something about it. . . . The crimes of news sources are no less reprehensible and threatening to the public interest when witnessed by a reporter than when they are not."

The majority's decision was not unchallenged. For Justice Douglas, this decision was a severe blow to the press's ability to "inform the people what is going on, and to expose the harmful as well as the good influences at work." As for the ability of reporters to gather news, Justice Douglas expressed concern that "if [the reporter] can be summoned to testify in secret before a grand jury, his sources will dry up and the attempted exposure, the effort to enlighten the public, will be ended. If what the Court sanctions today becomes settled law, then the reporter's main function in American society will be to pass on to the public the press releases which the various departments of government issue." But the harshest criticism of the decision came from Justice Stewart: "The Court's crabbed view of the First Amendment reflects a disturbing insensitivity to the critical role of an independent press in our society." This decision, he wrote, will invite "state and federal authorities to undermine the historic independence of the press by attempting to annex the journalistic profession as an investigative arm of government. Not only will this decision impair performance of the press' constitutionally protected functions, but it will, I am convinced, in the long run harm rather than help the administration of justice."

The newsmen in these cases wanted protection from being forced to testify. That was not Michael Smith's concern, however. Smith, a reporter for the *Charlotte Herald-News* in Florida, after testifying before a grand jury, wanted to write a book "about the subject matter of the investigation, a publication which would include [his] testimony and experiences in dealing with the grand jury."[19] Under Florida law, however, it was a criminal offense to disclose that information.

Smith sued Robert A. Butterworth, Jr., the attorney general of Florida, seeking a determination that the law was unconstitutional as a violation of the First Amendment. Federal District Judge Elizabeth A. Kovachevich granted judgment for the state. The court of appeals reversed, concluding that "the competing state interests were not sufficiently compelling to warrant the imposition of criminal sanctions on witnesses who revealed the content of their own grand jury testimony." A unanimous Supreme Court held that the Florida law violated the First Amendment.

Chief Justice Rehnquist, writing the opinion for the Court, recognized that "the grand jury has served an important role in the administration of criminal justice" but also found that "we must . . . balance [Smith's] asserted First Amendment rights against Florida's interest in preserving the confidentiality of its grand jury proceedings."

However, the justices did not believe that there was any need to keep the information secret after the grand jury's proceedings had been completed. Witnesses who feared retribution for their testimony could simply refuse to divulge it. And this law would have little effect upon an accused's attempt to suborn a witness, because under criminal procedure rules, witnesses' names must be revealed to the accused before trial. In response to the state's argument that an accused who has been exonerated by the grand jury could be held up to public ridicule by release of grand jury testimony, the Court noted that "reputational interests alone cannot justify the proscription of truthful speech."

The Chief Justice then explained the practical effect of Florida's statute:

> The effect is dramatic: before he is called to testify in front of the grand jury, [Smith] is possessed of information on matters of admitted public concern about which he was free to speak at will. After giving his testimony, [he] believes he is no longer free to communicate this information since it relates to the "content, gist, or import" of his testimony. The ban extends not merely to the life of the grand jury but into the indefinite future.

No Right of Access to All Information

*"The First Amendment does not guarantee the press a constitutional right to special access to information not available to the public generally."**

Questions relating to the extent that freedom of the press grants news personnel access to news and news sources have generally arisen when reporters have sought to obtain information about prisons or prisoners.

In *Pell v. Procunier,* discussed in Chapter VI,[20] a majority upheld a California prison rule that "the press and other media interviews with specific individual inmates will not be permitted."[21] The Court could find no support that "the Constitution imposes upon government the affirmative duty to make available to journalists sources of information not available to members of the public generally."

In recent years, conditions in our jails and prisons have frequently made the front page and have been included in newscasts. Penal institutions throughout the United States are overcrowded and understaffed, and prisoners are sometimes subjected to various kinds of physical punishment.

In 1975, after an inmate committed suicide at the Alameda County Jail, television and radio station KQED, operating in the San Francisco Bay area, requested permission to visit and take pictures in the jail. Sheriff Houchins denied the request. KQED and local branches of the NAACP petitioned the federal district court for preliminary and permanent injunctions against Sheriff Houchins. Shortly thereafter, the sheriff instituted a program of regular public tours of the facility, the first including a KQED reporter and other reporters. These tours, however, were a less than adequate response to the needs of the press. If a tour was filled with members of the public, no reporter could participate. Further, no photographs or tape recordings were permitted.

The parties therefore pressed their request in court and were met with the sheriff's assertion that "the unregulated access by the media would infringe inmate privacy, and tend to create 'jail celebrities,' who in turn tend to generate internal problems and undermine jail security."[22]

Judge Oliver J. Carter disagreed and issued an order "enjoin[ing] [Sheriff Houchins] from denying KQED news personnel and 'responsible representatives' of the news media access to the Santa Rita

*Branzburg v. Hayes, 408 U.S. 665, 684 (1972).

facilities.'" The court of appeals affirmed, and Sheriff Houchins appealed to the Supreme Court.

With only seven justices participating, the Court overruled the court of appeals and ordered the injunction set aside. Chief Justice Burger and justices White and Rehnquist rejected "the Court of Appeals' conclusory assertion that the public and the media have a First Amendment right to government information regarding the conditions of jails and their inmates and presumably all other public facilities such as hosptials and mental institutions." This, of course, does not leave the public without information about jail conditions. There are "citizen task forces and prison visitation committees," grand juries, and even courts that can monitor public institutions.

Because the decision had to be supported by at least four justices, Justice Stewart concurred in the judgment. However, he thought that the Court's opinion did not give sufficient consideration to the needs of the press. "I believe that the concept of equal access must be accorded more flexibility in order to accommodate the practical distinctions between the press and the general public." For Justice Stewart, it was no accident that the First Amendment contained separate rights to speech and to the press.

> That the First Amendment speaks separately of freedom of speech and freedom of the press is no constitutional accident, but an acknowledgement of the critical role played by the press in American society. The Constitution requires sensitivity to that role, and to the special needs of the press in performing it effectively. A person touring Santa Rita jail can grasp its reality with his own eyes and ears. But if a television reporter is to convey the jail's sights and sounds to those who cannot personally visit the place, he must use cameras and sound equipment. In short, terms of access that are reasonably imposed on individual members of the public may, if they impede effective reporting without sufficient justification, be unreasonable as applied to journalists who are there to convey to the general public what the visitors see.

The three dissenters, justices Stevens, Brennan, and Powell, thought that the Court's decision would make it possible for the government to conceal information. "An official prison policy," Justice Stevens argued, "of concealing ... knowledge from the public by arbitrarily cutting off the flow of information at its source abridges the freedom of speech and of the press protected by the First and Fourteenth Amendments to the Constitution."

Obscenity: *"I know it when I see it."*

*"But implicit in the history of the First Amendment is the rejection of obscenity as utterly without redeeming social importance."**

Concluding that obscenity was not entitled to First Amendment protection was much easier than defining it. But even after the Court gave *obscenity* a legal definition, the problem did not end; application of the definition to printed and film material remains fraught with difficulty.

Justice Stewart found that obscenity and hard-core pornography were the same, but he wasn't sure that he could define hard-core pornography. "I shall not today," he explained, "attempt further to define the kinds of material I understand to be embraced within that shorthand description; and perhaps I could never succeed in intelligibly doing so. But I know it when I see it, and the motion picture [*The Lovers*] involved in this case is not that." [23]

The terms *obscenity* and *pornography* are often used as if they were synonymous, but they are not. *Obscenity* has a legal definition, while *pornography* doesn't. *Pornography* is a term generally used by the public to encompass much sexually explicit material not considered legally obscene. Furthermore, "sex and obscenity are not synonymous. Obscene material is material which deals with sex in a manner appealing to prurient interest. The portrayal of sex, *e.g.,* in art, literature and scientific works, is not itself sufficient reason to deny material the constitutional protection of freedom of speech and press."[24]

The question of whether obscene material was entitled to any First Amendment protection came to the Court in two cases. Samuel Roth's business was selling books, magazines, and photographs. To promote sales, he mailed circulars and other advertising material that the government believed obscene. He was charged with violating a federal statute that "makes punishable the mailing of material that is 'obscene, lewd, lascivious, or filthy ... or other publication of an indecent character.'" He was convicted, and his conviction was upheld by the court of appeals.

David S. Alberts, also in the bookselling business, was "charged ... with lewdly keeping for sale obscene and indecent books, and with writing, composing and publishing an obscene advertisement of them, in violation of the California Penal Code." Alberts was convicted, and his conviction was upheld by a California appellate court.

Roth v. United States, 354 U.S. 476, 484 (1957).

The Supreme Court heard these cases at the same time and affirmed both convictions. These cases for the first time required the justices to determine the effect of the First Amendment upon allegedly obscene material. In approaching that issue, Justice Brennan, writing for the Court, engaged in some historical research. He found that "the guarantees of freedom of expression in effect in 10 of the 14 States which by 1792 had ratified the Constitution, gave no absolute protection to every utterance." Among the activities that could be punished were libel, blasphemy, and profanity, and as far back as 1712, it was a crime in Massachusetts to "publish 'any filthy, obscene, or profane song, pamphlet, libel or mock sermon' in imitation or mimicking of religious services." In addition, the idea that "obscenity [was] utterly without redeeming social importance" could be found in international agreements and federal and state statutes.

Having concluded that the First Amendment was no barrier to prosecution for mailing, selling, or distributing obscene material, the Court turned to the task of developing a test that courts could apply. After examining a number of lower court cases that had considered the problem, the majority determined that the proper test would be "whether to the average person applying contemporary community standards, the dominant theme of the material taken as a whole appeals to prurient interest." Because the trial courts in both of these cases had applied that test, the convictions were valid.

For justices Douglas and Black, this was a field that courts should not get involved in. In dissent, Justice Douglas expressed an absolutist view: "I would give the broad sweep of the First Amendment full support. I have the same confidence in the ability of our people to reject noxious literature as I have in their capacity to sort out the true from the false in theology, economics, politics, or any other field."

The Court's decisions in *Roth* and *Alberts* opened a Pandora's box of problems; the justices could not agree on the proper legal approach to obscenity. A per curiam opinion in a 1967 case summed up the situation:

> Two members of the Court have consistently adhered to the view that the State is utterly without power to suppress, control, or punish the distribution of any writings or pictures upon the ground of their "obscenity." A third has held to the opinion that a State's power in this area is narrowly limited to a distinct and clearly identifiable class of material. Others have subscribed to a not dissimilar standard, holding that a State may not constitutionally inhibit the distribution of literary material as obscene unless "(a) the dominant theme of the

material taken as a whole appeals to a prurient interest in sex; (b) the material is patently offensive because it affronts contemporary community standards relating to the description or representation of sexual matters; and (c) the material is utterly without redeeming social value," ... and that no such material can "be proscribed unless it is found to be *utterly* without redeeming social value." ... Another justice has not viewed the "social value" element as an independent factor in the judgment of obscenity.[25]

These divergent views regarding obscenity continued until 1973. At that time only justices Brennan and Douglas remained of those who participated in the *Roth* and *Alberts* cases in 1957, but "the intractable obscenity problem"[26] continued.

A Mr. Miller found himself caught up in the problem when he mailed literature offering "adult" material for sale.

> The brochures advertise four books entitled "Intercourse," "Man-Woman," "Sex Orgies Illustrated," and "An Illustrated History of Pornography," and a film entitled "Marital Intercourse." While the brochures contain some descriptive printed material, primarily they consist of pictures and drawings very explicitly depicting men and women in groups of two or more engaging in a variety of sexual activities, with genitals often prominently displayed.[27]

Miller was convicted by a jury of "knowingly distributing obscene matter" in violation of California law. At that time, California law defined *obscene* as follows:

> "Obscene" means that to the average person, applying contemporary standards, the predominant appeal of the matter, taken as a whole, is to prurient interest, i.e., a shameful or morbid interest in nudity, sex, or excretion, which goes substantially beyond customary limits of candor in description or representation of such matters and is matter which is utterly without redeeming social importance.

Miller's conviction was affirmed on appeal to a California appellate court, and he sought review in the Supreme Court.

California's definition of *obscenity* was in accord with what had evolved in Supreme Court decisions since 1957. But a new majority of justices thought the time had come for a more specific definition. Referring to the fact that the Court had previously held that "obscene material is unprotected by the First Amendment," Chief Justice Burger, for the majority, described the new test for obscenity:

> We now confine the permissible scope of such regulation to works which depict or describe sexual conduct. . . . A state offense must also be limited to works which, taken as a whole, appeal to the prurient interest in sex, which portray sexual conduct in a patently offensive way, and which, taken as a whole, do not have serious literary, artistic, political, or scientific value.

The Chief Justice then discussed whether a jury was to apply a "national" standard or standards of the community of the jury. The majority said it didn't make any difference. "It is neither realistic nor constitutionally sound," the Chief Justice explained, "to read the First Amendment as requiring that the people of Maine or Mississippi accept public depiction of conduct found tolerable in Las Vegas, or New York City." The Court then sent the case back to the California appellate court "for further proceedings not inconsistent with the First Amendment standards established by this opinion."

The *Miller* decision produced a dissent from Justice Douglas and one by Justice Brennan for himself, Stewart, and Marshall. Justice Douglas expressed concern that Miller might be sent to jail under standards that were not in effect at the time of the mailings. "Today we leave open the way for California to send a man to prison for distributing brochures that advertise books and a movie under freshly written standards defining obscenity which until today's decision were never part of any law."

Although Justice Brennan had written the opinion in the *Roth* and *Alberts* cases upholding punishment for sale or distribution of obscene material, the Court's problems with obscenity during the intervening years had caused him to reverse himself and take the position that writing a workable obscenity statute was impossible. He expressed his views in a case decided the same day as *Miller*.

> I am convinced that the approach initiated 16 years ago in *Roth v. United States,* . . . and culminating in the Court's decison today, cannot bring stability to this area of the law without jeopardizing fundamental First Amendment values, and I have concluded that the time has come to make a significant departure from that approach.[28]

His basic concern was that any statute that defined obscenity would be so vague that it would endanger constitutionally protected speech and press. He therefore concluded that "at least in the absence of distribution to juveniles or obtrusive exposure to unconsenting adults, the First and Fourteenth Amendments prohibit the State and Federal Governments from attempting wholly to suppress sexually oriented materials on the basis of their allegedly 'obscene' contents."

No matter which definition of obscenity the Court has used, the justices in most cases have had to make the final determination whether the material was obscene. Such was the situation when Billy Jenkins was convicted "for showing the film 'Carnal Knowledge' in a movie theater in Albany, Georgia," in March 1972.[29] When the case was heard by the Supreme Court, the justices unanimously voted to reverse the conviction. They did not do so for the same reasons. Justice Rehnquist, expressing his views and those of four other justices, held that "our own viewing of the film satisfies us that 'Carnal Knowledge' could not be found under the *Miller* standards to depict sexual conduct in a patently offensive way." The majority reached this conclusion even though

> the subject matter of the picture is, in a broader sense, sex, and there are scenes in which sexual conduct including "ultimate sexual acts" is to be understood to be taking place, the camera does not focus on the bodies of the actors at such times. There is no exhibition whatever of the actors' genitals, lewd or otherwise, during these scenes. There are occasional scenes of nudity, but nudity alone is not enough to make material legally obscene under the *Miller* standards.

The justices who usually dissented in obscenity cases did not do so here. By voting to reverse Jenkins's conviction, they were agreeing with the majority that the film was protected by the First Amendment.

Almost fifty years ago, the Court held that "the power of the state to control the conduct of children reaches beyond the scope of its authority over adults."[30] Using that statement as a point of departure, the Court was upheld "a New York criminal obscenity statute which prohibits the sale to minors under 17 years of age of material defined to be obscene on the basis of its appeal to them whether or not it would be obscene to adults."[31] Justice Stewart, concurring in the judgment in that case, summed up the constitutional rights of minors as follows:

> I think a State may permissibly determine that, at least in some precisely delineated areas, a child . . . is not possessed of that full capacity for individual choice which is the presumption of First Amendment guarantees. It is only upon such a premise, I should suppose, that a State may deprive children of other rights—the right to marry, for example, or the right to vote—deprivations that would be constitutionally intolerable for adults.

A majority of the justices have also allowed states to come down hard on persons producing and distributing "child pornography." They held that

> States are entitled to greater leeway in the regulation of pornographic depictions of children for the following reasons: (1) the legislative judgment that the use of children as subjects of pornographic materials is harmful to the physiological, emotional, and mental health of the child, easily passes muster under the First Amendment; (and) (2) the standard of *Miller v. California* . . . for determining what is legally obscene is not a satisfactory solution to the child pornography problem. . . ."[32]

More recently, the Court upheld a Ohio statute that "prohibits 'the possession or viewing of material or performance of a minor who is in a state of nudity, where such nudity constitutes a lewd exhibition or involves a graphic focus on the genitals, and where the person depicted is neither the child nor the ward of the person charged.'"[33]

Freedom of the Press — 1991 and Beyond

The justices should be given high marks for their interpretations of the freedom of the press provision of the First Amendment. Only under certain extenuating circumstances will the justices approve a "prior restraint" upon publication. Further, they have given similar protection to the publication of defamatory material against public officials and public figures. The justices believe that the threat of libel judgments "leads to self-censorship." Although recognizing a right to privacy, the Court's decisions hold that freedom of the press to publish truthful information, lawfully obtained, is more important.

Even when forced to balance the Sixth Amendment's right to a fair trial against the public's "right to know," the balance has been in favor of open trials, at least until alternatives to closure have been exhausted.

Extensive protection is also given the press and electronic media for the dissemination of sexually explicit material. The *Miller* test makes it difficult for prosecutors to obtain convictions under obscenity laws.

Three areas where the justices have permitted limitations on freedom of the press: (1) Persons who are not public figures or public officials may sue for libel without the heavy burden of proving that the publication was done with "malice" or "reckless disregard of the truth." (2) Reporters must testify before grand juries and reveal their news sources if asked to do so. (3) The press enjoys no greater right of access to information than the general public.

Because these principles of freedom of the press are so ingrained in First Amendment jurisprudence, it is unlikely that a majority of justices will permit much erosion thereof in the future.

X.
JUSTICE BRANDEIS AND THE FOUNDING FATHERS

"Those who won our independence believed that the final end of the State was to make men free to develop their faculties; and that in its government the deliberative forces should prevail over the arbitrary. They valued liberty both as an end and as a means. They believed liberty to be the secret of happiness and courage to be the secret of liberty. They believed that freedom to think as you will and to speak as you think are means indispensable to the discovery and spread of political truth; that without free speech and assembly discussion would be futile; that with them, discussion affords ordinarily adequate protection against the dissemination of noxious doctrine; that the greatest menace to freedom is an inert people; that public discussion is a political duty; and that this should be a fundamental principle of the American government. They recognized the risks to which all human institutions are subject. But they knew that order cannot be secured merely through fear of punishment for its infraction; that it is hazardous to discourage thought, hope and imagination; that fear breeds repression; that repression breeds hate; that hate menaces stable government; that the path of safety lies in the opportunity to discuss freely supposed grievances and proposed remedies; and that the fitting remedy for evil counsels is good ones. Believing in the power of reason as applied through public discussion, they eschewed silence coerced by law—the argument of force in its worst form. Recognizing the occasional tyrannies of governing majorities, they amended the Constitution so that free speech and assembly should be guaranteed.

"Fear of serious injury cannot alone justify suppression of free speech and assembly. Men feared witches and burnt women. It is the function of speech to free men from the bondage of irrational fears. To justify suppression of free speech there must be reasonable ground to fear that serious evil will result if free speech is practiced. There must be reasonable ground to believe that the danger apprehended is imminent. There must be reasonable ground to believe that the evil to be prevented is a serious one. . . .

"Those who won our independence by revolution were not cowards. They did not fear political change. They did not exalt order at the cost of liberty. To courageous, self-reliant men, with confidence in the power of free and fearless reasoning applied through the processes of popular government, no danger flowing from speech can be deemed clear and present, unless the incidence of the evil apprehended is so imminent that it may befall before there is opportunity for full discusion. If there be time to expose through discussion the falsehood and fallacies, to avert the evil by the processes of education, the remedy to be applied is more speech, not enforced silence. Only an emergency can justify repression. Such must be the rule if authority is to be reconciled with freedom. Such, in my opinion, is the command of the Constitution. It is therefore always open to Americans to challenge a law abridging free speech and assembly by showing that there was no emergency justifying it."*

*Justice Brandeis, concurring in *Whitney v. California*, 274 U.S. 357, 375–377 (1927).

NOTES

A note regarding citations of court cases: "X v. Y, 25 U.S. 372, 376 (19nn)" means that the X v. Y opinion appears in volume 25 of the *United States* reporter at page 372, and the quotation appears on page 376, and that the case was decided in 19nn. Quotations without a footnote number are generally taken from the same source as the preceding quotation which bears a footnote number.

Preface

1. *San Diego Tribune,* February 19, 1990, p. A-6.
2. Charles Warren, *The Supreme Court in United States History* (Boston, Toronto: Little, Brown, 1922), v.1, p. 2.
3. Earl Warren, *A Republic If You Can Keep It* (Quadrangle Books, 1972), p. xi.

Chapter I

1. For a more detailed review of the history surrounding the adoption of the Constitution and the Bill of Rights, see *1787 The Grand Convention,* Clinton Rossiter; *The Birth of the Bill of Rights,* Robert Allan Rutland; *Constitution of the United States,* Senate Document 99-16, Historical Note, pp. xxix–xxxv, 949–51, 1982; *The Bill of Rights, a Documentary History,* B. Schwartz; *The Framing of the Constitution,* Max Farrand.
2. Madison to Jefferson, Phila., August 12, 1786. Robert A. Rutland, *The Papers of James Madison,* v. 9, p. 95.
3. Madison to Jefferson, Orange, June 19, 1786. Robert A. Rutland, *The Papers of James Madison,* v. 9, p. 77.
4. Fred W. Friendly and Martha J.H. Elliott, *The Constitution, That Delicate Balance* (New York: Random House, 1984), p. 111.
5. Ellwood P. Cubberly, *Public Education in the United States,* 1947, p. 15.
6. Samuel Eliot Morison, *The Oxford History of the American People,* (New York: Oxford University Press, 1965), p. 288.
7. Sylvia R. Frey and Marian J. Morton, *New World, New Roles* (Greenwood Press, 1986), p. 98.
8. Linda Grant De Paww and Conover Hunt, *Remember the Ladies* (Viking Press, 1976), p. 45.

9. John C. Fitzpatrick, ed. *Diaries of George Washington 1749–1799*, v. IV, pp. 37–38.

10. L.H. Butterfield, et al., eds., *The Book of Abigail and John, Selected Letters of the Adams Family, 1762–1784* (Cambridge, Mass.: 1975), p. 121.

11. *Ibid.* at pp. 121–22.

12. Selma R. Williams, *Demeter's Daughters* (Anthenum, 1976), p. 242.

13. *Ibid.* at p. 243.

14. *Ibid.* at p. 243.

15. Barbara Mayer Werthiemer, *We Were There* (Pantheon Books, 1977), p. 30.

16. Merl R. Eppse, *The Negro Too, in American History* (National Education Publishing Co., 1938), pp. 78–79.

17. George Washington to Robert Morris, Mt. Vernon, April 12, 1786, Jared Sparks, *The Writings of George Washington*, v. IX, p. 159.

18. Jefferson to Brissott de Warville, Paris, February 11, 1788, Julian P. Boyd, *The Papers of Thomas Jefferson*, v. 12, pp. 577–78.

19. Robert A. Rutland, *The Papers of James Madison*, v. 10, p. 157.

20. *Ibid.* at p. 157.

21. Letter to George Washington, *The Works of Alexander Hamilton in Twelve Volumes*, federal edition, v. 9, p. 418.

22. Madison to Jefferson, Phila., June 6, 1787, Robert A. Rutland, *The Papers of James Madison*, v. 10, p. 29.

23. *Benjamin Franklin*, federal edition, v. 11, p. 379.

24. Words of George Mason, *Notes of Debates in the Federal Convention of 1787*, reported by James Madison, p. 630.

25. Robert A. Rutland, *The Papers of James Madison*, v. 11, p. 175.

26. *Ibid.*, v. 12, at pp. 196–97.

27. M. Pusey, *Charles Evans Hughes* (1963) p. 204; speech at Elmira, New York, May 3, 1907.

Chapter II

1. Justice Bernard Botein, *Trial Judge* (New York: Simon and Schuster, 1952), p. 3.

2. Everett Lloyd, *Law West of the Pecos, The Story of Roy Bean* (San Antonio, Tex.: The Naylor Company, 1941), p. 71.

3. *Ibid.* at p. 121.

4. For a detailed review of the federal judicial system, see Charles A. Wright, *The Law of Federal Courts*, 4th ed., pp. 1–21.

5. Glenn Shirley, *Law West of Fort Smith: A History of Frontier Justice in the Indian Territory, 1834–1896*, p. 35.

6. Quentin Reynolds, *Courtroom: The Story of Samuel S. Leibowitz* (New York: Farrar, Straus and Company, 1950), p. 372.

7. Kenneth Smemo, *Against the Tide, The Life and Times of Federal Judge Charles F. Amidon, North Dakota Progressive* (New York and London: Garland Publishing, 1986), p. 128.

8. *Ibid.* at p. 128.

9. Robert Francis Kennedy, Jr., *Judge Frank M. Johnson: A Biography* (G.P. Putnam's Sons, 1978), p. 31.

10. 461 U.S. 171 (1983).

11. *Ibid.* at p. 177.

12. Joseph Ulman, *A Judge Takes the Stand* (New York: Alfred A. Knopf, 1933), p. 261.

13. *Ibid.* at p. 265.

14. 754 F.2d 1311 (1985).

15. *Ibid.* at 1318–19.

16. Florence Ellinwood Allen, *To Do Justly* (Cleveland, Ohio: Western University Press, 1965), p. 148.

17. Florence E. Allen, *This Constitution of Ours* (New York: G.P. Putnam & Sons, 1941), p. 124.

18. Henry J. Abraham, *Justices and Presidents, a Political History of Appointments to the Supreme Court* (New York: Oxford University Press, 1974), p. 75.

19. "In Memoriam, Earl Warren," 88 *Harvard Law Review*, 1, 3 (1974).

20. Earl Warren, *A Republic, If You Can Keep It* (Quadrangle Books, 1972), pp. 109–10.

21. Yates v. United States, 354 U.S. 298, 344 (1957).

22. Leon Jaworski, *Confession and Avoidance* (Garden City, N.Y.: Anchor Press/Doubleday, 1979), p. 200.

23. *Ibid.* at p. 202.

24. 403 U.S. 713 (1971).

25. United States v. Nixon, 418 U.S. 683 (1974). Justice William Rehnquist, who had been appointed by President Nixon, did not participate in this case.

26. *Ibid.* 711–12.

27. 372 US. 335 (1963).

28. *Ibid.* at 337.

29. *Ibid.* at 344.

30. 1 Cranch 137 (1803).

31. *Ibid.* at 154.

32. *Ibid.* at 163.

33. *Ibid.* at 177–78.

34. Moragne v. States Marine Lines, 398 U.S. 375, 403 (1970).

35. 316 U.S. 455 (1942).

36. Louis Nizer, *Reflections Without Mirrors* (Garden City, N.Y.: Doubleday and Company, 1978), p. 268.

37. Quentin Reynolds, *Courtroom, the Story of Samuel S. Leibowitz* (New York: Farrar Straus, 1950), pp. 418–19.

38. The Honorable William J. Brennan, Jr., "In Honor of Walter V. Schaefer," 74 *Nw. Law Review* 677 (1979).

39. "In Memoriam—Roger John Traynor," 71 *California Law Review* 1037, 1039, 1053, 1060 (1983).

40. Danskin v. San Diego Unified School Dist., 171 P.2d 885, 888 (1946).

41. *Ibid.* at 892.

42. Howard Simmons and Joseph A. Califano, Jr., eds., *The Media and the Law,* (New York, Washington, London: Praeger) pp. 36–37. See also Fred

W. Friendly and Martha J.H. Elliott, *The Constitution — That Delicate Balance* (Random House, 1984), p. xiii.

Chapter III

1. Barron v. Mayor and City Council of Baltimore, 32 U.S. 243, 247 (1833).
2. Chicago, Burlington & Quincy R.R. v. City of Chicago, 166 U.S. 226 (1897).
3. See *Constitution of the United States,* Senate Document, 99-16, pp. 951–58.
4. Gitlow v. New York, 268 U.S. 652 (1925).
5. Malloy v. Hogan, 378 U.S. 1, 10–11 (1964).
6. Adamson v. California, 332 U.S. 46, 89 (1947).

Chapter IV

1. Everson v. Board of Education, 330 U.S. 1, 11 (1947).
2. 333 U.S. 203 (1948).
3. 343 U.S. 306 (1952).
4. 370 U.S. 421 (1962).
5. 374 U.S. 203 (1963).
6. 397 U.S. 664 (1970).
7. 403 U.S. 602 (1971).
8. Wolman v. Walter, 433 U.S. 229, 262 (1977).
9. 413 U.S. 756 (1973).
10. 474 U.S. 481 (1986).
11. Tilton v. Richardson, 403 U.S. 672, 686 (1971).
12. Roemer v. Maryland Public Works Board, 426 U.S. 736, 745–746 (1976).
13. 449 U.S. 39 (1980).
14. Lynch v. Donnelly, 465 U.S. 668, 671 (1984).
15. County of Allegheny v. American Civil Liberties Union, 109 S. Ct. 3086, 3098–99 (1989).
16. 472 U.S. 38 (1985).
17. Scopes v. State, 289 S.W. 363 (1927).
18. Epperson v. Arkansas, 393 U.S. 97, 107 (1968).
19. 482 U.S. 578 (1987).
20. 463 U.S. 783 (1983).
21. 366 U.S. 420 (1961). See also Two Guys from Harrison-Allentown v. McGinley, 366 U.S. 582 (1961); Braunfeld v. Brown, 366 U.S. 599 (1961); Gallagher v. Crown Kosher Super Market, 366 U.S. 617 (1961).
22. 42 USC 2000e ff.
23. 483 U.S. 327 (1987).
24. Selective Draft Law Cases, 245 U.S. 366, 390 (1918).
25. 401 U.S. 437 (1971).
26. County of Allegheny v. American Civil Liberties Union, 109 S. Ct. 3086, 3138 (1989).

Chapter V

1. 98 U.S. 145 (1879).
2. See Murphy v. Ramsey, 114 U.S. 15 (1885); Davis v. Beason, 133 U.S. 333 (1890); Mormon Church v. United States, 136 U.S. 1 (1890).
3. Davis v. Beason, 133 U.S. 333, 342 (1890).
4. 329 U.S 14 (1946).
5. Prince v. Massachusetts, 321 U.S. 158, 176 (1944).
6. Douglas v. Jeannette, 319 U.S. 157, 167 (1943).
7. Lovell v. Griffin, 303 U.S. 444, 448 (1938).
8. Cantwell v. Connecticut, 310 U.S. 296, 301-2 (1940).
9. Murdock v. Pennsylvania, 319 U.S. 105, 108-9 (1943).
10. Communist Party v. Subversive Activities Control Board, 367 U.S. 1, 137 (1961).
11. Kunz v. New York, 340 U.S. 290 (1951).
12. Marsh v. Alabama, 21 So.2d 558, 561 (1945).
13. Marsh v. Alabama, 326 U.S. 501, 509 (1946).
14. Heffron v. Int'l. Soc. of Krishna Consc., 452 U.S. 640, 647 (1981).
15. United States v. Schwimmer, 279 U.S. 644 (1929); United States v. Macintosh, 283 U.S. 605 (1931).
16. 328 U.S. 61 (1946).
17. Hamilton v. Regents, 293 U.S. 245, 251-52 (1934).
18. In re Summers, 325 U.S. 561, 574 (1945).
19. Gillette v. United States, 401 U.S. 437, 461 n. 23 (1971).
20. 415 U.S. 361 (1974).
21. Thomas v. Review Bd., Indiana Empl. Sec. Div., 450 U.S. 707, 717-18 (1981).
22. Sherbert v. Verner, 374 U.S. 398, 404 (1963).
23. Frazee v. Illinois Dept. of Empl. Security, 109 S. Ct. 1514, 1517 (1989).
24. 366 U.S. 599 (1961).
25. Board of Education v. Barnette, 319 U.S. 624, 628-29 (1943).
26. Minersville District v. Gobitis, 310 U.S. 586 (1940).
27. Board of Education v. Barnette, 319 U.S. 624, 638 (1943).
28. Torcaso v. Watkins, 162 A.2d 438, 440 (1960).
29. Torcaso v. Watkins, 367 U.S. 488, 496 (1961).
30. Wisconsin v. Yoder, 406 U.S. 205, 211 (1972).
31. United States v. Lee, 455 U.S. 252, 257 (1982).
32. Employment Div., Dept. Human Res. v. Smith, 110 S. Ct. 1595, 1597 (1990).
33. Wooley v. Maynard, 430 U.S. 705, 707 (1977).
34. 322 U.S. 78 (1944).
35. Quaring v. Peterson, 728 F.2d 1121, 1123 (1984).
36. Jensen v. Quaring, 472 U.S. 478 (1985).
37. Bowen v. Roy, 476 U.S. 693, 695 (1986).
38. Goldman v. Weinberger, 475 U.S. 503, 505 (1986).
39. O'Lone v. Estate of Shabazz, 482 U.S. 342, 345 (1987).
40. Watson v. Jones, 80 U.S. 679, 727 (1871).
41. 443 U.S. 595 (1979).

Chapter VI

1. Stromberg v. California, 283 U.S 359, 361 (1931).
2. Schenck v. United States, 249 U.S. 47, 48–49 (1919).
3. 250 U.S. 616 (1919).
4. Pierce, et al. v. United States, 252 U.S. 239 (1920).
5. Gilbert v. Minnesota, 254 U.S. 325, 326 (1920).
6. Gitlow v. New York, 268 U.S. 652, 673 (1925).
7. John Bartlett, *Familiar Quotations,* ed. Emily Morison Beck (Boston, Toronto, London: Little Brown, 1980).
8. 341 U.S. 494 (1951).
9. *Ibid.* at 496.
10. United States v. Dennis, 183 F.2d 201, 226 (1950).
11. 341 U.S. at 509.
12. 354 U.S. 298 (1957).
13. Brandenburg v. Ohio, 395 U.S. 444, 445–46 (1969).
14. Hague v. C.I.O., 307 U.S. 496, 515 (1939).
15. Cantwell v. Connecticut, 310 U.S. 296 (1940).
16. Schneider v. State, 308 U.S. 147, 162 (1939).
17. Cox v. Louisiana, 379 U.S. 559 (1965).
18. Cox. v. Louisiana, 379 U.S. 536, 540 (1965).
19. 379 U.S. at 562.
20. 408 U.S. 104 (1972).
21. Frisby et al. v. Schultz et al., 108 S. Ct. 2495, 2498 (1988).
22. Boos v. Barry, 485 U.S. 312, 316 (1988).
23. Flower v. United States, 407 U.S. 197 (1972).
24. Chess v. Widmar, 635 F.2d 1310, 1313, (1980).
25. Widmar v. Vincent, 454 U.S. 263, 271 (1981).
26. Airport Comm'rs. v. Jews for Jesus, Inc., 482 U.S. 569, 571 (1987).
27. Adderley v. Florida, 385 U.S. 39, 46 (1966).
28. Greer v. Spock, 424 U.S. 828, 831 (1976).
29. Renton v. Playtime Theatres, Inc., 475 U.S. 41, 44 (1986).
30. Mutual Film Corp. v. Ohio Indust. Com., 236 U.S. 230 (1915).
31. 475 U.S. at 47.
32. Northern Cinema, Inc. v. City of Seattle, 585 P.2d 1153, 1155 (1978).
33. 475 U.S. at 52.
34. Terminiello v. Chicago, 337 U.S. 1, 4 (1949).
35. *Ibid.*
36. Chicago v. Terminiello, 79 N.E.2d 39, 42 (1948).
37. 337 U.S. at 3.
38. 340 U.S. 315 (1951).
39. State v. Chaplinsky, 18 A.2d 754, 758 (1941).
40. Chaplinsky v. New Hampshire, 315 U.S. 568, 569 (1942).
41. Lewis v. New Orleans, 415 U.S. 130, 132 (1974).
42. Cohen v. California, 403 U.S. 15, 16–17 (1971).
43. F.C.C. v. Pacifica Foundation, 438 U.S. 726, 729 (1978). "The original seven words were, shit, piss, fuck, cunt, cocksucker, motherfucker, and tits.

Those are the ones that will curve your spine, grow hair on your hands and . . . maybe even bring us, God help us, peace without honor . . . um, and a bourbon." *Ibid.* at 751.

44. 109 S. Ct. 2829 (1989).
45. Schad v. Mount Ephraim, 452 U.S. 61, 65 (1981).
46. Halter v. Nebraska, 205 U.S. 34, 41 (1907).
47. Spence v. Washington, 418 U.S. 405, 406 (1974).
48. Smith v. Goguen, 415 U.S. 566 (1974).
49. 105 L. Ed.2d 342 (1989).
50. United States v. Eichman, 110 S. Ct. 2404, 2405 (1990).
51. Staub v. City of Baxley, 355 U.S. 313, 321 (1958).
52. 394 U.S. 147 (1969).
53. Schaumburg v. Citizens for Better Environment, 444 U.S. 620, 624 (1980).
54. United States v. Auto Workers, 352 U.S. 567, 572 (1957).
55. 2 USC Sections 431ff.
56. Buckley v. Valeo, 424 U.S. 1, 39 (1976).
57. 470 U.S. 480 (1985).
58. Citizens Against Rent Control v. Berkeley, 454 U.S. 290, 291 (1981).
59. Austin v. Michigan Chamber of Commerce, 110 S. Ct. 1391, 1392 (1990).
60. F.E.C. v. Massachusetts Citizens for Life, Inc., 479 U.S. 238, 241–242 (1986).
61. 110 S. Ct. at 1398.
62. 486 U.S. 414 (1988).
63. Ex Parte Curtis, 106 U.S. 371, 372 (1882).
64. United Public Workers v. Mitchell, 330 U.S. 75, 91 (1947).
65. C.S.C. v. Letter Carriers, 413 U.S. 548, 556 (1973).
66. Broadrick v. Oklahoma, 413 U.S. 601, 602 (1973).
67. Connick v. Myers, 461 U.S. 138, 141 (1983).
68. 483 U.S. 378 (1987).
69. Tinker v. Des Moines School Dist., 393 U.S. 503, 504 (1969).
70. Tinker v. Des Moines Ind. Com. School Dist., 258 F. Supp. 971, 972 (1966).
71. 393 U.S. at 508.
72. Bethel School District No. 403 v. Fraser, 478 U.S. 675, 687 (1986).
73. Adler v. Board of Education, 342 U.S. 485, 492 (1952).
74. Pickering v. Board of Education, Dist. 205, 225 N.E.2d 1, 10 (1967).
75. Pickering v. Board of Education, 391 U.S. 563, 568 (1968).
76. In re Grimley, 137 U.S. 147, 152 (1890).
77. Parker v. Levy, 417 U.S. 733, 736–37 (1974).
78. Brown v. Glines, 444 U.S. 348, 350 (1980).
79. Martinez v. Procunier, 354 F. Supp. 1092, 1095 (1973).
80. Procunier v. Martinez, 416 U.S. 396, 405–6 (1974).
81. Hillery v. Procunier, 364 F. Supp. 196, 197 (1973).
82. Pell v. Procunier, 417 U.S. 817, 822 (1974).
83. 482 U.S. 78 (1987).
84. First National Bank v. Bellotti, 435 U.S. 765, 767 (1978).
85. 447 U.S. 530 (1980).

86. Consolidated Edison v. Pub. Ser. Comm'rs., 390 N.E.2d 749, 751 (1979).

87. 447 U.S. at 533.

88. Pacific Gas & Elec. Co. v. Pub. Ser. Com., 475 U.S. 1 (1986).

89. Valentine v. Chrestensen, 122 F.2d 511, 512 (1941).

90. Valentine v. Chrestensen, 316 U.S. 52, 54 (1942).

91. Cammarano v. United States, 358 U.S. 498, 514 (1959).

92. Bigelow v. Virginia, 421 U.S. 809, 812–13 (1975).

93. Virginia Pharmacy Bd. v. Virginia Consumer Council, 425 U.S. 748, 749–50 (1976).

94. Linmark Associates, Inc. v. Willingboro, 431 U.S. 85, 95 (1977).

95. 447 U.S. 557 (1980).

96. Metromedia Inc. v. San Diego, 453 U.S. 490, 538, 539 (1981).

97. Bolger v. Youngs Drug Prod. Corp., 463 U.S. 60, 62 (1983).

98. Bates v. State Bar of Arizona, 433 U.S. 350, 354 (1977).

99. Ohralik v. Ohio State Bar Assn., 436 U.S. 447, 449 (1978).

Chapter VII

1. Louis B. Wright, *Magna Carta and the Tradition of Liberty* (Am. Revolution Bicentennial Administration, 1976), p. 29.

2. Bernard Schwartz, *The Roots of the Bill of Rights* (New York: Chelsea House, 1980), v. 4, p. 842.

3. Osborn v. Pennsylvania-Delaware Ser. Sta., 499 F. supp. 553, 556 (1980).

4. Adderley v. Florida, 385 U.S. 39, 49–50 (1966).

5. United States v. Harriss, 347 U.S. 612, 615 (1954).

6. McDonald v. Smith, 472 U.S. 479, 481–82 (1985).

7. Brown v. Louisiana, 383 U.S. 131, 136 (1966).

8. 15 United States Code Section 1.

9. 365 U.S. 127 (1961).

10. Noerr Motor Freight v. Eastern R. Pres. Conf., 155 F. Supp. 768, 827 (1957).

11. 365 U.S. at 138.

12. California Motor Transport v. Trucking Unlimited, 404 U.S. 508, 511 (1972).

13. United States Postal Service v. Hustler Magazine, Inc., 630 F. Supp. 867 (1986).

14. State of Missouri v. Nat. Organization for Women, 620 F. 2d 1301, 1302 (1980).

15. Smith v. Silvey, 149 Cal. App. 3d 400, 403 (1983).

16. Aknin v. Phillips, 404 F. Supp. 1150, 1152 (1975).

17. 299 U.S. 353 (1937).

18. State v. De Jonge, 51 P.2d 674, 675 (1935).

19. 299 U.S. at 355.

20. Thomas v. Collins, 323 U.S. 516, 518 (1945).

21. City of Cincinnati v. Coates, 255 N.E.2d 247, 248 (1970).

22. Coates v. City of Cincinnati, 402 U.S. 611 (1971).
23. 448 U.S. 555, 558 (1980).

Chapter VIII

1. Whitney v. California, 274 U.S. 357, 358 (1927).
2. 278 U.S. 63 (1928).
3. Communications Assn. v. Douds, 339 U.S. 382, 385–86 (1950).
4. NAACP v. Alabama, 357 U.S. 449, 452 (1958).
5. NAACP v. Button, 371 U.S. 415, 419 (1963).
6. Brotherhood of Railroad Trainmen v. Virginia Bar, 377 U.S. 1, 2 (1964).
7. United Mine Workers of America v. Illinois Bar Association, 389 U.S. 217, 218 (1967).
8. Adler, et al. v. Board of Education, 342 U.S. 485, 492 (1952).
9. 367 U.S. 203 (1961).
10. 389 U.S. 258 (1967).
11. N.A.A.C.P. v. Claiborne Hardware Co., 458 U.S 886, 889 (1982).
12. Barenblatt v. United States, 360 U.S. 109, 114 (1959).
13. 366 U.S. 82 (1961).
14. Shelton v. Tucker, 364 U.S. 479, 480 (1960).
15. Buckley v. Valeo, 424 U.S. 1, 64 (1976).
16. Brown v. Socialist Workers '74 Campaign, 459 U.S. 87, 99 (1982).
17. Elrod v. Burns, 427 U.S. 347, 350–351 (1976).
18. 445 U.S. 507 (1980).
19. 110. S. Ct. 2729 (1990).
20. Anderson v. Celebrezze, 460 U.S. 780 (1983).
21. Kusper, et al. v. Pontikes, 414 U.S. 51 (1973).
22. Democratic Party of U.S. v. Wisconsin, 450 U.S. 107, 109 (1981).
23. Tashjian v. Republican Party of Connecticut, 479 U.S. 208 (1986).
24. Bd. of Dirs. of Rotary Int'l. v. Rotary Club, 481 U.S. 537, 544, 545 (1987).
25. Roberts v. United States Jaycees, 468 U.S. 609 (1984).
26. Healy v. James, 408 U.S. 169, 171 (1972).

Chapter IX

1. Patterson v. Colorado, 205 U.S. 454, 458–59 (1907).
2. Near v. Minnesota, 283 U.S. 697, 702 (1931).
3. 403 U.S. 713 (1971).
4. 427 U.S. 539, 556 (1976).
5. Freedman v. Maryland, 380 U.S. 51 (1965).
6. New York Times Co. v. Sullivan, 376 U.S. 254 (1964).
7. Curtis Publishing Co. v. Butts, 388 U.S. 130, 132 (1967).
8. Gertz v. Robert Welch, Inc., 418 U.S. 323, 325–26 (1974).

9. Hustler Magazine v. Falwell, 485 U.S. 46, 52 (1988).

10. Cox Broadcasting Corp. v. Cohn, 420 U.S. 469, 487 n. 16 (1975). (See Warren and Brandeis, "The Right to Privacy," 4 *Har. L. Rev.* 193 [1890].)

11. Time, Inc. v. Hill, 385 U.S. 374, 413 (1967).

12. 420 U.S. at 474.

13. Smith v. Daily Mail Publishing Co., 443 U.S. 97, 99 (1979).

14. Richmond Newspapers, Inc. v. Virginia, 448 U.S. 555, 560 (1980).

15. Globe Newspaper Co. v. Superior Court, 457 U.S. 596, 598 (1982).

16. Press-Enterprise Co. v. Superior Court, 464 U.S. 501 (1984).

17. Press-Enterprise Co. v. Superior Court of Cal., 478 U.S. 1 (1986).

18. Branzburg v. Hayes, et al. Judges, 408 U.S. 665, 667–68 (1972).

19. Butterworth v. Smith, 110 S. Ct. 1376, 1379 (1990).

20. See discussion in text, Chapter VI, at notes 81–83.

21. Pell v. Procunier, 417 U.S. 817 (1974).

22. Houchins v. KQED, Inc., 438 U.S. 1, 5 (1978).

23. Jacobellis v. Ohio, 378 U.S. 184, 197 (1964).

24. Roth v. United States, 354 U.S. 476, 487 (1957).

25. Redrup v. New York, 386 U.S. 767, 770–71 (1967).

26. Interstate Circuit, Inc. v. Dallas, 390 U.S. 676, 704 (1968).

27. Miller v. California, 413, U.S. 15, 18 (1973).

28. Paris Adult Theatre I v. Slaton, 413 U.S. 49, 73–74 (1973).

29. Jenkins v. Georgia, 418 U.S. 153, 154 (1974).

30. Prince v. Massachusetts, 321 U.S. 158, 170 (1944).

31. Ginsberg v. New York, 390 U.S. 629, 631 (1968).

32. New York v. Ferber, 458 U.S. 747 (1982).

33. Osborne v. Ohio, 110 S. Ct. 1691, 1698 (1990).

INDEX

23.91